History of the Boilermakers' Society

Volume 1   1834–1906

History of the Boilermakers' Society

Volume 1   1834–1906

by J. E. Mortimer

London   George Allen & Unwin Ltd
Ruskin House   Museum Street

Printed in Great Britain
in 11 *point Times Roman*
by Clarke, Doble & Brendon Ltd
Plymouth

Preface

This book was written for members of the Boilermakers' Society. It is intended to be read by working men and I hope, therefore, that its style makes for easy reading. I hope, too, that readers outside the trade union movement will find it of interest. I have tried to do justice to the first seventy years or so in the stirring story of one of Britain's proudest unions. Some critics may feel that there is an absence of carefully compiled tables of statistics, references and footnotes which are sometimes, though not always, an indication of scholarly research. I accept the criticism, but reply that my purpose was the more important one of writing a book which platers, welders, caulkers, riveters and other structural steel tradesmen might be persuaded to read in their leisure hours after a hard day's work in a shipyard, engineering workshop or on a construction site.

The members of the Boilermakers' Society belong to an organisation which has shared in almost every advance and suffered in almost every defeat of the British trade union and labour movement. To study its history is to study the history of British labour. It is also a history of democratic endeavour, of the strivings, aspirations, successes, failures and unfulfilled objectives of a band of working men stretching through a succession of generations. In one way or another they have sought through their Society to influence eventually virtually everything affecting their working lives.

If objectivity means – as in my view it should mean – a readiness to present issues as they really are and not to gloss over weaknesses or to present only that which is favourable, I have tried to be objective. If, however, objectivity is taken to imply a lack of commitment then I acknowledge that in this sense I have not even tried to be objective. This book has been written in the very firm belief that trade unionism is and has been a tremendous force for social progress, for the improvement of workers' conditions, for enlightened legislation on a wide range of issues, and for the enlargement of democracy. As with no other social movement it has provided working men and women with an opportunity to help in shaping the environment within which they labour. The Boilermakers' Society has a very special place in the history of British trade unionism and every chapter in this book has been written not with clinical detachment but with the kind of fundamental sympathy that only a sense of commitment can provide.

Critical appreciation of the successes and failures of a developing organisation is fully compatible with a commitment to its fundamental purpose. Most certainly this is not an uncritical book. Indeed, part of the fascination of writing it was to study the influences, exemplified in the history of the Boilermakers' Society, which gave to British trade unionism a number of its characteristic weaknesses. Business unionism – that is, a narrow concern with occupational advantages derived from protective practices, collective bargaining, and generous provident benefits – was well established in British nineteenth-century craft unionism before it became fashionable and better publicised in the U.S.A. The Boilermakers' Society in the latter part of the last century was an effective business union. But business unionism did not provide an answer to all the problems of shipbuilding workers. Nor did it offer a way forward in response to repressive legal judgements which took from trade unionists a number of rights essential for the effective functioning of their unions. Even less did business unionism based on craft exclusiveness provide guiding inspiration for the millions of unskilled and semi-skilled workers who were still outside the unions by the 1880s. In the ultimate, the welfare of boilermakers – whether in relation to the prosperity of the industries in which they work, their social security, the civil rights which they enjoy and their opportunity to influence events – could not be divorced from the welfare of the rest of the British people and primarily of the rest of the working class. How boilermakers reacted to and learnt from these experiences forms the real substance of this book.

Inevitably, a substantial part of this book deals with the part played in the Boilermakers' Society by Robert Knight, one of the most distinguished trade unionists, not only in the history of the Society but also in the history of the British trade union movement. He served as General Secretary for nearly thirty years in the period of great expansion of British shipbuilding. He was for many years

8

influential in the TUC and occupied its presidential chair. I have
tried to make a fair judgement of Robert Knight's contribution
to trade unionism. He was by any standards a commanding figure
with outstanding attributes. I hope that I have given him the credit
he deserves for his immense contribution in developing the administration of the Society and for his single-minded devotion to
the welfare, as he saw it, of the members of the Society. I have tried
also to show how in very important respects Robert Knight's views
corresponded, at the time, to the needs and wishes of the membership. In some respects also he was in advance of the membership
as, for example, in his early recognition of the need for a federation
of engineering unions.

Despite all this, my final conclusion – as readers will see – is
critical of much that Robert Knight came eventually to represent.
His grip had to be loosened to make possible a revival of democracy
within the Society. Moreover, in the great debates that overtook the
trade union movement in the final ten years of his period of office
he was a leading figure in the rearguard action of the 'old' leadership within the TUC against the 'new' unionists and the socialists.
Nevertheless, this did not prevent the Boilermakers' Society from
occupying a very early place in the formation of the Labour Party.
The struggles and internal controversies within the Boilermakers'
Society towards the end of the last century are indicative of the
changes that had to take place as an essential preliminary for the
emergence of a labour movement with both a political and an industrial wing.

The Boilermakers' Society has always had for me a very special
interest, even though it has never been my privilege to be a member of it. I first learnt something about it when I started work as
an apprentice ship-fitter in an Admiralty Dockyard and when I was
a member of the then Amalagamated Engineering Union. From
men who had worked not only for the Admiralty but also in shipbuilding on the north-east coast, the Clyde, the Mersey and at
Barrow I was told that the Boilermakers' Society was a very un-
usual organisation. It had a very long history, it was tightly organised and exclusive, it was militant, it had a pronounced tendency
to insist on trade demarcation and its members showed great
solidarity one with another.

Later, when I became an active member and official of the then

Association of Engineering and Shipbuilding Draughtsmen, I was to learn more of the Boilermakers' Society. I spent many hours in the company of Gavin Martin, who was then the General Secretary of the Confederation of Shipbuilding and Engineering Unions. Gavin was a former shipbuilding worker from the Caledon shipyard in Dundee. He was a full-time official of the Boilermakers' Society before his election as General Secretary of the CSEU. He asked me on many occasions to help in the preparation of policy statements and wage claims for the CSEU and this gave me the opportunity to meet him frequently. I listened on many occasions to his stories of the Boilermakers' Society, told in his rich Scottish accent and with the intelligence and discernment which he always displayed. His stories were of innumerable struggles, of strikes, lock-outs, demonstrations, unemployment, family hardships, controversies and amusing incidents.

Gavin Martin exemplified many of the characteristics of the Boilermakers' Society. He was class conscious in the sense that he always looked at important national issues from the standpoint of the industrial working class, and he never pretended that the interests of employers and workers were always the same. He was proud of the Boilermakers' Society, of its tradition and above all of its solidarity. At the same time he sometimes displayed a narrowness of outlook in relation to semi-skilled and unskilled workers. He preferred particularly to limit the influence inside the Confederation of the two general workers' unions, the Transport and General Workers' Union and the National Union of General and Municipal Workers. It should, of course, be remembered that during Gavin's time as General Secretary the two general workers' unions stood firmly on the right wing of the trade union movement, whereas his personal views favoured what could best be described as responsible and disciplined militancy. It would have been interesting to observe the effect on his attitude of subsequent changes towards the left in the leadership of the Transport and General Workers' Union. Regrettably, Gavin died before these changes so significantly altered the balance of power in the trade union movement. Many of Gavin's views on the importance of rank-and-file democracy and workers' participation were similar to those expressed more recently by Jack Jones, the present General Secretary of the Transport and General Workers' Union.

Most trade union officials who knew Gavin Martin closely were deeply influenced by him. I was one of them. I remember him with admiration and affection. Together with Harry Brotherton, of the sheet-metal workers, who for about ten years presided over the CSEU, he provided outstanding qualities of leadership to Britain's engineering and shipbuilding workers. Their task was made all the more difficult by divisions between the unions affiliated to the CSEU, by internal disputes and by inconsistencies from time to time in the policies of some of the unions in the Confederation.

Throughout the twenty years I served as a full-time official of the draughtsmen's union (now the technical section of the Amalagamated Union of Engineering Workers), I learnt more and more about the Boilermakers' Society. I saw the union in operation in Britain's shipyards and factories, where its members frequently worked side by side with members of the draughtsmen's union. Between the two unions there was the respect and goodwill which skilled men could be expected to show to each other.

I came to know a succession of officials of the Boilermakers' Society and I heard their spokesmen at the TUC, at the Confederation of Shipbuilding and Engineering Unions, and at the Labour Party conference. There were Mark Hodgson, Ted Hill, Alf Whitney and Finlay Hart of an earlier generation; Danny McGarvey, John Hepplewhite, John Chalmers, Ted Williams, and Albert Chalkley – to mention only a few – of a later generation. From all of them at some time or another I picked up something of the lore of the Boilermakers' Society.

There was also, of course, one other figure in the history of the boilermakers who, through his written and spoken words, conveyed to many others, including myself, a glimpse of the special traditions of the Society. It was Harry Pollitt. Though I met him on occasions, I never had the opportunity to talk to him about the union of which he held life-long membership. No one, however, who heard him speak or who read his many articles or his autobiographical essay, *Serving My Time*, could fail to note the influence on him of his membership of and activity in the Boilermakers' Society.

Of the men of my own generation in the Boilermakers' Society the one I know closest of all is Danny McGarvey. I have enjoyed his friendship for many years. At different times I have spent many

11

hours in his company and discussed with him almost every major problem facing the trade union and labour movement during the past twenty-five years. Danny is utterly dedicated to the interests of the members of the Boilermakers' Society and from him I have learnt much of the history, practices and policies of the organisation of which he is now the President.

I wish also to acknowledge the help I have been given from time to time by John Hepplewhite. John is widely read and I have often gained valuable information from conversations with him. He has also assisted in providing source material and photographs for this book.

Finally I wish to thank the Boilermakers' Society for giving me the opportunity to write this book. It would be too much to hope that others will gain as much from reading it as I gained in understanding from writing it. I hope, nevertheless, that it will help members and others to a fuller appreciation of the role of generations of boilermakers in the development of the British trade union and labour movement.

The main sources of material for this book were the monthly and annual reports of the Society and the seventieth anniversary volume on the Society prepared by the then General Secretary, Mr. D. C. Cummings.

J. E. MORTIMER

Contents

Illustrations

Chapter 1

The Formation of the Union

The first recorded trade union meeting of boilermakers took place on 20 August 1834. The meeting place was Manchester. A decision was taken to form a Society of Friendly Boiler Makers and fourteen members were enrolled.

Some two months later another branch of the Society was established. This time it was in Bolton. Four boilermakers were present at the inaugural meeting. A secretary, James Cooper, was elected to conduct the affairs of the branch and to maintain regular communication with the parent body in Manchester. Before long a branch president was elected, James Warbrick, and he is credited with organising regular discussion meetings on Sunday evenings to stimulate the interest of members in the aims and activities of the young Society. The active members of the Bolton branch, and particularly the secretary James Cooper, also sought recruits in neighbouring towns, including Bury and Blackburn.

In the spring of 1835 a General Council of the Society was formed. As was the custom in the early days of trade unionism, it was not a delegate or representative committee elected by the various branches but was drawn from the parent branch of the organisation. The first General Council of the Society of Friendly Boiler Makers consisted of fourteen members, with Abraham Hughes as chairman and William Hughes as secretary. William Hughes can thus be regarded as the first General Secretary of the Boilermakers' Society.

From the early records of the Society it is clear that William Hughes was a deeply religious man. As the first secretary he was charged with the task of drawing up an opening ceremony for branch meetings, an initiation procedure for the introduction of new members and a series of 'lectures', which were printed and were intended to inform and educate members about the purposes of the Society and the ideals on which it was based. William Hughes also arranged for the design of an emblem for the Society. The design included an uplifted hand with a hammer, representing the 'sign' of the Society, and four sketches illustrating the work and brother-hood of boilermakers. The design carried a motto, HUMANI NIHIL ALIENUM (To humanity nothing hostile).

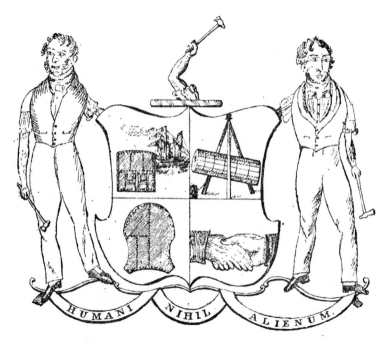

BRANCH CEREMONY

The branch-opening ceremony drawn up by William Hughes and approved by the General Council provided for a prayer to be said by the branch president. All members were required to stand. The words of the prayer were:

> 'ALMIGHTY God who disposest of man in the way which seemeth best to thy Godly wisdom, so fit and prepare our hearts, that while we remain together we may receive thy good gifts with thankfulness, through Jesus Christ our Lord. Amen.'

18

At the conclusion of the prayer the branch president was required to declare, 'Brothers, I declare this lodge to be duly opened under the title of The Order of Friendly Boiler Makers.'

The initiation ceremony for a new member took the form of an oath. The new member was required to promise, 'before God and this assembly', that he would keep inviolable 'all the secrets or transactions that I do hear, see or receive relative to this Order, namely the Order of Friendly Boiler Makers, especially the grip, words, signs or counter-signs of a Friendly Boiler Maker, whom I believe to be a true and faithful brother amongst us . . .'

When the new member had given this vow he was then addressed by the branch president. The standard form of address reminded the new member that a vow 'is a solemn appeal to Almighty God, desiring his mercy and protection no otherwise than in the matter or thing vowed to be true or false . . .' The sacredness with which the initiation vow was regarded can be measured by the concluding two sentences of the standard address to the new member:

> If thou vow a vow unto the Lord thy Lord, thou shall not slack to pay for it, for the Lord will require of thee, and that which is gone out of thy lips, thou shalt keep and perform according as thou hast vowed unto the Lord, and which thou hast promised with thy mouth. And JEPHTHAH, a Judge of the Israelites, rather than break his vow sacrificed his only daughter.

The written 'lectures' for the education of the Society's members stressed the value of brotherhood and unity, and outlined the functions of branch officers. Members were also expected to familiarise themselves with the ritual for gaining admission to a branch meeting room. This ritual was of special importance because it provided protection against intruders who might be informers or spies on behalf of employers or the authorities. Frequent reference was made in the 'lectures' to Biblical events. The 'lectures' were also written in the form of questions and answers.

To the question: 'Can you give me an instance of the good effect of unity?' the reply was 'Yes, worthy president, we understand from Holy Writ that between David and Jonathan there was a unity subsisted, to the end that it was the saving of David's life.' The 'lecture' then went on to describe how Jonathan saved David's life by giving him timely notice of the jealousy and evil intent of Saul.

19

This, the 'lecture' stressed, should 'teach both you and I to give a brother in unity timely notice of any impending danger, if in our power'.

The ritual for gaining admission, described in the lecture, consisted of four distinct raps at the door of the lodge by the member wanting to gain entry. The member was then required to listen for a response of four raps from the inside of the door. The member also had to give the first part of the sacred word or sign – which was changed every three months – to the outside door-keeper. If, however, the member had forgotten or did not know the secret word or sign for the current quarter, the outside door-keeper reported the presence of the person claiming to be a member to the inside door-keeper who in turn reported to the branch secretary. It was then for the branch secretary to determine from his books whether the person claiming to be a member was, in fact, a member.

When a member had been admitted through the door of the branch room he had still not finished his ritual for admission to the meeting. The door was closed behind the member and he was then required to give the second half of the secret password or sign to the inside door-keeper.

Two of the elected officers of the branch were known as inspectors. It was their job to be present at the lodge meeting place before the branch opened. Upon the order of the president they were required immediately before the opening ceremony 'to rise from their seat and to go round and examine every person in the room'. If the inspectors found in the meeting room a person who was not a member of the Society they had to report the fact to the branch president who would then ask the non-member to leave the room. If, however, the non-member refused to leave the president had the right to order the inspectors 'to compel him to leave the room'.

The president of the branch was endowed with very considerable power. He was regarded as the principal officer of the branch and it was his duty to propose the business with which the branch was called upon to deal. He could also 'call to order any refractory member and, if not obeyed in due time', could 'levy such fines or penalties as the rules will permit'. The president was also charged with the responsibility of ensuring that all other officers of the branch fulfilled their duties.

Careful arrangements were made to ensure that the contributions

20

of members were properly recorded and that the money received was safeguarded. Contributions were paid to a steward and entered into the book by the secretary. Another steward checked the entries made by the secretary. The two stewards were then responsible for conveying the cash to the treasurer in the presence of the president. The treasurer had to enter the amount received in the cash-book and the stewards then conveyed the cash to the president. It was the president's job to lock away the cash and he then had to give the key to the treasurer. These arrangements were made to ensure that no one official had the responsibility of handling the Society's money. The possibility of loss or theft was reduced by the sharing of responsibility for recording and handling the cash.

There were two other elected officials of the branch. They were known as the marshals or hosts. It was their job to order the beer. Threepence of the four-weekly subscription of 1s 9d was allocated for the purchase of beer. The marshals were required to distribute the beer with impartiality among the members assembled at the meeting. If they ordered more than was allowed by the Society's custom they were required to pay for the excess.

The preface to the lectures drawn up by the secretary, William Hughes, opened with words that were to become the traditional form of address in the Boilermakers' Society. They were: 'Worthy President, Vice, Officers and Brothers All'.

By 1836 the Society was beginning to reach beyond the Manchester and Bolton area. On 27 July 1836 a branch of fourteen members was opened in Bristol. One of its early recruits was John Allen, who was later to become the General Secretary of the Society. Three years later, in 1839, the Society opened its first branch in London.

THE FIRST RULE BOOK

It was in this same year, 1839, that the Society drew up its first rule book. It was done under the direction of the General Council of the parent branch in Manchester. Before 1839 there was no formal written constitution but decisions were made from time to time to serve as rules for the conduct of the Society. It was decided that these various decisions should be revised and consolidated into a book of rules. A special committee was elected for the purpose and it submitted its findings to three general meetings of members held in Manchester. The last of these meetings, at which the proposed rules were confirmed, was held in March 1839.

The preamble to the first book of rules carried the title 'Let Brotherly Love Continue'. It said that the members had united 'to administer to each other's necessities and to relieve each other in sickness and poverty'. It went on:

> You are not only united in brotherly love to administer to the necessities of the sick and afflicted, but those who are in poverty and distress for want of employment or other unforeseen circumstances.

The rule book as approved by the three general meetings of members was a lengthy document of fifty-one pages, indicative of the thoroughness with which the constitutional committee had discharged its task. The emphasis of the constitution was on the provision of provident benefits. There was very little, if anything, concerning the trade union function of collective bargaining.

The constitution of the Society was framed to make it an exclusive organisation of craftsmen. The entrance fee was fixed at the very high sum of £1 1s. Of this amount 10s 6d had to be paid by the applicant on the night on which his membership was proposed and the remaining 10s 6d had to be paid four weeks later on the night of admission. The lower age limit for membership was eighteen and the upper age limit was forty-five. It was thus an organisation of the younger craftsmen. The upper age limit was fixed because of the generous benefits provided under the rules. Older members would have been a burden on the funds.

Contributions to the Society were fixed at 1s 9d for every four weeks, of which 3d was allocated for beer. Sick pay was 10s per week for six months, 5s for the second six months and 3s 6d for the remaining period of sickness. This was, by the standards of 1839, an extremely generous rate of benefit. Members were required to pay their contributions to the Society whilst receiving sick benefit.

Members who were sixty years of age and who had been in membership for twenty years were entitled to superannuation at the rate of 3s 6d per week. It is significant that as long ago as 1839 the members of the Society decided that a workman should be eligible for a pension payment at sixty years of age. Even today nearly all members are required to continue working until they are sixty-five

22

years of age before qualifying for either a State pension or a pension granted under a private industrial scheme. Funeral benefit on the death of a member amounted to £8 and on the death of a member's wife to £7. For the relief of unemployment two special kinds of benefit were provided. When a member was thrown out of work the members who remained in employment in the same branch were required to claim 1s extra per day from their employer. This money was then used to assist the unemployed members. If an employer refused to pay the extra 1s per day, the members at other work-shops and yards had to be informed. They were expected not to take new employment with the firm or firms where the extra pay-ment for the relief of the unemployed was not being made. It was also stipulated that night work and Sunday work was to be paid at double the normal rate of payment. This was to encourage em-ployers to give jobs to unemployed members and to discourage overtime.

The second method of assisting unemployed members was by the provision of what was known as travelling or tramping benefit. An unemployed member who had been in the Society for at least twelve months and who was up-to-date with his contributions could obtain a certificate from his branch secretary which he could present to the secretary of a branch in another town. He would then be provided with supper, a pint of beer and a bed for the night. If the unemployed member had been in the Society for at least two years he was entitled, in addition, to a payment of 1d for each mile he had travelled by land or water since he was last assisted. If he crossed from England to Ireland or from Ireland to England he was entitled to a payment of 5s. 'Tramping members' were required to call at the nearest branch in their search for work, and could not ask for relief more than once in six months from any one branch.

The rules stipulated that 'political discourse, seditious sentiment, indecent songs', cursing, swearing, obscene language and betting should not be introduced at meetings. A member who broke this rule or who refused to take his seat or be silent when ordered to do so by the president was liable to a fine of 3d for the first offence, 6d for the second offence and expulsion from the meeting for any subsequent offence.

Provision was also made in the rules for a method of settling disputes between members and branch officers. Disputes were usually

23

concerned with the interpretation of rules on eligibility for benefit. The rules required that five arbitrators should be elected by the members. The arbitrators were to be nominated from persons who had no direct interest in the funds of the Society. When a dispute arose an arbitration panel of three was drawn by lot from the names of the five elected arbitrators. The arbitration panel was empowered to give a decision on the point of dispute. The losing side had to pay the arbitrators' expenses, which were not to exceed 10s, together with the expenses of any necessary witnesses.

The first rule book stipulated that committee meetings of the General Council should be held quarterly in Manchester. The General Council was given power at these meetings to alter the rules of the Society.

Chapter 2

The Social Background

It was no accident that the Boilermakers' Society came into existence in 1834. This was a year of unprecedented trade union agitation. The early trade union movement reached a new high peak of activity. It lasted only for a brief period but the formation and continued existence of the Boilermakers' Society was one of the permanent gains to emerge from it.

THE INDUSTRIAL REVOLUTION

The craft of boilermaking was made necessary by the Industrial Revolution, a period which covered most of the second half of the eighteenth century and the first half of the nineteenth century. It was a period when tremendous changes took place in the manner of producing goods and in the way in which people earned their living. Handicraft production gave way to workshop manufacture. Machines were introduced, tasks were broken down to allow for the division of labour, and workers were employed together in larger numbers in factories. The range of goods which could be manufactured in this way was greatly increased and productivity was much higher. Before the Industrial Revolution nearly everyone in Britain worked on the land. A small minority worked in towns and villages as hand craftsmen. With the coming of the Industrial Revolution a growing proportion of the population was employed in factories.

The manufacture of goods by machinery in factories was made possible by the development of steam power. The steam engine was steadily improved through the period of the Industrial Revolution.

This enabled the muscle power of human beings to be replaced by power generated by the heating of water into steam. Steam occupies a far greater volume than the water from which it is boiled and it is this transformation which enables mechanical work to be performed through the medium of a steam engine.

In order to make factory production possible other industrial developments were also necessary. Iron had to be obtained for the making of machinery, coal had to be mined to provide power for the new steam engines, new roads and railways had to be built to transport the raw materials to the factories and then to take the finished goods from the factories, and new skills had to be learnt for the preparation, shaping, cutting and fabrication of metal and metal products, for the mining of coal, and for the operation of machinery of all kinds.

The Industrial Revolution brought into existence two new social classes, the industrial employers and the industrial workers. The employers owned the factories, the machinery and most of the tools necessary for production. They also owned the finished product which had been manufactured, not for their own personal use, but for sale on the market. The difference between the price obtained for the sale of the product and the cost of production was the profit of the employer. Some of this profit was generally used to give the employer a very much higher standard of living than that of the workers, but much of it was often used to expand business. New factory buildings were constructed, new machinery was acquired, and more raw materials were bought. The accumulation of industrial wealth as a source of ever-increasing future profit became the dominant motive of employers. More profits could be made and more wealth accumulated by keeping the wages of the workers as low as possible.

The industrial workers, in contrast, owned virtually nothing other than their own ability to work. They had to sell this ability to work to an employer in order to obtain a livelihood. By competing one against another for the available jobs, the workers were at a serious disadvantage when bargaining with an employer about the level of wages to be paid and about their other conditions of employment. The workers who were without any kind of skill suitable for the new industries were forced by the employers to live at a very low level of subsistence. Workers who had acquired one of the new in-

26

dustrial skills were more fortunate and were able to obtain a higher wage. Even they, however, could be reduced to destitution through unemployment during trade depression or if they were away from work for a long period because of sickness or injury.

THE BOILERMAKER'S CRAFT

The craft of boilermaking developed with the evolution of the steam engine. An essential part of a steam engine is a boiler. This is a vessel in which water is heated to boiling point to produce steam. A boiler had to include a furnace for the combustion of coal or other fuel, and it had to provide as large a heating surface as possible so that the heat released by the combustion of the fuel could be transmitted to the water. The water had to be contained in a separate compartment or, at a later stage, in tubes. The boiler had to be sufficiently strong to withstand the high steam pressures generated when the furnace was at full blast. Boilers were made of plates of metal which were cut and bent to shape. The plates had then to be joined together and made steam tight. The methods of marking out plates, of making templets (essentially a templet is a pattern), of cutting and shaping plates and then of joining them together have changed with the development of new techniques, but all the operations involved, both then and now, form part of the boilermaker's craft. They include plating, templet making, rolling, planing, punching, shearing, bending, welding, flanging, drilling, riveting, caulking and tubing. It is part of the boilermaker's trade to fabricate metal structures or machines of the most diverse kinds from plates, angles, tee-pieces, channels and joist sections. Originally, some boilermakers were also expected to be able to shape metal by the process of forging (that is, to change the shape of a piece of metal by heating it and then striking it with a hammer). This, however, is a separate craft – that of the blacksmith – and demands a high level of skill. The blacksmiths developed their own trade union, and it was not until many years later that their union amalgamated with the Boilermakers' Society.

The craft of boilermaking as it originally developed was an extremely wide one, calling for considerable skill in many different operations. It was not surprising, therefore, that a measure of specialisation began to develop even at an early stage. The employer recognised that specialisation would help productivity. Some who today criticise the tradition of specialisation among boilermakers overlook or are, perhaps, unaware of the circumstances in which it originated and developed. It was introduced and extended as a means to promote higher productivity.

The great name in the development of the steam-engine was that of James Watt. His was not the first steam-engine to be made, but Watt was responsible for the invention of an engine which was both more efficient and more economical in the use of fuel than anything that had been produced before. Watt collaborated with Mathew Boulton, a production engineer of outstanding ability, and in the final quarter of the eighteenth century they established a successful business for the manufacture of steam-engines. Even then the total number in operation in the infant British industries was less than 300. At first the steam-engines were used for pumping water in the coal-mines. Soon, however, they were applied as a source of power in the textile industries, above all in cotton.

The first quarter of the nineteenth century brought further important developments in engineering. The development of the modern metal lathe, with a slide rest and lead screw, dates from about 1800. The planer followed fairly quickly afterwards, to be followed by the shaper, slotter and borer. A new group of workers was coming into existence, the mechanics of modern industry. They included turners, fitters, moulders, smiths and boilermakers. Frequently these mechanics were known by the general title of millwrights, though strictly the millwrights of old worked with hand tools rather than with the new machines.

The mechanics were not only needed for the production and maintenance of steam engines and the new kinds of metal machinery installed in the textile industry, but were also soon to be needed for railroad and locomotive construction, for metal bridge-building and for shipbuilding. The first iron railroad to be constructed was in 1767, but it was not intended for a steam-powered locomotive. It was used only for a transport wagon to be hauled by men or by horses. By the end of the eighteenth century there were a number of such short railroads which served as feeders for canal transport. More such railroads were constructed in the first quarter of the nineteenth century and on some of them experiments were con-

28

ducted for the pulling of tubs or wagons by cable wound round drums driven by stationary steam-engines.

In 1825 a steam-locomotive designed by Stephenson was used for haulage purposes on the Stockton and Darlington Railway. The great era of railway construction, with steam-locomotives, had begun. By 1850 more than 6,600 miles of railway had been built. A very important new area of employment for boilermakers was opening. Steam-locomotives could not be constructed without the skill of the boilermakers. The development of the railways also brought into existence another new opening for the employment of boiler-makers. This was in the construction of metal bridges. The building of metal bridges involved the use of heavy sections and plates of metal which had to be marked out, drilled, cut, shaped and joined together. All this was part of the boilermaker's trade. The first metal railway bridge was constructed in 1823 for the Stockton and Darlington Railway Company. It spanned a small tributary of the River Wear and formed part of the railroad when it was opened in 1825. Since that time thousands of metal bridges have been con-structed.

The development of steam-powered ships built of metal instead of wood also dated from the first half of the nineteenth century. Iron and steel shipbuilding was to provide employment for tens of thousands of platers, riveters, drillers, templet-makers, markers-off, caulkers and other tradesmen with the various skills associated with boilermaking. They were required not only for the manufacture of marine boilers, but also for the construction of ships' hulls. So important was shipbuilding to become for boilermakers that for many years the Boilermakers' Society was thought of primarily as a shipbuilding union.

Soon after the early development of the steam-engine by Watt attempts were made to apply it to the propulsion of ships. By 1802 a steamship, the *Charlotte Dundas*, was working on the Forth and Clyde Canal. Ten years later a passenger steamship, the *Comet*, ran on the Clyde. In 1819 a steamship, the *Savannah*, crossed the Atlantic, and in 1825 another steamship, the *Enterprise*, completed a voyage to India.

The earliest steamships were built of wood, and steam power was used to turn paddles placed at the side of the ship. In 1838, however, Messrs Laird & Company of Birkenhead launched a small steamship with a screw propellor. Ocean navigation by steam-driven, screw-propelled iron ships soon became a possibility. By the last quarter of the nineteenth century steel had replaced iron as the main metal for ship construction. Passenger and cargo fleets, with a total displacement of millions of tons, travelled by mechanical propulsion across the oceans of the world. For many years Britain was by far the world's largest builder of ships.

The Robert F. Stockton,
built by Laird & Co., 1838

TRADE UNION ORGANISATION

Trade union organisation among the new mechanics, brought into existence by the Industrial Revolution, began to be established on something like a firm basis in the 1820s. In his book *The Story of the Engineers* – a history of the Amalgamated Engineering Union and of the earlier unions that formed the AEU – James Jefferys pointed out that, although the Friendly Society of Ironmoulders had been formed in 1809 and the Friendly and Benevolent Society of Vicemen and Turners in London in 1818, it was not until the first half of the 1820s that firm roots of trade union organisation began to be sunk. In 1822 the Mechanics' Friendly Union Institution was formed in Bradford, and in November 1824 the first branch of the Steam Engine Makers' Society was formed in Liverpool. Two years later this Society was able to hold its first delegate meeting in Manchester, and five branches were in existence. Another union of engineers formed in 1826 in Manchester was the Friendly Union of Mechanics. Jefferys emphasised in his book that these were not the

30

only unions of mechanics to have been formed at that time, but they appear to have been the strongest.

In the early 1820s trade unions were still illegal. At the turn of the century legislation had been passed to strengthen the provisions of the law against combination for trade purposes. Even before the Combination Acts of 1799 and 1800, trade combinations were often regarded as illegal both under existing statute and under common law. Moreover, the doctrine of *laissez-faire* was becoming increasingly popular in ruling circles and this strengthened common-law conceptions against trade unionism. According to the doctrine of *laissez-faire* the maximum public good would be achieved – this was usually identified with the maximum production of wealth – if each individual citizen was permitted to pursue his own economic interest without any kind of State intervention or other interference in the free operation of market forces. Thus, a combination of workmen to improve wages or working conditions was held to constitute interference in the free operation of the labour market.

One purpose of some of the earliest trade combinations was, in fact, to request that the State, through the local magistrates, should fix wages. This it had the power to do under the Statute of Artificers (1563). This power, however, had fallen increasingly into disuse in the eighteenth century, particularly under the impact, from about 1760 onwards, of the development of the new industries. This power given to magistrates to fix wages was finally repealed in 1813–14.

The strengthening of the law against trade combinations at the turn of the century was prompted not only by fears about trade unionism but also by a desire on the part of the Government and those whom it represented to suppress anything which might serve as instruments for the importation into Britain of the democratic doctrines associated with the French Revolution. In the 1790s there had been a new political ferment in Britain. Societies, drawing their support from artisans and progressive thinkers, came into existence for the study and propagation of democracy, republicanism and the rights of man. In the same period a powerful movement of rebellion developed in Ireland and its most advanced leaders, notably Wolfe Tone, expressed strong sentiments in favour of democracy and in support of the labouring poor against the propertied classes. In 1797 there were also extensive mutinies in the British Navy. All these events persuaded the powers that be in Britain that radicalism should be denied open means of expression. Despite the repressive legislation of the 1790s and 1800, radicalism could not be stamped out in Britain.

Industry developed rapidly in the first quarter of the nineteenth century. The harsh conditions of life for those employed in the new industries inevitably produced movements of resistance. Trade combinations of various kinds – some of a temporary nature, others with a more permanent existence – came into being in many different areas. In some areas the magistrates sought to suppress the early unions with the utmost severity. In other areas the unions were treated with near-toleration. Some employers found it preferable not to incur the hatred of workers by instigating prosecutions.

The Combination Laws were finally repealed in 1824. A select committee of the House of Commons reported that they had not prevented the foundation of trade combinations, but instead had a tendency 'to produce mutual irritation and distress, and to give a violent character to the combinations, and to render them highly dangerous to the peace of the community'. The select committee recommended that employers and workers 'should be freed from such restrictions, as regards the rate of wages and hours of working, and be left at perfect liberty to make such agreements as they eventually think proper'.

The repeal of the Combination Laws was due, first and foremost, to the thousands of workers who had persisted, despite the law, in forming and belonging to trade unions. But for this resistance there would have been no move to repeal the Combination Acts. Secondly, the repeal was due to the recognition by some employers and by sections of the House of Commons that repression was not achieving its purpose and was more likely to worsen than to improve relations between masters and men. Thirdly, it was due to the very able way in which the parliamentary moves for repeal were handled by the radical London tailor, Francis Place.

The repeal of the Combination Acts coincided with a period of brisk trade and was followed by an outburst of trade union activity. A new parliamentary select committee was appointed as a result of expressions of alarm in Government circles at the extent and practices of trade unionism. This was followed by a new law in 1825, which confirmed the repeal of the Combination Acts but narrowed the legality of trade combinations to questions of wages and hours

RULES AND REGULATIONS

TO BE OBSERVED BY

THE WORKMEN

IN THE EMPLOY OF

ROBT. STEPHENSON & CO.

WORKING HOURS.

1. The Bell will be rung at 6 o'clock in the Morning and at 6 o'clock in the Evening throughout the Year for a Days Work, except during the Months of November, December, and January, when work will commence at 7 o'clock in the Morning, and close at 6 o'clock ; and on Saturdays the Day's Work will end at 4 o'clock.

2.—The Meal Times allowed from 1st of February to the 31st of October are, from ½ past 8 to 9 for Breakfast, and from 1 to 2 for Dinner, during which period the First Quarter of a Day will end at ½ past 8, the Second at ½ past 11, the Third at 2, and the Last at 6 o'clock. From 1st of November to 31st January the Meal Times are from 9 to ½ past 9 for Breakfast, and from 1 to 2 o'clock for Dinner ; during this period the First Quarter of a Day will end at 9 o'clock, the Second at 12, the Third at ½ past 3, and the Last at 6 o'clock.

3.—Overtime to be reckoned at the rate of Eight Hours for a Day, but no Overtime to be entered until a whole Week of regular time has been worked.

4.—Every Workman to write on his Time-board, with his Time, the Name of the Article or Articles he has been working at during the Day, and what Engine or other Machinery they are for.

5.—Every Workman to be provided with a Drawer for his Tools with Lock and Key. The Drawer and Key to be numbered, and all his Tools to be marked with the same Number and the Letters R. S & Co. The Key to be left in the Store-house every Night when the Man is done Work. To be accountable for his Tools when leaving the Employ, and, in case of Loss, the amount to be deducted from his Wages.

		s.	d.
6.—Any Workman who does not return his own Time-board to the Office when done Work, and, on the Evening previous to the pay at 6 o'clock, to be fined		0	3
7.—Any Workman either putting into the Office or taking out of the Store-house any other Board than his own, to be fined for each Board		0	3
8.—Any Workman neglecting to leave the Key of his Drawer in the Store-house when done Work to be fined		0	3
9.—Any Workman leaving his Candle burning, or neglecting to shut his Gas Cock, to be fined		1	0
10.—Any Workman enlarging, or in any way altering or damaging his Gas Burner, to be fined		1	0
11.—Any Workman leaving his Work without giving Notice to one of the Foremen to be fined		0	6
12.—Any Workman opening the Drawer of another, or taking his Tools without leave, to be fined		0	6
13.—Any Workman taking Tools from a Lathe, or other Piece of Machinery, to be fined		0	6
14.—Any Workman not returning Taps or Dies, or any other general Tool to the Person who has the charge of them, as soon as he is done with them, to be fined		0	6
15.—Any Workman coming to, or returning from Work, who comes in or goes out at any Door other than that adjoining the Office, to be fined		0	6
16.—Any Workman taking Strangers into the Manufactory without leave, or talking to such as may go in, to be fined		0	6
17.—Any Workman interfering with, deranging or injuring any Machinery or Tool, to pay the cost of repairing the damage, and to be fined		1	0
18.—Any Workman washing himself, putting on his Coat, or making any other preparation for leaving Work before the Bell rings, to be fined		1	0
19.—Any Workman creating tumult or noise in the Manufactory, at any time, to be fined		1	0
20.—Every Workman to provide himself with One Pair of Compasses, One Pair of Callipers, One Two-foot Rule, One Plumb and Line, and One Square, or the same will be supplied to him by his Employers, and the Value deducted from his Wages.			
21.—Any Workman smoking in the Manufactory during Working Hours, to be fined		1	0

22.—No Workman to leave the Employ without giving a Week's Notice, and the same to be given by Robert Stephenson & Co., to any Workman whose services they may cease to require.

No Beer or Spirits allowed to be taken into the Works without Leave.

NOTE.—Every Workman on entering the Employ of Robt. Stephenson & Co. will be expected to put his Name at the back of these Rules and Regulations in testimony that he will conform to them.

ALL FINES TO GO TO THE SICK FUND.

1st. November, 1838.

[handwritten: To Mr A L White from T.H. Scott who did not receive these regulations whilst serving his apprenticeship]

Newcastle-upon-Tyne : Printed by M. BENSON, Dean Street.

[handwritten: Rules of Working Hours in 1 Week 59. 40. 50. Months — 59 Hours p Week. Months — 61 do. do.]

1. Workshop rules 1838

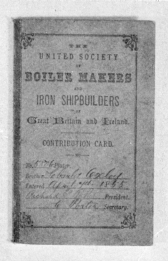

CHARLES OXLEY
JOINED SOCIETY IN 1855

BARKER OXLEY
JOINED SOCIETY IN 1867

CHARLES JACOB OXLEY
JOINED SOCIETY IN 1890

JAMES BARKER OXLEY
JOINED SOCIETY IN 1914

2. Membership cards of four generations of boilermakers

of labour. The new law also introduced stringent provisions against 'intimidation, molestation, or obstruction'. Professor G. D. H. Cole in his *A Short History of the British Working Class Movement* said of the 1825 Act:

> It remained, indeed, lawful to form trade unions, but under conditions which made it very difficult for any body of workers to take effective action without incurring penalties either under statute or under common law.

TRADE UNION AND POLITICAL UPSURGE

The ten-year period between 1824 and 1834 – immediately preceding the formation of the Boilermakers' Society – was one of growing trade union and political activity. Indeed, although it was to end in defeat for the workers, it was one of the periods of militancy in British working-class history. The origin of the Boilermakers' Society undoubtedly owed much to the great outburst of working-class activity which culminated in the formation of the Grand National Consolidated Trades Union in 1834.

In the years immediately following 1825 trade union organisation was extended through the textile industries of Yorkshire and Lancashire, to the coal-mines, particularly in the north-east, to the building industry, to the potters, the clothiers and many smaller trades.

The early 1830s was also a period of intense political agitation for parliamentary reform, particularly for the extension of the franchise, for more parliamentary representation for the new towns, and for the abolition of the parliamentary seats with only a handful of voters. These seats gave assured representation to local squires and landlords. The agitation for parliamentary reform came originally from political radicals but as the new industrialists gained in strength they joined the movement for reform. They demanded a greater share in political power to correspond with the realities of economic power. The Reform Bill, first introduced in 1830 by the Whigs, met the demands of the rising middle-class industrial interests. It provided for the redistribution of seats, swept away many of the country seats with very few voters, and extended the franchise to the middle class in the towns. It was at first rejected by the Commons. It was then re-introduced and rejected by the Lords. There was tremendous agitation throughout the country and many big demonstrations were held in support of reform. A third Reform Bill was thrown out by the Lords, but by now the popular movement was too strong to resist. At last the Lords gave way and the Reform Bill was passed.

Thousands of workers had participated in the movement for reform but the new Reform Act – as many of the radicals pointed out – made no concessions to industrial workers. Because of the property qualification under the new Act, the workers were still without the vote and, therefore, had no means of ensuring independent labour representation. Nevertheless, the participation of many workers in the reform agitation helped to develop the political consciousness of the emergent working class. In the first half of the nineteenth century the early working-class movement did not distinguish to anything like the extent that it did in later years between trade union and political means of advance.

GRAND NATIONAL CONSOLIDATED TRADES UNION

The independent workers' movement reached its highest point in this new upsurge in the Grand National Consolidated Trades Union of 1833–4. This was more than a newly created centre for trade unionism. It was a movement, formed with the inspiration of Robert Owen, which was based on the working class and which regarded trade unionism not only as an organisation of struggle for improved working conditions, but as an instrument through which a new society could be built, based on productive guilds operated by the workers themselves. Recruitment to the new body proceeded apace, and it was estimated that at the height of its influence the Grand National Consolidated Trades Union, together with independent unions, had a total membership – for only a very short period, it is true – of more than a million.

The employers and the Government replied savagely. In a number of towns, workers who belonged to the Grand National were locked out. Despite efforts by the Grand National to raise money, the workers in most cases were eventually forced into defeat. Meanwhile the Government decided to prosecute six Dorset agricultural labourers who, in the village of Tolpuddle, had formed a lodge of

34

the Friendly Society of Agricultural Labourers, one of the constituent organisations of the Grand National Consolidated Trades Union. They were found guilty of administering unlawful oaths, namely the initiation ceremony of the Society, and were sentenced to seven years' transportation to the penal colony in Australia. This sentence led to widespread protests. Nevertheless, the Tolpuddle martyrs, as the Dorset labourers came to be called, were transported and it was not until four years later, following continued protests, that they were finally brought back to Britain.

The great upsurge in trade union activity came temporarily to an end in 1834. The employers, showing confidence derived from their growing economic strength, struck ruthlessly at the new independent movement of the working class. The workers themselves were ill-prepared for the realisation of the ambitious objectives of the Grand National Consolidated Trades Union. They had developed the first stage of consciousness of the need for radical social change, but had not yet developed either the stable industrial or political organisations necessary to wage the struggle over a long period of time. Nor had they worked out a theory of social change with which to guide the day-to-day struggle.

THE BOILERMAKERS

The small group of boilermakers who came together in Manchester in August 1834 to form the Society of Friendly Boiler Makers would certainly have heard of the Grand National Consolidated Trades Union. No one will now ever know how many of them were inspired by, or had participated in, the great struggles of the preceding years. There can be no doubt, however, that the formation of the Boilermakers' Society was one of the permanent gains left by the upsurge of trade union and political activity on the part of the industrial working class in the ten year period following the repeal of the Combination Acts.

In one important respect, nevertheless, the boilermakers of 1834, together with others who were the mechanics of the new industrial system, were *not* typical of the majority of the labouring poor. They were very highly skilled workers and the demand for their labour, despite occasional trade recessions, was expanding. Their wages and their standard of living were considerably higher than

35

that of the vast majority of the working class. In his *British History in the Nineteenth Century and After: 1782–1919*, G. M. Trevelyan says that any picture of the earliest and worst stage of the Industrial Revolution is too black if it omits the life of the mechanics. The fact that the highly skilled workers formed an 'aristocracy of labour' is a key to the understanding of important features of the British trade union movement and to the development of the Boilermakers' Society in the second half of the nienteenth century.

Chapter 3

A National Organisation

The 1840s was the decade of Chartism, a period in which there was intense working-class political agitation and activity. It was also the decade in which the Boilermakers' Society established itself as a national organisation with a firm foundation and stable structure.

Among the active members of the Boilermakers' Society were a number who were also strong supporters of Chartism. One such member was John Roach of Manchester, one of the pioneers of the Society, and a member of the committee in 1839 which drew up the first rule book. When he died in 1847 a memorial card was printed and sold to members throughout the Society. It contained verses in tribute to John Roach. Among the verses were the following:

> An honest man! One whom we knew full well,
>   Who lov'd his country with a patriot's zeal,
> Whose ardent actions did his strength excel,
>   In braving danger for our labour's weal;
>   Whom nought could conquer, save resistless death
>   Hath yielded unto God his latest breath.

> Shall we forget with what undaunted brow,
>   Thou dar'd resist the foes of labour's rights?
> Shall we neglect those virtues to avow
>   Which shone in thee, and are men's chief delights?
>   No! No! a thousand times our nature cries,
>   And in the echo all that's just replies.

These humble lines, though vulgar and uncouth,
  Are dedicated unto thy worth, dear Roach:
Thou friend of man, of justice, and of truth:
  The stranger when he doth thy grave approach,
    Shall see no lofty tomb nor monumental bust,
    But thou shalt sleep in peace, thou honest man and just!

John Roach was reported to have been an enthusiastic propagandist for the Boilermakers' Society, and a stirring speaker. It was an indication of his strong Chartist connections that he named his son Feargus O'Connor Roach, after the Chartist leader Feargus O'Connor.

CHARTISM

Chartism, it has often been pointed out, was a movement whose basic strength was derived from the protest of working people against very bad economic conditions, but whose programme was expressed exclusively in political terms. Chartism developed as an independent movement towards the end of the 1830s. A few years earlier many workers had been drawn into the mass movement for parliamentary reform, but the 1832 Reform Act did not fulfil their expectations. It gave to the new industrial employers and middle class in the towns a share in political power but it left the working class as powerless as ever.

The Chartist movement included various trends and interests. Much of the inspiration for it came from politically active skilled artisans in the London area who organised themselves, together with a number of middle-class radical sympathisers, into the London Working Men's Association. Another important trend was represented by the radicals of the Birmingham Political Union. This included a working-class section, but the leadership remained in middle-class hands. The third, and socially the most significant, element in Chartism was the new industrial working class of the West Riding of Yorkshire and of Lancashire. This generally represented the more militant trend within Chartism. Whereas in London the radical artisans were among the better paid workers, many of the factory workers of Yorkshire and Lancashire lived in acute

38

LINES

Sacred to the Memory of

JOHN ROACH,

BOILER-MAKER LATE OF MANCHESTER,

A SON OF LABOUR—A TRUE DEMOCRAT—A FIRM FRIEND—A DE-
TERMINED ADVOCATE—AN UNPAID PATRIOT
A PURE PHILANTHROPIST—AND

AN HONEST MAN!

The task is mournful, yet 'tis pleasing too,
 To speak in praise of dear departed worth
But when that praise is pure—deserving—true—
 Our inmost heartfelt sentiments come forth:—
 Then speak we as we find—and feeling just—
 From candid men we feel no mean mistrust.

An honest man! one whom we knew full well,
 Who lov'd his country with a patriot's zeal,
Whose ardent actions did his strength excel,
 In braving danger for our labour's weal;
 Whom nought could conquer, save resistless death
 Hath yielded unto God his latest breath..

JOHN ROACH! the echo of thine honest name,
 Inspires the humble muse to try the stream;
Where it may waft thee down the tide of fame—
 And though it fail, yet still the pleasing theme,
 Which brings thee back to memory once more,
 Gives joy to bless thee from the true heart's core.

Our once beloved friend! and yet not ours alone.
 But friend to every man whom he could aid;
Whose breast responded to misfortune's moan,
 Did good unask'd, unpray'd for, and unpaid;
 Whose very life was one eternal round
 Of shielding weakness wheresoe'r 'twas found

Shall we forget thy kind but anxious eye,
 When thou wert bent upon a generous deed?
It seemed as if thy onward soul would fly,
 To help the poorest mortal in his need,
 Like Charity, impatient to be there,
 Where poverty had made the most despair.

Shall we forget with what undaunted brow,
 Thou dar'd resist the foes of labour's rights?
Shall we neglect those virtues to avow
 Which shone in thee, and are men's chief delights?
 No! no! a thousand times our nature cries,
 And in the echo all that's just replies.

Of noble birth thou boasted not the seeds,—
 Thine was a life we dearly love to prove,—
Blending true friendship with the noblest deeds,
 And working out the principles of love,
 Using thy every energy for good—
 Putting to shame high-born ignoble blood.

These humble lines, though vulgar and uncouth.
 Are dedicated unto thy worth, dear Roach:
Thou friend of man, of justice, and of truth:
 The stranger when he doth thy grave approach,
 Shall see no lofty tomb nor monumental bust,
 But thou shalt sleep in peace, thou honest man
 and just!

BENJAMIN STOTT.

poverty and miserable squalor. They were the victims of cruel exploitation.

There were three main waves, extending over a period of about eleven years, in the rise and ultimate decline of Chartism. All were concerned with gaining support, in the form of popular petitions, for a six point Charter. The six points were:

1 Universal manhood suffrage.
2 Vote by ballot.
3 Equal electoral districts.
4 Payment of Members of Parliament.
5 Abolition of the property qualification for Members of Parliament.
6 Annual Parliaments.

The winning of these political demands was seen as the key to economic change. The workers who gave their support to Chartism, who signed its petitions and who attended its meetings and huge demonstrations, were looking for an improvement in their conditions of life. Parliamentary reform on the lines of the Charter was seen as a means to an end, and not as an end in itself.

The Chartist movement ended in apparent defeat. None of the three great surges of activity, in 1838–9, in 1842 and again in 1847–8, achieved their objective. Nevertheless, Chartism contributed a great deal to the development of the workers' movement and to the struggle for civil rights. It showed that an independent workers' movement was possible; it underlined the necessity both for political *and* industrial struggle; and it proved the need, if only through its weakness, for the workers' movement to have a social and economic perspective and to be guided by clear ideas on its objectives.

If these were some of the lessons for the labour movement, there were also lessons learnt by the ruling class from the experience of Chartism. They began to understand that, if revolution was to be averted, some improvement had to be made in working-class conditions, and some of the economic benefits of the new industrial system had to be more widely shared. They also learnt, in due course, that the demand for the extension of political rights to workers could not be permanently denied and that other means must be found – through the influence of the press, the control of the education system, and changes in the traditional political parties

– to ensure that the workers did not use their new political rights to demand a thorough social transformation. Chartism, thus, had a very important influence on the subsequent course of British history.

The growth of the Boilermakers' Society in the second half of the nineteenth century, the greater readiness of the employers to negotiate and to make concessions, and the success of the Society, despite occasional setbacks, in ensuring that its members should be treated as an 'aristocracy of labour' is explained not only by the strength of organisation among boilermakers themselves but also by the experiences and lessons learnt during the stormy years of the Chartist movement.

NEW BRANCHES

In the 1840s the Boilermakers' Society extended its membership to become, in fact as well as in aspiration, a national trade union. Branches were opened in Leeds in 1840, in Belfast in 1841, in Bradford in 1842, and in Liverpool, Hull and Newcastle in 1843. In 1842 a first attempt was made to bring together the branches which had been formed or were about to be formed in various parts of the country. At this meeting a first attempt was also made to introduce a limited measure of centralisation in relation to branch funds. Until that time each branch had financial autonomy. In 1842 it was agreed that each branch should submit a statement on its membership and financial reserves. Its reserves per member could thus be calculated. The branches with a higher than average level of reserves could then be instructed to remit money to branches with a lower than average level of reserves. This was not a strict method of central financial control, because everything depended upon each branch providing an accurate statement of its reserves. Nevertheless, it showed that the various branches in the Society recognised the need for some form of central control. The need for this control was underlined by a trade depression in 1842. Unemployment caused a severe drain on the finances of branches. Authority was given to what was then known as the acting branch to stop travelling allowances. The acting branch served as the Executive Council of the Society. It was a branch, selected by the other branches, to take decisions between annual meetings on issues which affected the whole Society. It was a form of executive control

41

often used in the early trade union movement before executive committees, drawn from various areas, had been established.

In the second half of the 1840s the annual meetings of the Society became prolonged affairs. Much time was spent discussing contributions and benefits. A new secretary, John Roberts, was elected in 1842 and took office during the following year. At the outset he was paid 12s per week and he performed his duties in the evenings and on Sundays. By 1845 he had been appointed as a full-time secretary on a wage of 36s per week. He was paid 5s 6d a day extra, plus travelling expenses, when he was away from home on the Society's business. Two years later his pay was increased to £2 2s per week and his additional payment when away from home was increased to 6s per day.

THE CONSTITUTION TAKES SHAPE

In 1845, the year in which the General Secretary became a full-time official, the annual meeting of the Society lasted for no less than seven days instead of the customary two days. The thirty-three delegates represented thirty-five branches and made a thorough review of the constitution of the Society. The name was changed from the Friendly Boiler Makers' Society to the United Friendly Boiler Makers' Society. The inclusion in the title of the word 'United' was indicative of the trend towards the integration of the separate branches into a more closely knit national organisation. This meeting also introduced a new benefit. Members who were totally disabled as a result of an accident at work were entitled to what was known as a 'bonus gift' to be financed by a levy of 1s on every member. Branches were also required by decision of the 1845 annual meeting to establish a protection fund into which all income had to be put after the payment of sick, funeral and disablement benefits and normal branch management expenses. From this fund the branches met the cost of dispute, unemployment, 'travelling' and superannuation benefit. Travelling or tramping benefit was again introduced to assist unemployed members, following its suspension during the depression of the early 1840s. It was fixed at $\frac{1}{2}$d per mile, and 1s 3d was paid for bed and supper for an overnight stay. Superannuation benefit remained unchanged at 3s 6d per week for members who were sixty years of age, who had been members of the Society continuously for at least twenty years, and who were unfit for work. The meeting also decided that holders-up should be eligible for membership providing that they had worked continuously at the trade between the ages of twenty and twenty-five. They were, however, prohibited from working as riveters unless permission to do so had been given to them by the Society's members. Similarly, riveters were prohibited from working as platers unless sanction had been given.

In 1847 the annual meeting, which on this occasion lasted eleven days, decided that the rules should make provision for the Society to have an Executive Committee of five members. The five members were to be drawn from the 'head lodge', or what had been formerly known as the 'acting branch' of the Society. There was, then, still no provision for the election of an executive committee drawn from and elected by all the branches in the Society. The rules specified the duties of the new Executive Committee. They were 'to transact all the general business of the Society and determine all appeals from any lodge when the rules of the Society are silent upon the matter'; to authorise the opening of new branches; to audit the accounts of the general secretary; and to 'give all instructions to the general secretary in the duties of his office'. The Executive Committee were also empowered to take a vote of the whole membership on issues on which the opinion of the members had to be obtained.

The fact that the rules of the Society during its formative years made provision for the payment of dispute benefit clearly indicated that strikes and lock-outs were not unknown among the Society's members. There is, however, little remaining record of local disputes. At the 1845 annual meeting reference was made to a dispute at Smethwick. Apparently there had been a dispute in one of the boiler shops and the labour of the Society's members had been withdrawn. The 1845 annual meeting decided that members should again be permitted to work in the shop where the dispute had taken place, providing that they obtained the wage rates paid in the locality.

In 1845 a strike of members at Dukinfield was authorised by the Executive Committee. The employers, said a letter sent by the Executive Committee, 'had broken their word'. The Executive Committee agreed that the members should give a week's notice of strike action. The members were urged 'to wage war to the knife' and to spare no expense to win. There is no record, unfortunately, of whether the strike succeeded or failed.

FURTHER CHANGES

The 1848 annual meeting was held in Liverpool and lasted for twelve days, even though on this occasion there were only twenty-one delegates. Among the delegates was John Allen, who later was to become the General Secretary of the Society. The annual meeting took note of the continued financial difficulties of the Society and reduced the scale of financial benefits. Tramping or travelling allowances were stopped for a period of twelve months from August 1848, and the disablement levy was reduced from 1s to 6d per member. It was also decided to create a new class of membership open to persons who were not eligible, because of age or ill health, to qualify for sickness or funeral benefits. The new category was to be known as Protective Fund members with a subscription rate of 1s 3d for every four weeks. They were entitled to dispute benefit and disablement benefit only. The rate of dispute benefit for all members was fixed at 12s per week for married men, together with 6d per week for each child under ten years of age. Single men received 10s per week. This meeting was the first to discuss at length the growing practice of piece-work. A resolution was adopted stating that piece-work 'has in all instances a tendency to be injurious to our trade, and that it is the unanimous opinion of the meeting that each member belonging to the Order should use his united efforts to suppress and if possible to abolish it entirely'. The resolution went on to advise all branches to use their efforts to abolish piece-work. It also said that any member who accepted piece-work without his being compelled to do so by circumstances over which he had no control should be fined 10s for the first offence, £1 for the second offence and thereafter should be expelled. The meeting also decided that, in the future, regular annual delegate meetings need not be held. The Executive Council was, however, empowered to take a vote of the entire membership if and when it was thought that it would be helpful to convene a delegate meeting.

Following the 1848 annual meeting, a new and revised rule-book was issued. The new rules contained a number of significant changes.

The purpose of the union was redefined. Instead of being concerned exclusively with the provision of benefits for members, the Society was given a new objective, namely the unity of members 'for the support of their trade'. This represented the recognition of a wider trade union purpose. The new rules also provided for a new and reduced scale of entrance fees. The fee for new members aged twenty to twenty-five was fixed at 10s; for new members aged twenty-five to thirty at 15s; for new members aged thirty to thirty-five at £1, and for new members aged thirty-five to forty at £1 5s. Persons aged over forty were ineligible for new membership. It was stipulated that all apprentices should serve at least five years before the age of twenty-one. Youths who were not apprentices were required to work at the trade for five years before reaching the age of twenty.

In addition to embracing full members the new rules provided for the admission of protective fund members. These were persons ineligible to qualify for sick and funeral fund benefit. Protective fund members were admitted to the Society provided they had five years at the trade. The entrance fee for them was fixed at 10s and the four-weekly contribution at 1s 3d. They were not to be admitted to normal branch meetings, but they had the right to attend meetings called exclusively for trade purposes. Protective fund members had to pay their contributions in a separate room from that in which the normal branch business was being transacted. The contribution for a full member was 2s 6d every four weeks. Of this sum, 1s 3d was allocated to the sick and funeral fund, 1s to the protective fund, and 3d for the general expenses of the branch. Each branch secretary, who was to be elected annually, was entitled to a payment of 10d per year for each member. The rate of sickness or accident benefit for members who had been in the Society for at least twelve months and who were up-to-date with their contributions was fixed at 10s per week for the first six months, 5s per week for the second six months and 3s 6d per week thereafter. This benefit was paid providing that the illness was not brought on by intoxication, venereal disease or other 'improper conduct'. Funeral benefit was fixed at £10, to be paid to the widow on the death of a member, and £7 to a member on the death of his wife. If a member died who had no known relatives, the officers of the branch were charged with providing a funeral for him. It was stipulated that the

45

funeral should be 'decent and moderate'. Members who reached the age of sixty and who had paid contributions for at least twenty years were entitled to a superannuation benefit of 3s 6d per week.

The president and vice-president of each branch were elected during March and September of each year. The other officials of the branch, apart from the secretary, held office for periods of three months, and every member was required to serve in rotation. A member who refused to serve as a steward, guardian, marshal or inspector could be fined 2s 6d for each offence. Each branch was also required to elect a committee of ten members whose duty was to consider any disputes which might arise in the branch. One of the principal responsibilities of the committee was to consider claims made by members for benefits under the rules. The rules stated that members should be admitted to branch meetings only after giving the password. The president was charged with preserving decency and good behaviour at branch meetings, and any member who introduced indecent songs, swore, promoted gaming, used obscene language, ate, slept or refused to keep silent when called upon by the president to do so could be fined 3d for the first offence, 6d for the second offence and expelled from the branch meeting for the evening for the third offence. It was significant that this rule on preserving good behaviour at branch meetings did not, in contrast to the original rules of 1834, insist that members should not engage in political discourse or utter seditious sentiments. No member was, however, allowed to speak more than three times on one subject and he was expressly forbidden from interrupting, laughing at, or mocking other members. Members were also forbidden to disclose to non-members any of the private transactions of the Society. If a member broke this rule he was liable to a fine of 10s for the first offence, £1 for the second offence and expulsion from the Society for the third offence.

Provision was made within the rules for the holding of general meetings to which all members could be summoned. The rules stated that a summons should be duly served to each member, except that, where ten or more members worked in a workshop, one summons should be forwarded for every ten members. Members who did not attend a summoned meeting could be fined 6d. The rule also stated that no member should be allowed to leave the branch room without the president's permission for the first two hours after the opening of the meeting.

One of the rules set out the procedure for the election of the general secretary of the Society. At that time he was sometimes known as the corresponding secretary. The rules stated that a general secretary should be elected annually 'or oftener' by all the branches. He was required to devote the whole of his time to the business of the Society. It was stated that he 'shall be under the control of the Executive Committee at the Head Lodge, who shall have the power, in case of death or removal, or violation of laws, to appoint another temporary until the whole of the lodges are made acquainted'. All members of the Society were eligible to apply for the position of general secretary. The rule stipulated that the general secretary should be elected by a majority of the Society, and required that the general secretary should keep a general register into which the names of all the Society's members should be entered. The register was to indicate when and where each member was admitted, his age, the trade in which he was employed, and whether or not he was married. This requirement of the rules was, in fact, not carried out. Some of the leading members of the Society considered that it would be dangerous to compile a register of members' names and addresses. The legality of trade unionism was still very uncertain, and the possibility that such a register might fall into the hands of hostile authorities was viewed with apprehension.

The Executive Committee of the Society continued to consist of five persons in the Head Lodge. This was another name for the 'acting branch' referred to earlier. The Executive Committee was required to transact all the general business of the Society and to determine appeals made by a branch or branches on matters on which the rules of the Society were silent. The Executive Committee held office for a period of one year. The rules stated that the Executive Committee should 'also give all instructions to the general secretary in the duties of his office'.

ANOTHER GENERAL SECRETARY

Early in 1849 a new general secretary was appointed. He was John Pennie. He had acted in that capacity for a period before his official appointment. The previous general secretary, John Roberts, left

England somewhat mysteriously towards the end of 1848. He sailed from Southampton as a member of the crew of a P & O steamer. John Pennie was to remain as the general secretary of the Society until 1853, when he emigrated to the United States. During the period of office of John Pennie, honorary membership of the Society was extended to the world-famous engineer, George Stephenson. When a bridge was built across the Menai Straits a branch of the Boilermakers' Society was opened at Menai. The last rivet was put in the bridge, on completion, by George Stephenson. It was then that he was made an honorary member of the Boilermakers' Society and, in return, he made a donation of £3 3s to the Society.

In June 1850 the levy of 6d per member for the payment of disablement benefit was abolished. A new rule was introduced which provided a fixed sum of £60 for total disablement through accident. Half of this sum was to be met from the general funds of the Society and the other half was to be raised by a levy.

3. Membership certificate 1844

4. General Council of the Society 1895. It was this Council which proposed that the locally elected lay Executive Council should be replaced with a nationally elected full-time Executive Council. This proposal was intended to curtail the power of the General Secretary, Robert Knight. A leading figure in this revolt from below was D. C. Cummings of London, one of the youngest members of the General Council. Four years later he was elected to succeed Robert Knight as General Secretary

Chapter 4

Craft Unity But Not an Engineering Amalgamation

Events in the 1840s had underlined the need for unity among members of the Boilermakers' Society. Unity was needed so that members in the towns where there was nearly full employment could provide financial assistance to members who were out of work in towns where trade was depressed. The development of a more closely knit national organisation made it possible for these transfers of money to take place. But even more important was the need for unity to resist attacks by employers on wages and conditions during periods when trade was slack, and to obtain improvements when trade was buoyant.

AN ENGINEERING AMALGAMATION

The importance of trade union strength and unity had become apparent not only to many boilermakers but also to many others among the 'new mechanics'. In 1850 discussions were opened about the possibility of amalgamation between a number of trade societies organising mechanics, millwrights, steam-engine makers, patternmakers and blacksmiths. The Boilermakers' Society was invited to participate but decided not to do so. The moulders also stood aloof. The boilermakers had developed their own generous scale of benefits and many members were apprehensive lest these benefits might have to be reduced in any scheme of amalgamation. The Boilermakers' Society was also more interested in extending its organisation to cover all who were already eligible to join rather than to submerge its identity in a broader organisation. The amalgamation discussions led, despite considerable difficulties and

D

some opposition within the participating societies, to the formation of the Amalgamated Society of Engineers, Machinists, Smiths, Mill-wrights and Patternmakers. At its formation in January 1851 its membership was only about 5,000. Some of the branches of the participating societies refused at the outset to amalgamate. The new Society was, however, well and energetically led and within eighteen months of its formation it had just about doubled its membership. Within the Boilermakers' Society there were a number of active members who were sympathetic to the principle of amalgamation and disagreed with the decision of the boilermakers' leadership not to join in the amalgamation discussions. At least two of the branches, Bury and Swindon, were known strongly to favour amalgamation. Indeed, so strong was their advocacy of amalgamation that it was feared that they might break away from the Boilermakers' Society and apply to join the new Society. In the late summer of 1851 the Boilermakers' Executive Committee wrote to the new Amalgamated Society to enquire whether there was any truth in reports which they had received that the Bury and Swindon branches were about to transfer to the new organisation. A reply was received stating that there was no truth in such reports. The letter of reply did, however, contain the comment: 'At the same time I may as well mention that the subject has been before the Executive Council, and they have decided that it is a question that can only be settled at our next Delegate Meeting.'

This sentence certainly seemed to imply that the Amalagamated Society was aware that a number of branches of the Boilermakers' Society favoured amalgamation. In the outcome, nevertheless, none of the branches of the Boilermakers' Society broke away.

CRAFT UNITY

The amalgamation discussions had an important indirect influence on the Boilermakers' Society, even though the Society itself did not participate in them. They gave an impetus to the movement for the creation of one all-embracing organisation of craftsmen engaged in the various skills associated with boilermaking. On the Clyde and in London more and more craftsmen were being employed on iron shipbuilding and ship-repairing. They were using techniques and skills associated with boilermaking. A separate Scottish society of boilermakers had existed for a number of years and it was not until 1849 that the English society opened its first branch in Scotland. This was at Greenock. The immediate effect was to worsen the hitherto friendly relations between the English and the Scottish societies. Subsequently, however, the relations between the two bodies again improved and there was a strong body of opinion in favour of amalgamation among the active members in Scotland.

In London, even though branches of the existing Boilermakers' Society were already in existence, a new organisation for boiler-makers was formed in 1849. It was known as the Amicable and Provident Society of Journeymen Boiler Makers of Great Britain. Its main difference from the existing Boilermakers' Society was that it placed even greater emphasis on the provision of financial bene-fits to members who suffered unemployment or who retired from work because of old age.

In 1852 both the Scottish Society and the London Society applied to join as part of the Boilermakers' Society. The applications were considered by the 1852 delegate meeting and were approved. Repre-sentatives of the Scottish Society addressed the delegate meeting. As a gesture to the number of members of the Scottish and London societies who were employed in shipbuilding, the title of the amalga-mated society was changed to the United Society of Boiler Makers and Iron Shipbuilders. The recruitment of the Scottish and London societies added no more than about two hundred members to the parent society. At the end of 1851 the membership of the Society was 1,781 enrolled in forty-five branches. By the end of 1852 the membership had risen to about 2,000 enrolled in fifty-two branches. One important development in the structure of the Society, promp-ted by the amalgamation of the Scottish and London societies, was the provision for the establishment of district committees with power to make bye-laws for their district.

THE IMPORTANCE OF PROVIDENT BENEFITS

At the 1852 delegate meeting the rules of the Society were again revised. A preface was introduced which stressed that the purpose of the Society was to provide for mutual relief in sickness and un-employment and to establish funds for other benevolent purposes. The preface said:

These views can be carried into effect by uniting together, while in employment, and subscribing a small sum per week, which, under wholesome laws and economical management, will be capable of affording, at least, some assistance to those who occasionally have the misfortune of being out of employment, to keep the gaunt wolf from the door, and prevent, in a great measure, the painful sensation of hunger.

The preface said nothing at all about collective bargaining, nor was there even a hint of any struggle against employers. The wording, with its entire emphasis on provident benefits, was largely taken from the preamble to the rules of the former London society.

The revision of rules in 1852 increased the rate of subscription from 2s 6d to 3s every four weeks. The entrance fees were reduced by about 25 per cent but were still very high in relation to wages. They varied, according to the age of the entrant, from 5s to £1. The different funds of the Society, namely the sickness and funeral fund and the protective fund, were consolidated into one general fund. Provision was made for the periodic 'equalisation' of funds between branches. Unemployment benefit was fixed at 8s per week for ten weeks, 6s per week for a further ten weeks, with a maximum payment of £7 in any one year. Dispute benefit was fixed at 12s per week, and provision was made for the payment of what would now be called victimisation benefit to any member who lost his job because of activities on behalf of the Society. This benefit was made equal to half normal pay. The full scale of benefits for which members were now eligible in return for their contribution of 9d per week was as follows:

Sickness benefit:
Twenty-six weeks at 10s per week
Twenty-six weeks at 5s per week
Thereafter 3s 6d per week as long as sickness continued.

Funeral benefit:
At member's death   £10
At member's first wife's death   £7
At member's second wife's death   £7

Disablement benefit:
Total disablement through accident   £60
Total incapacity through apoplexy, epilepsy, paralysis and
blindness   £30

Unemployment benefit:
For ten weeks each year   8s per week
For ten weeks each year   6s per week

Superannuation benefit:
Members over sixty years of age with twenty years' membership
3s 6d per week

Victimisation benefit:
Half-pay

Travelling benefit:
Unemployed members sent by the Society to jobs in another
town were allowed 'the cheapest fare whether by railway, stage
coach, or steam boat . . .'

In 1853 the General Secretary, John Pennie, decided, after only
four years in office, to emigrate to the United States. He was replaced by George Brogden of Hull who had been a delegate at the
1852 delegate meeting. Unfortunately George Brogden was also
destined to have only a short period of office. He died after a
short illness in March 1857. George Brogden did, however, officiate
at another delegate meeting, in 1856, when the rules of the Society
were again revised. A new rule was introduced to make clear the
main principles of the structure of the Society. It consisted of
members working at 'boilermaking and iron shipbuilding'. They
were to be organised into 'an indefinite number of branches, each
branch to consist of the members residing in its neighbourhood'.
The rule laid it down explicitly that 'all the funds of the society
shall belong to the whole society'. From time to time there was to
be 'an average equalisation of the funds of the several branches'.
Each branch was to receive the contributions of its own members
and to pay sickness and unemployment benefit. The Executive
Council was to be responsible for the payment of funeral and
accident benefits. Each branch was required to forward to the
Executive Council a sum equal to 1s per member per quarter.

The 1856 annual delegate meeting met during the early stages of another trade depression. Certain economies were, therefore, made in the use of the funds. The disablement benefit was changed to a scale of payments depending upon the length of membership. The scale started at £20 after twelve months' membership and rose to £60 after five years' membership. If, however, the disablement resulted from epilepsy, apoplexy, paralysis or blindness, the scale of benefit rose from £20 after two years' membership to £30 after three years' membership.

The size of the Executive Council was increased to seven and the Council was charged with the general management of the Society. The members of the Executive Council were to be elected for six months by a branch or group of branches to be determined every two years by all members of the Society. Three of the seven members of the Executive Council were to be elected after three months and the remaining four after six months. This rota of three-monthly elections was then to be maintained. In addition to being responsible for the general management of the Society, the Executive Council was empowered to 'determine all appeals when the rules of the Society are silent upon the matter', to authorise the opening of new branches, and to 'give instructions to the General Secretary in the duties of his office'. The General Secretary (the title corresponding secretary was now dropped completely) was to be elected every two years; he was to devote the whole of his time to the business of the Society; and he was to be under the control of the Executive Council.

Thirty-nine delegates, together with the chairman and the General Secretary, were present at the 1856 delegate meeting. Four of the branches, Stockport, Huddersfield, Chepstow and Middlesbrough, were represented by delegates from other branches. The branches represented by their own delegates were Manchester Nos. 1 and 2; Dukenfield; London Nos. 1, 3 and 4; Woolwich (also known as London No. 2); Bristol; Liverpool Nos. 1, 2 and 3; Birkenhead; Crewe; Leeds; Hull; Dublin; Belfast; Bradford; Newcastle Nos. 1 and 2; Bolton; Wolverton; Southampton; Bilston; Warrington; Bury; St Helens; Lincoln; Swindon; Wigan; Portsmouth; Greenock; South Shields; Heywood; Dumbarton; Glasgow; Stockton-on-Tees; Deptford and Newport. The meeting reaffirmed the Society's hostility to piece-work and decided that an essay competition should be organised, with a first prize of £10 and a second prize of £5, on the evils of piece-work and the best way to combat it. The meeting also decided that former members, who had been employed as foremen and who had been compelled to leave the Society by their employers, should be eligible to rejoin, providing that during their period of foremanship they had acted fairly to the Society's members. This was intended as a counter-measure to the practice of many employers who required their foremen to resign from the Society.

JOHN ALLEN

In 1857, following the death of George Brogden, the Society elected John Allen as its new General Secretary. He was then fifty-two years of age and he was to hold office for nearly fourteen years. John Allen was born in Ireland and learnt his craft as a boilermaker in the U.S.A. He returned to the British Isles and worked in the Bristol area. He was for many years the secretary of the Bristol branch and he represented the branch at the 1856 delegate meeting. He could not have been elected to office at a more difficult time. Trade was bad and was getting worse. Hundreds of members suffered unemployment. Unemployment benefit had to be reduced early in 1858 because the Society's funds were running low. A number of other administrative economies were also made. Between September 1857 and September 1858 the Society paid out more than £6,000 in unemployment benefit, equivalent to more than £2 per member. By the autumn of 1858 John Allen had no alternative but to recommend the Executive Council to suspend the payment of unemployment benefit. The debts of the Society exceeded its assets by about £180. The effect of the depression on the trade union activity of the Society can be judged from a statement circulated by the Executive Council to all members in October 1858. It said that the 'employers are taking every advantage of us in our present weak, and we may say, dejected state'. The suspension of unemployment benefit stopped the reduction in the funds, even though it caused suffering and distress among many of the Society's members. By the end of 1858 the funds had to some extent recovered and there was a balance of £1,778. The Society now had 3,453 members organised in no less than sixty-nine branches. Trade recovered rapidly in 1859 and by the summer there were less than twenty members out of work. This new prosperity continued during 1860 and 1861. By the time of the 1862 delegate meeting, the funds of the Society had risen to more than £7,250. All the debts had been cleared and the payment of benefits had been restored. The Society had proved that it could exist not only in times of prosperity but also in times of severe unemployment. It had withstood an economic blizzard.

Chapter 5

A New Militancy

The close of the 1850s and the opening of the 1860s saw one of the most bitterly-fought struggles in the history of British trade unionism. The London building employers made a determined attempt to crush trade unionism among their employees. The immediate cause of the dispute was the sacking of a building tradesman who had participated in a deputation to his employer in favour of a reduction in the basic hours of work to nine per day. His fellow tradesmen withdrew their labour against the victimisation of one of their spokesmen. Other London building employers then locked out their workers and stated that they would not re-employ them unless each worker signed a document which stated:

> I declare that I am not now nor will I during the continuance of my engagement with you become a member of, or support, any society which, directly or indirectly, interferes with the arrangements of this or any other establishment, or with the hours or terms of labour, and I recognise the right of employer and employed individually to make any trade agreement on which they may choose to agree.

Early in 1860, after the dispute had lasted for more than six months, a settlement was secured. The claim for a nine-hour day was dropped and, in return, the employers withdrew their 'document'.

SOLIDARITY

Active trade unionists in many other industries and occupations recognised the vital importance of the fight of the London building-

57

trade workers. It was not an ordinary dispute about wages or hours of work; it was a struggle in which the very right of workers to belong to a trade union was being challenged by an organised and strong group of employers. Many other unions contributed to the funds of the London building-trade workers. Among them was the Boilermakers' Society, and in the early stages of the London building-trade dispute the Executive Council called for a voluntary donation of 1s per member to assist the building-trade workers, to be followed by a voluntary levy of 6d per week. The monthly Trade Report for September 1859 circulated by the Executive Council stated that £95 1s 8d had already been received for the fund from Boilermakers' branches. The Trade Report stated:

> We would in the first place beg to remind you that there were between eleven and twelve thousand men involved in this affair of signing a document which was intended to crush trade societies and unions among the workmen; and that the men for resisting such an attempt were turned from their work by their employers, thereby depriving them of the means of living, so that they may be starved into humble and degraded submission . . . the working classes find that the employers are about to shackle them in debased slavery and wretchedness, by signing a document which will render labour so powerless and capital so rampant that it can at any future time commit upon the employed acts of injustice with impunity . . .

The following month's issue of the Society's Trade Report again dealt at length with the building-trade dispute. It described the document which building-trade workers were being pressed by their employers to sign as 'a blow to destroy all trades unions'. It reported that already sixty-four deaths had occurred in the families of locked-out building-trade workers 'wholly attributable to their destitution and suffering'. The Trade Report urged support for the voluntary levy of 6d per week. The campaign to collect money for the building-trade workers continued long after the dispute had ended. The original donation equal to 1s per member (on average wages of from 25s to 30s per week) had been made by the Executive Council and the branches were then expected to collect 1s from each member and forward it to the central funds. The Society's Trade Report for October 1861 recorded that £176 15s 10d had been collected to replace this original donation. Only four branches, Bolton, Bury, Wigan and Heywood, had failed to contribute.

Less than four years later the Society again introduced a levy to support other workers involved in a trade dispute. This time it was a dispute involving the iron-workers of Staffordshire. The Executive Council made a donation of £100 to the iron-workers and then took a ballot of the branches as to whether a further £100, to be raised by a 6d levy, should be given. The voting in favour of the further donation was 3,797 to 901. The Society's Trade Report for April 1865 said of these donations:

> We think as many others do that we have done right in support-
> ing the men so far as the £100 goes, and that we shall be doing
> right in giving them another £100, so as to let employers see that
> union among the working classes is strong, and capable of
> resisting oppression when sought to be fixed upon them.

Other appeals for assistance for workers involved in trade disputes were received by the Society. The Executive Council was, however, reluctant to extend aid without clear authority from the members and unless the issue of the dispute was of importance. Nevertheless, they were conscious that on occasions appeals had been turned down which ought to have been supported. The London branches of the Society, for example, had urged support for an appeal from London type-founders who had been locked out by their employers when they had asked for a wage increase. Other appeals had been received from cotton spinners in Manchester, letterpress printers in Manchester and glass cutters in Wolverhampton.

In the autumn of 1865 the Executive Council balloted the branches on a proposal that they should be authorised to make grants to other unions involved in dispute without having to seek separate approval for each donation. In their appeal for support the Executive said:

> We have often refused them (ie appeals for assistance) when we
> have known the cause that they were struggling for was a just
> cause, and one they ought to succeed in. We have seen in these
> appeals different bodies of unionists in their struggle with capital
> losing ground, getting the worst of the contest, for the want of a
> little timely assistance, which we, who heard these appeals and
> statements would gladly assist and render to them if we could . . .

59

By 3,429 votes to 2,139 the branches voted in favour of the Executive Council's proposal. Many of the branches were in favour of permitting donations to be made up to a sum of £20. The Executive Council decided, however, to limit each donation to not more than £15 without a vote of the branches.

RELATIONS WITH THE ASE AND SHIPWRIGHTS

Relations with other trade unions were not, however, always friendly. There was frequent friction with the Amalgamated Society of Engineers and with the unions catering for carpenters and ship-wrights. The ASE claimed that their members who were angle-smiths were entitled to work in any branch of the metal industries where their skill could be utilised, including boilermaking and ship-building. They further claimed that they did not seek to prevent members of the Boilermakers' Society from working on engine forgings. The Boilermakers' Society contended, on the other hand, that all angle-smiths employed in shipbuilding and boilermaking should be their members. They pointed out that they did not claim the right to organise angle-smiths employed on engine-work.

These differences might not have been very serious if they had not affected the conduct of a number of strikes in which members of the Boilermakers' Society were engaged. There were a number of cases, notably one at the firm of Wigram's in London, where an angle-smith belonging to the ASE remained at work, apparently with the approval of his union, when members of the Boilermakers' Society were on strike. Members of the Boilermakers' Society who had left Wigram's were, however, prevented from obtaining work by members of the ASE in shops organised by the ASE. Difficulties also occurred in disputes at a Deptford firm, at Chatham Dockyard and in a number of railway workshops. Attempts were made by direct discussions between the two unions to smooth out the diffi-culties. They were unsuccessful. In the early winter of 1865 the Boilermakers' Society issued a pamphlet, written by the General Secretary, setting out their side of the case in the frequent disputes with the ASE.

Relations with the shipwrights were, if anything, even worse. Throughout the 1860s there were frequent disputes about the division of work in shipbuilding. The shipwrights sought to establish their right to work on metal construction. The Boilermakers' Society insisted that plating and the associated tasks with metal were for their members only. The shipwrights, they argued, were craftsmen in wood. 'Wooden men' was the term usually applied to them. The dispute with the shipwrights reached its most serious proportions in the Admiralty Dockyards. The shipwrights were well established in these yards, where they had been engaged on the construction and repair of wooden ships for many years. Despite the strong efforts of the Boilermakers' Society, the shipwrights were able to maintain their control of ship construction, whether in wood or in metal. In the private shipbuilding and ship-repairing yards the shipwrights were much less successful. Though there was a constant struggle for the control of work, the outcome in most cases was favourable to the boilermakers.

RANK-AND-FILE MILITANCY

The tradition of rank-and-file militancy in the Boilermakers' Society was already beginning to take shape in the 1860s. In April 1862 the Executive Council considered it necessary to rebuke many of the branches for supporting strikes which had not been given the Executive Council's approval. It pointed out that the rules gave the Executive Council sole authority to sanction strike pay of 12s per week. It complained that on many occasions branches had paid strike benefit contrary to its wishes. When it had remonstrated with the branches it had 'been abused and unheeded'. Branches, said the Executive Council, had been acting in 'open defiance of the Executive'.

Not all strikes, of course, were refused authorisation by the Executive Council. Support was given in the autumn of 1861 to a strike at a firm in the Old Kent Road, London. Members were requested in the monthly Trade Report 'to keep from Mr England's shop, Old Kent Road, London'. In December 1861 a levy of 4d per week on all members was introduced to support the strike at Wigram's, London, where a foreman carpenter had been put in charge of all ship construction and carpenters had been introduced to do work claimed by the Boilermakers' Society. The Executive Council described the dispute at Wigram's as 'the heaviest blow ever aimed at us'. The dispute dragged on for many months and most of the members of the Boilermakers' Society eventually found work elsewhere. In the summer of 1862 the levy in support of the strike was reduced to 1d per week. The strike at Wigram's had what at first sight might be regarded as an indeterminate outcome. The Society did not win the dispute but Wigram's ran into financial difficulties because of it. This served as a warning to other ship-builders and ship-repairers not to introduce carpenters to do 'iron work'.

MOVEMENT FOR HIGHER WAGES

Early in 1863 there was a ferment of activity among shipyard workers on the North-East coast. Trade in the shipbuilding in-dustry was booming and wages on the Tyne tended to be lower than in some of the other shipbuilding centres. For some inexplic-able reason Messrs Hawthorn's of Newcastle chose this time of prosperity to reduce the wages of their platers, riveters and holders-up. The wages of the platers were cut from 29s to 28s per week, of the riveters from 26s to 24s and 23s per week, and of the holders-up to 19s per week and less. The firm also proposed to introduce a grading scheme under which different rates of wages were to be paid. The 'iron-men' at Hawthorn's were not all mem-bers of the Boilermakers' Society but the action of the firm united members and non-members alike in their opposition. When the strike began the Executive Council of the Society withheld official support. It was prepared to support the members who had with-drawn their labour but – in accordance with the rules of the Society – it was not able to sanction financial assistance to the non-members. Fortunately, the members on the Tyne rallied magnificently to give money to support the strike. It was this support which, as the Executive Council subsequently acknowledged, enabled the strike to be brought to a victorious conclusion.

The victory at Hawthorn's and the rank-and-file support which it aroused electrified feeling right along the Tyne. The strike at Hawthorn's was quickly followed by a strike at Stephenson's, where the wages were even lower. At yard after yard, increases were won as a result of the new enthusiasm for trade unionism. The Executive Council decided to send the General Secretary to the Tyne and he reported that 'the men on the Tyne, extending to Shields, are in one perfect state of excitement; all determined to act together and become one united body of our Society, for the purpose of raising the wages and placing themselves on a level with any other part of the three kingdoms'.

On 28 February 1863 the Newcastle branch held an open recruitment meeting for members and non-members. It was enthusiastic and very well attended. A few days later a mass meeting was organised and it was filled to capacity. Resolutions were passed pledging support to the Boilermakers' Society. The following night another mass meeting was held, this time convened by the Newcastle No. 2 branch. On succeeding nights there were big meetings arranged in Jarrow, Howdon and Shields. Although there was no branch of the Boilermakers' Society in Shields, the men there were already on strike for higher pay and against the introduction of carpenters on iron-work. The movement also spread to the nearby Wear, and at a special meeting held in Sunderland no less than fifty-seven new members were recruited to the Society. Altogether, the activity on the Tyne and Wear, sparked off by the proposed wage reductions at Hawthorn's, resulted in the recruitment of hundreds of new members for the Society and widespread wage increases. It also strengthened the claim of the Boilermakers' Society that only their members should be employed on iron structural work in shipbuilding.

In 1863 two members of the Boilermakers' Society in Hull were sentenced by a local magistrate to three months' imprisonment for alleged intimidation arising out of a strike. From the issues of the Trade Report published at the time, it appears that evidence against the two members, O'Neill and Galbraith, was given by another boilermaker named Longman. The December 1863 issue of the Trade Report described him as 'traitor Longman – words which probably will be heard of by children not yet born . . .' The Society decided to support an appeal to the Queen's Bench Division against the sentences. The appeal was successful. Moreover, a counter-claim for costs was submitted. An award was made which, however, by no means met the whole of the costs incurred by the Society. A sum of approximately £200 was not recovered. To meet this cost a levy of 9d per member was imposed throughout the Society.

At the beginning of 1864 a new rank-and-file movement for wage increases began to develop. The first area to move into action was that of Liverpool and Birkenhead. After a strike lasting only two days, increases were obtained at a number of firms. At Laird's of Birkenhead where, according to the Executive Council, Mr Laird 'is well known for his principles of crushing the workmen' the strike lasted four days. Laird's sought to prolong the resistance of the Mersey employers but they failed. Shortly after the victory at Liverpool and Birkenhead wage increases were secured for members employed in Hull. Both on the Mersey and at Hull the new rate for riveters was 30s per week.

The wages movement quickly spread to almost every other part of Britain. By the end of April 1864 the Executive Council was congratulating the membership on the wage increases which had been achieved. They reported, however, that they had been criticised for not sanctioning strike action in support of wage claims, even though no less than between twenty and thirty strikes had taken place. The payment of strike benefit was not authorised in any of these disputes. The Executive Council stated that if they had paid strike benefit 'we might at this moment have hundreds of men out on strike agitating the whole country and drawing upon the funds of the Society'. The Executive Council advised the membership to seek wage increases by negotiation.

In the early summer one of the district claims led to a protracted dispute. The employers in Leeds resisted the claim for wage increases for members of the Society. A national ballot of the branches was taken and it was agreed that, if necessary, support should be given to a strike in the Leeds area. Further negotiations proved abortive and a strike was called. A considerable amount of money was raised locally from voluntary collections. More than half of it was used to pay the return fares of non-members who were recruited by the firms from other areas to work in the strike-bound shops. Strike benefit was paid to the Society's members involved in the dispute. A national levy of 9d per member was imposed to help meet the cost of the dispute. Unfortunately, the available records do not indicate whether the dispute was won or lost. There was, however, much bitter feeling aroused because of blacklegging by a small number of ASE members.

AN EMPLOYERS' OFFENSIVE

There were reports of a number of strikes through the winter of 1864–5, but by the summer of 1865 trade was declining. It was the employers who were now on the offensive. On the Clyde, employers pressed for wage reductions of from 3s to 5s per week, and at Hull there was a strike against a decision of an employer to reduce the piece-work price on rivets by 6d per hundred. The strike was settled but the principle of a reduction in the piece-work price had to be accepted. In August there were strikes of members on the Clyde at Govan, Partick and Dumbarton. All were against proposed wage reductions. There was also a strike of platers at Sunderland against a wage cut and the men at Hartlepool were threatened with a reduction. In Middlesbrough there was a strike against the introduction of shipwrights on to 'iron-work'. There was also a strike at Heywood in Lancashire, and at Belfast the employers broke an agreement with the Society by stopping certain allowances which in some cases amounted to as much as 1s per day.

During the autumn the trade depression deepened. In Dublin there was a strike of boilermakers against a wage cut of 2s per week, and in Liverpool members were on strike against reductions imposed both on time-workers and piece-workers. In Birkenhead the riveters struck against a proposal by the employers that each man should put twenty-five more rivets into position each day without any increase in pay. At the end of October 1865 the Executive Council of the Society said of the situation:

> When the dark and ominous clouds of depression lower around us and threaten almost the very existence of our Society; when capitalists, like prowling wolves, snatch eagerly at every chance, or every shadow of a chance to grind us to the earth . . . it is time not only to think but also to act.

The Executive Council also warned members not to sign contracts of employment which would limit their right to strike. At Birkenhead the platers had stopped work within twenty-four hours of being asked to do so, in support of the riveters whose piece-work burden had been increased. The employer then took legal action against them for breach of contract. Eleven platers were summoned to appear at a local court. Fortunately, they were discharged. Ac-

E

cording to a statement issued at the time by the Executive Council, the defence lawyer argued that the men ought not to have been brought before a criminal court but that the case should have been heard in the County Court. The local court apparently decided, nevertheless, to hear the case, but happily, according to the Executive Council's statement, they were finally convinced that 'they had really no jurisdiction'.

AGITATION FOR SHORTER HOURS

Though there was no easing of the trade depression in the winter of 1865–6, an agitation started for the introduction of a nine-hour working day. The initiative for this movement came from the northeast coast and, in particular, from ASE members at the Palmer Shipbuilding Company. It was argued that in a period of trade depression a reduction in working hours would create employment. The Executive Council of the Boilermakers' Society was very cautious in its attitude towards the agitation for a nine-hour day. In view of the trade depression they urged that the agitation for it should be peaceful and 'by no means to assume anything like hostility to our employers so as to cause strikes'.

The new movement was, however, already gathering strength. In Hartlepool a victory was secured and a nine-hour day was established. Members at Stockton then sought, but were refused, the support of the Executive Council to take strike action for a nine-hour day in their own area. They decided, nevertheless, to come out. The employers retaliated by legal action. A number of platers were taken to court for breach of contract. They lost the case and were sentenced to imprisonment. Meanwhile the employers at Hartlepool decided to revoke the nine-hour agreement. They locked out the members of the Boilermakers' Society and of other unions. There was also a lock-out in the Middlesbrough area. By the end of March there were over 500 men on strike and about 2,750 men locked out in the Tees area. They included boilermakers, smiths, moulders, joiners and engineers. The movement ended in defeat for the men.

The claim for shorter hours was next taken up by the men on the Clyde. The employers responded by forming the Clyde Shipbuilders and Engineers' Association. The new Association issued

66

revised conditions of employment to the workmen of their constituent firms. One of these conditions was:

> That the workmen in our employ sign a declaration binding themselves to renounce all unions of workmen, and that they will neither assist morally nor pecuniarily, directly or indirectly, any workmen who may be locked out, or who may be on strike in opposition to the interests of the employers.

The Clyde employers were determined to break trade union organisation among the shipbuilding and engineering workers. They indicated that unless these new conditions were accepted the workers would be locked out. The unions did not, of course, capitulate to the new demands of the Clyde employers. On the contrary they resisted the union-breaking efforts of the employers. The result was that more than 20,000 workers were locked out.

A controversy then arose within the Boilermakers' Society about the payment of dispute benefit. The crux of the dispute was that about 800 members on the Clyde were not entitled to benefit, either because they had only recently joined the Society or because they were in arrears. There were also charges and counter-charges between the Executive Council and the Clyde District Committee about an alleged delay in appealing to members in other parts of Britain for funds to assist those who were involved in the dispute but who, according to the rules of the Society, were not entitled to benefit. The result of this internal controversy was that extremely bad feeling was created between the Executive Council and the Clyde membership. The opinion was widely held on the Clyde that the leadership in England cared little whether the Scottish members remained in the Society or not.

The lock-out on the Clyde lasted for a number of weeks. A return to work was eventually arranged but under terms which represented a victory for the employers. The employers did not withdraw their requirement that their workers should sign a 'non-union' document. On the other hand, a number of employers did not apply this requirement rigorously. The defeat of the workers led to the near collapse of trade union organisation in a number of workshops.

SETBACK ON THE CLYDE

During the dispute on the Clyde the Executive Council had sent a full-time official, William Swan, to assist in organising resistance to the lock-out. Mr Swan had been elected in 1864 following a decision by the Society to appoint one of their members as a 'lecturer' to promote trade union organisation among boilermakers who were not members of the Society. Before the lock-out started on the Clyde Mr Swan had spent some time there on an organising mission. He was highly successful and at the beginning of 1864 it had been reported that 864 new members had been made for the Society in the Clyde area.

In the controversy between the Executive Council and the Clyde membership William Swan took the side of the Clyde members. Mutual recrimination continued through the winter of 1866–7, and by the spring of 1867 relations came to a point of crisis. More than 600 members had left the Society on the Clyde and the wages of boilermakers were as low as from 17s to 24s per week. The remaining members on the Clyde, encouraged by William Swan, refused to pay the full contributions of 4s per month then in force and insisted on paying only 3s 6d per month. Eventually the Executive Council decided to suspend all benefits to Clyde members. When they were challenged they submitted their action, for approval or disapproval, to a vote of the branches. The branches upheld the decision of the Executive Council.

By 1868 the Society could claim only 156 members in Scotland. They were divided between no less than nine branches, all of them with a mere fraction of their former strength. Even the largest branch, Glasgow No. 2, had only forty-one members and one of the branches, Paisley, had only two members. It was estimated that well over 90 per cent of the eligible workers on the Clyde were now unorganised.

William Swan had meanwhile been discharged from his employment by the Society. His support of the Clyde members was, no doubt, an important factor in his dismissal, but the ostensible reason was that trade was depressed and the Society could not afford to maintain a 'lecturer'. Indeed, one other 'lecturer' had also been elected – Mr J. Edwards of Liverpool – and he too was discharged in 1868. Following his dismissal William Swan sought to organise a new union on Clydeside. It was named the National Association of Operative Boiler Makers and Iron Ship Builders. William Swan acted as its General Secretary and it was said of it that it enjoyed the benevolent regard of the Clyde employers. The new union offered generous scales of benefit in return for a weekly contribution of no more than 7½d. Unemployment benefit was fixed at 8s per week, sickness benefit at 10s per week and superannuation benefit at 5s per week. In addition, the advertised scale of benefits included payments for disablement and for the death of a member's wife, a member's child and the member himself. Needless to say, it would have been impossible to maintain benefits at this rate from a weekly subscription of 7½d. There is no record that the new union evoked any kind of favourable response among the Clyde shipbuilding workers.

THE GENERAL SECRETARY

The defection of William Swan and the events surrounding it were the most significant but not the only controversial points concerning the full-time officials of the Society in the 1860s. In the early 1860s, before a 'lecturer' was elected, the General Secretary was the only full-time official of the Society. In 1861 on a vote of the branches his wage was increased. 270 members voted against an increase, 16 voted for 2s per week increase, 47 for 4s, 165 for 5s, 553 for 6s, 789 for 10s and 160 for 12s. It was decided in the light of this vote to increase the General Secretary's wage from £1 10s to £1 16s per week. The following year the members were asked to approve another wage increase for the General Secretary. The 1862 delegate meeting proposed that his wage should be increased by a further 6s. to £2 2s per week. There was a good case for this proposition. The General Secretary of the ASE, it was said, received £2 15s per week, together with 7s for the assistance of his son. In addition he was accommodated rent free and payment was made for his coal and gas. It was also pointed out to the delegate meeting of the Boilermakers' Society that a wage of £2 2s per week had been paid to the previous General Secretary. Nevertheless despite these facts – or perhaps because most of the members were unaware of them – the proposed increase was turned down on a vote of the branches by 1,627 to 1,367. The General Secretary,

John Allen, thereupon tendered his resignation. He complained that not only had the proposed wage increase been rejected but also his duties had been increased as a result of the decisions of the 1862 delegate meeting. A number of branches urged the Executive Council to persuade John Allen to stand again in the election for the ensuing vacancy. Allen agreed to do so but only on condition that it was made clear that he would not accept the job at less than £2 2s per week. In the subsequent ballot between three candidates Allen received 2,660 votes, his nearest rival 1,519, and the third candidate 155.

NEW RULES

The 1862 delegate meeting added a new rule on the formation of district committees. The rule provided for the division of the Society into districts and for the election of district committees from the constituent branches. It was left to the Executive Council to draw up the boundaries of the various districts and to arrange, where appropriate, for the election of district committees. A new rule was also adopted recognising the existence of piece-work. It was so worded as to imply that members would accept piece-work only when compelled to do so. The new rule provided for a dispute benefit of 7s per week, 'after being out six days', to piece-workers who resisted a reduction in piece-work prices.

The 1862 delegate meeting decided by thirty-three votes to two to oppose any further discussions on amalgamation with the ASE. The delegates also decided to appoint one or two delegates 'for the purpose of lecturing and organising the trade in all parts where deemed necessary and beneficial'. The pay for this job was fixed at 6s per day when the delegate was at home 'and 3s 6d extra when travelling'. John Pendlebury of Manchester was elected as 'lecturer' by the delegates but before the delegate meeting ended he had already resigned. The election of another 'lecturer' was then left to the Executive Council. It was not until 1863 that William Swan was elected as the first of the Society's 'lecturers' or full-time organising delegates.

The 1862 delegate meeting was attended by thirty-eight delegates. Its discussions ranged widely over the affairs of the Society. It lasted for a number of weeks and some of the delegates claimed expenses

70

for twenty-seven working days and four Sundays. The cost of the meeting was nearly £475. Delegates were allowed 9s 6d per working day and 6s for each Sunday.

During the 1860s, up to the time of the virtual collapse of the Society in Scotland, the membership and funds had increased rapidly. At the beginning of the 1860s the membership was not much more than 3,500. By 1866 it had risen to more than 9,000. The funds also increased. By 1866 they were nearly £20,000. The disputes of 1866–8 and the trade depression of the period resulted in a rapid drain of the funds. By 1868 the balance had again fallen to less than £1,000.

Chapter 6

Formation of the TUC and Trade Union Law Reform

In 1865 the treasurer of the Bradford branch of the Boilermakers' Society defaulted with a sum of £25. The Society took legal action to recover the money, but the Bradford magistrates held that the rules of the Society were unlawful because at common law a trade union was an organisation in restraint of trade. The Society lost the case but decided to appeal in view of the importance of the principle involved. It had been thought that trade union funds were protected under the Friendly Societies Act, 1855, and that unions would be able to recover their money from defaulting officials or branch officers. The Executive Council of the Boilermakers' Society was convinced that the decision of the Bradford magistrates was the result of prejudice. They were reinforced in this view because, only a few weeks earlier, they had taken successful legal action in the neighbouring city of Leeds to recover money taken by the Leeds branch secretary. The January 1866 issue of the Trade Report of the Executive Council said of the Bradford case:

> 'The Bradford magistrates were two iron masters who were the principals in the Yorkshire lockout of the iron makers, and, we may say, were strongly opposed to ours and all other trade unions as was made plain in their hearing of the case.'

The Executive Council said in the Trade Report that it was necessary that an appeal should be lodged. It was essential, if there was any possibility at all, to punish 'the villain who would rob us and then make a public laughing stock of our Society and its representatives'. The Society was, however, short of money. The necessary funds could be raised only by introducing a levy of 1s per member.

72

This was done, and the case was eventually taken to the Court of the Queen's Bench. It was all to no avail. The higher court, in effect, confirmed the decision of the Bradford magistrates. It was held that trade unions were not protected by the Friendly Societies Act and had no right of legal action to recover money from defaulting officials.

THE HARSHNESS OF THE LAW

This decision caused widespread concern throughout the trade union movement, not least to the unions of craftsmen which placed such importance on the protection of their funds used primarily for benevolent purposes. It was clear that the financial stability of the unions was threatened unless the law could be changed. There was also a growing demand to change the law affecting the contractual relationship between employer and worker. This was then known as the law of master and servant. If a worker broke his contract of employment, he could be taken to court on a criminal charge and, if convicted, could be sentenced to imprisonment. On a number of occasions the Executive Council of the Boilermakers' Society had appealed to members to exercise caution not to break contracts of employment in industrial disputes nor to enter into contracts which required them to give long periods of notice to terminate them. The law of master and servant had been made a very live issue in the Boilermakers' Society when, in 1866, a number of members were sent to prison for breach of contract arising out of a dispute on hours of work in the Tees-side towns. (See last chapter.)

Members of many other unions were also affected by the harshness of the law of master and servant. Professor B. C. Roberts in his history of *The Trades Union Congress 1868–1921*, pointed out that the Glasgow Trades Council had obtained information showing that over 10,000 cases under the law of master and servant came before the courts each year. Efforts made by trade unionists to change the law did much to stimulate co-operation between different unions and to assist the formation and early development of trades councils in a number of the bigger cities. Partly as a result of a campaign conducted by the unions some improvement was secured by the passing of new legislation in 1867.

NEED FOR TRADE UNION CO-OPERATION

It was, however, another event which did more than anything else to impress upon trade unionists the need for some kind of joint and continuing organisation to represent their interests. In October 1866 an attempt was made to coerce a non-unionist in the Sheffield cutlery trade by exploding gunpowder in his house. Opponents of trade unionism said that this was typical of the trade union movement. The outcome was that the Government appointed a Royal Commission to investigate trade unionism and, in particular, to find out the real facts about the Sheffield outrage. The appointment of an official enquiry was supported by most of the trade union leaders of the time. Indeed, they had agreed that there should be an enquiry, for they were concerned to defend the name of the trade union movement and to make it clear that the violence in Sheffield was not typical of the methods of the unions.

In June 1866 a conference of trade union representatives had been held in Sheffield to form The United Kingdom Alliance of Organised Trades. This was before the violent incident in Sheffield, and the unions were mainly interested in forming an organisation for mutual assistance in lock-outs. The Boilermakers' Society was represented at the conference. There was considerable disagreement between the unions about what constituted a lock-out as distinct from a strike, and subsequently the Boilermakers' Society and most other unions withdrew from the Alliance. Its life was brief.

Strong support for the Sheffield conference was given by the newspaper, *Beehive*. This newspaper was published by a company which had raised much of its capital in share clubs based on trade union branches. The inspiration for *Beehive* came from George Potter, who first came into prominence as an official of a small London union of carpenters at the time of the building-trade dispute in 1859. George Potter had exceptional talents and a vigorous personality. In general, his point of view on most trade union issues was more radical than that of the leadership of the bigger amalgamated unions based on London. Some of the leaders of these unions – who later were described by the historians, Sidney and Beatrice Webb, as the 'Junta' – were frequently at odds with George Potter and *Beehive*.

The presentation of trade union evidence to the Royal Commission and the conduct of the campaign to clear the name of the trade union movement were very much in the hands of the 'Junta'. They carried out their task very competently. They were able to show that the bigger amalgamated unions were run efficiently; that they did much to protect their members against the hazards of unemployment and sickness; that they favoured conciliation and the peaceful settlement of trade disputes; and that their methods had nothing in common with the violence which had occurred in Sheffield. George Potter and his colleagues, on the other hand, were not able officially to attend the hearings of the Royal Commission, after one of their trade union nominees had been excluded for making a public attack on one of the Commissioners who was continuing to voice anti-trade union sentiments.

The Royal Commission published its findings in March 1869. There was both a Majority and a Minority Report. The Majority Report recommended that conditional legal recognition should be given to trade unions. The unions were, however, not to pursue actions which would lead to a breach of contract nor to discriminate against non-unionists. Protection was to be given to their funds, subject to their rules not containing provisions for limiting the number of apprentices; limiting or preventing the introduction of new machinery; prohibiting piece-work or the employment of union members with non-union men. Unions were also to be required not to support members of other unions involved in a trade dispute. The Minority Report, in contrast, urged that legal recognition should be given to trade unions without introducing new conditions. Unions would be given the cover of the Friendly Societies Acts, so that their funds would be protected.

The publication of the findings of the Royal Commission had confirmed that the trade unions were not engaged in violent activities. For the most part the unions were performing a valuable service in protecting their members against the worst effects of unemployment, sickness and accidents, and even in their collective-bargaining functions they were more concerned to resolve than to promote disputes.

The trade union movement conducted a vigorous campaign in support of the recommendations of the Minority Report. The Executive Council of the Boilermakers' Society strongly supported the campaign for the reform of trade union law. The Trade Report of April 1869 said of the Majority Report of the Royal Commission:

> Shall those Commissioners who reported, and who wish to oppress trade unionists, be allowed to go forward in their career of class legislation, to the injury of labour and the ruin of every trade unionist who stands determined to protect his home, his family and himself by an honest remuneration for his labours.

The Executive Council urged members to petition their Members of Parliament in favour of reform. 'Be alive to your own interests,' said the Executive Council. 'Your freedom or slavery now depends upon your own action.'

THE TUC

The campaign for the protection of the good name of trade unionism and for law reform underlined to many trade unionists the need for the holding of a congress of trade unionists for the purpose of discussion and the formulation of proposals to advance the interests of the movement. In 1868 the Manchester Trades Council decided to convene a trades congress which they hoped would be the first of a series of annual meetings. At these annual meetings it was suggested, according to the letter of invitation, that 'previously carefully prepared papers' should be discussed 'with a view to the merits and demerits of each question being thoroughly ventilated through the medium of the public press'.

The 1868 Congress was representative mainly of trades councils – except those of London and Glasgow – together with a small number of delegates direct from trade societies. The London 'Junta' did not participate in the Manchester Congress and, indeed, regarded it with some suspicion. George Potter, on the other hand, was present at the Manchester Congress. Many of the delegates at Manchester reciprocated the suspicions of the 'Junta'. Nevertheless, despite these mutual suspicions the proceedings of the 1868 Congress and of the following annual congresses did much to bring about a reconciliation between factions and to provide eventually for the emergence of a united leadership for the movement. Late in 1870 the Boilermakers' Society decided to be represented at the annual Trades Congress or, as it has since become known, the TUC. Shortly afterwards, in 1871, they decided also to support the Labour Representation League which had been formed in 1869 to 'secure the return to Parliament of qualified working men . . .'

After the initial Trades Congress in Manchester in 1868, the Congress for the following year was held in Birmingham. It, too, was largely representative of trades councils, including this time the London Trades Council. The London Trades Council was charged with the task of convening the next Congress. It did not do so, however, until March 1871. This Congress was, for the first time, really representative of the British trade union movement. It was also the first Congress at which the Boilermakers' Society was represented. The 1871 accounts of the Society contain two items of expenditure which probably refer to the 1871 Congress. The first is for £1 to 'G. Potter'. This may have been a donation to Potter's *Beehive*, but it is more likely that it was to do with the 1871 Congress. Potter was the elected chairman of the Congress. The second item of expenditure was 10s for 'share of conference room, London'. It was listed immediately beneath the entry 'G. Potter'. It was probably the Boilermakers' share of the expenses for the 1871 TUC.

The Government's Trade Union Bill, following the report of the Royal Commission, had been published shortly before the 1871 Congress. It provided for the registration of trade unions and gave legal protection to their funds. On the other hand, it affirmed that trade unionists were liable to criminal prosecution for a wide variety of actions designed to coerce or intimidate employers. Trade unionists were quick to recognise that the effect of this provision would be to make a criminal offence of almost any kind of pressure on employers exerted in the course of a dispute. Whilst it could be argued that this was no worse than the existing law, trade unionists were apprehensive that the codification of offences within a new statute would result in more vigorous oppression.

The 1871 TUC appointed a Parliamentary Committee to continue the representations made by the trade union movement against the objectionable section of the Government's proposed new legislation. A campaign was also conducted to stir public opinion to support the trade union movement. This campaign was not immediately successful but the Government were, nevertheless, persuaded to divide their proposals into two separate measures. The first, the

Trade Union Act, contained the clauses which gave legal recognition to trade unions and enabled them to protect their funds. The second contained the objectionable clauses on criminal offences.

The Boilermakers' Society supported the continuing efforts of the TUC Parliamentary Committee for more favourable trade union legislation. In 1871 a donation of £5 was made towards the cost of the work of the Parliamentary Committee. When the Trade Union Act 1871 was passed, the Boilermakers' Society was among the first to take advantage of its provisions for registration. It was the third trade union to register. The date of registration was 2 January 1872.

A year later in the annual report for 1872 an appeal was made to all members of the Boilermakers' Society to appoint deputations to candidates at the next General Election to press for the amendment of trade union law. The report said:

We wish to be placed as trade unionists on an equal footing in the eyes of the law as all other classes, and do not wish to be granted any special favours. We wish to obtain justice and this we must have. As our rules are registered according to Act of Parliament, and an annual return made of income and expenditure, we have nothing to cloak or hide from public view. Let us, therefore, give our votes to such as will do for us all in their power in the direction in which we are aiming, and then we may confidently hope that in the end we shall obtain that which we seek.

NEW INJUSTICES

At the end of 1872 there was a legal case, involving a number of gas-stokers in London, which underlined the need for further trade union law reform. Five gas-stokers, who were participating in a trade dispute, were sentenced to twelve months' imprisonment. The judge, in passing sentence, said that they had left their employment in a conspiracy and that by misleading others they had been guilty of a 'wicked conspiracy'. An appeal for money to help the families of the gas-stokers was issued by a committee of leading trade unionists and other sympathisers. It was published in the Trade Report of the Boilermakers' Society, together with the comment that the law had been strained 'to raise a beacon terror to frighten all trades unionists into their employers' terms'.

In May 1873 the Trade Report of the Boilermakers' Society warned that the employers were organising to resist any change in the law. A circular issued by the General Association of Master Engineers, Shipbuilders, Iron and Brassfounders was reproduced. The circular said that measures should be taken 'to resist the trades unionists in their attempts to efface from the statute books such laws as experience is daily showing to be of paramount importance for the safety of capital, the protection of labour and the property of the country'.

The agitation for trade union law reform was carried to an even higher pitch when, in the spring of 1873, sixteen women, wives of agricultural labourers, were sentenced to hard labour for picketing 'blacklegs' who had taken the jobs of their locked-out husbands. The story can best be told in the words of the Boilermakers' Trade Report:

> The climax was reached a few days since when the magistrates of Chipping Norton, in the County of Oxford, sent sixteen women to prison for from seven to ten days each for – what do you think? – intimidating men! The facts are these: A few weeks ago, owing to an agitation among the agricultural labourers for an increase of wages, the farmers around the village determined on a lock-out. The result was that men with families, who have barely managed to keep body and soul together on 10s a week, were suddenly deprived of that small pittance; and had it not been for the union they must have sued for forgiveness for the shocking sin of 'asking for more' – or have died. At this point a whisper went around the village that a farmer was about to bring in 'new hands', which was done. The men themselves, who were thus supplanted, appeared not to have interfered in any way with the interlopers; but the women could not sit down contented and see their husbands deprived of their employment, and they and their families starving, without striking at least one blow for freedom. As the thought, so was the act. Sixteen women went out to meet, as they came from their work, the men who had interposed to ruin their husbands, and the men betook themselves to flight, and here the matter ought to have ended. But no; the

79

cowardly farmer summoned the women, under the Criminal Law Amendment Act, and the whole of them were sent to hard labour, some with their infants at their breasts.

A big demonstration of trade unionists was held in London on Whitsuntide Monday 1873 to protest against these injustices. The Boilermakers' Society supported the demonstration and again urged all members to press candidates at the forthcoming General Election for the repeal of the Criminal Law Amendment Act, the reform of the Master and Servant Act so that breach of contract should no longer be a criminal offence, and the elimination of the crime of 'conspiracy' in relation to trade disputes.

LAW REFORM

Trade unionists were active in petitioning candidates at the 1874 General Election and many of them gave their support to candidates – either Liberal or Conservative – who pledged their support for trade union law reform. In addition, there was a small number of independent workers' candidates who stood in the election. Two trade unionists were elected to Parliament. One of them, a miners' leader, Alexander McDonald, had been sponsored by a local Working Men's Radical Association and by the Labour Representation League to which the Boilermakers' Society had given its support some few years earlier. The election resulted in the overthrow of the Liberal Government. The new Prime Minister was the Conservative, Disraeli. The new Government appointed a Royal Commission on the Labour Laws but its work was largely ineffective. Nevertheless, in 1875 the Government introduced new legislation which went a very long way towards meeting trade union demands for law reform. The Criminal Law Amendment Act was repealed and a new law, the Conspiracy and Protection of Property Act, 1875, was passed. This removed many of the objectionable features of the law of conspiracy in relation to trade disputes and gave a measure of protection for peaceful picketing in trade disputes. The new Act also repealed the Master and Servant Act, 1867, and other enactments which had made breaches of contract a criminal offence. The only exceptions were breaches of contract likely to lead to loss of life, serious injury or serious damage to property, or breaches of contract by workers employed in certain public utilities.

80

Robert Knight

D. C. Cummings

James Cooper

John Allen

James Conley

John Hill

Robert Knight – General Secretary 1871–1899

D. C. Cummings – elected General Secretary 1899

James Cooper – one of the earliest active members of the Society

John Allen – General Secretary 1857–1871

James Conley and John Hill – stood as Labour candidates in 1906 General Election

6. The General Offices, Lifton House in its original state

The 1875 annual report of the Boilermakers' Society welcomed the 'great improvements in the laws relating to labour'. It warned, however, that time alone would show 'how far these amendments are calculated to give us as trade unionists that complete justice which we claim as a right'.

Chapter 7

A New Phase and a New General Secretary

The period of change in trade union law, 1870–5, was also a period of change for the Boilermakers' Society. By 1870 the General Secretary, John Allen, was at the age of sixty-five. For some time there had been a growing feeling among active members that when he reached this age he should retire. There had been criticism of his administrative methods or alleged lack of method. It was eventually agreed that John Allen should retire in March 1871 and that he should be granted a pension of £1 per week.

ROBERT KNIGHT

In the election for a new General Secretary the successful candidate was Mr Robert Knight of Devonport. He was thirty-seven years of age when elected and he had been a member of the Society for thirteen years. He was an angle-iron smith by trade. He had been an active member of the Society, a frequent correspondent to local newspapers in defence of boilermakers' interests, and he had shown a keen interest in the development of education. Robert Knight was also a strong co-operator and had served both as chairman and secretary of a co-operative society. He was also a Sunday-school teacher.

Robert Knight was fortunate in being elected General Secretary at a time when trade was prosperous. It made it easier for him to put the administration of the Society on a sounder footing. He took the opportunity which the circumstances provided. His first annual report was a model of efficiency and tidiness. He was able to point out that at no time in the history of the Society had there been such full employment. Many employers had made concessions on wages and on hours of labour. The nine hour day, he pointed out, had now become generally recognised for the Society's members.

Robert Knight was to be the General Secretary of the Boilermakers' Society for almost the remainder of the nineteenth century, a period of about twenty-nine years. Despite periodic fluctuations in trade and a serious depression which lasted through part of the seventies and eighties, it was a period of expansion for the main industry, shipbuilding, in which boilermakers were employed. From 1885 until the end of his career over 70 per cent of the world's new tonnage was being launched from British shipyards. In some years Britain's proportion rose to over 80 per cent. In one of the main centres, the Wear, where output in 1870 was only about 10 per cent higher than thirty years earlier, the growth of the shipbuilding industry was rapid. From a figure of 70,000 tons in 1870, output rose to 295,000 tons in 1901 and was to grow even further in years ahead.

Robert Knight epitomised both the strength and the weakness of trade unionism among the aristocracy of labour in the heyday of British capitalism. He was efficient in administration and was concerned always to protect the funds of the union. His policy was one of conciliation towards the employers. This policy provided gains when trade was good, and when it was depressed the financial strength and provident benefits of the union helped to protect members. It answered to the occupational needs – as they saw it – of most members of the Boilermakers' Society. Nevertheless, it did not provide an adequate answer to some of the wider economic and social changes which took place during Robert Knight's period of office, particularly towards the end of the century. British capitalism was to be challenged by newer capitalist powers, and within Britain a new trend was to develop, both industrially and politically, within the working-class movement.

THE WINNING OF THE NINE HOUR DAY

The nine hour working-day of which Robert Knight spoke in his first annual report was not achieved without struggle. At the centre of the struggle were the engineering workshops and shipyards on the Tyne and Wear. The initiative came mainly from members of the Amalgamated Society of Engineers in Sunderland. In April 1871 engineering workers in Sunderland came out on strike in favour of a claim for a nine hour working day. The strike was condemned by the leadership of the ASE but it proved, nevertheless, to be successful. The employers conceded the full demand of the men, and the shorter working day was introduced from 2 May. The movement then spread to Newcastle. The claim of the workers was rejected by the employers and towards the end of May thousands of workers withdrew their labour, including the boilermakers employed on the Tyne. The strike lasted nearly five months and ended, as in the struggle at Sunderland, in a victory for the workers. The employers agreed to introduce a nine hour working day from 1 January 1872.

At the beginning of the strike the members of the ASE received strike benefit of 3s per week. This, however, was subsequently increased, and, by the last week of the strike, the payment of benefit had risen to 12s per man and 1s for each child. Many donations were made to the strike fund from other unions.

The Boilermakers' Society was able to give much more generous financial support to its members. All members received 18s per week, made up of dispute benefit paid in accordance with the rules, supplemented by benevolent grants. Hundreds of pounds were contributed by branches of the Boilermakers' Society towards the central strike fund to assist strikers who were not members of any trade union, or who had only recently joined and were not, therefore, eligible for benefit.

The winning of the nine hour day in 1871 as direct result of the strike of workers on the Wear and the Tyne was the most successful mass action of engineering workers and boilermakers since their respective unions had been formed.

PROSPERITY

The prosperity in trade and the improvement in administrative efficiency as a result of the election of a new General Secretary led to a considerable strengthening of the Boilermakers' Society. No less than thirteen new branches were opened in 1871, including one as far afield as Constantinople. Membership went up by 1,722 in the course of twelve months, and at the end of 1871 nearly 9,000 members were on the books of the Society. The funds of the Society also increased by nearly £5,000.

In his annual report Robert Knight included a summary of expenditure on the main financial benefits to members for the previous five years. This showed that the average sum paid per member for the whole of the five year period for sickness, funeral, medical, unemployment, superannuation and accident benefit was £8, in contrast to only 3½d per member paid in dispute benefit. Robert Knight said:

> The result at once shows that most of our demands (if just) can be obtained without strikes, which no one deplores more than myself. I am aware that disputes will arise between masters and men as long as human nature remains as it is; but experience teaches me that nine tenths of these disputes can be settled by conciliation . . .

The annual report also contained a table of wages paid and hours worked in boilershops and shipyards in all branches of the Society. This table revealed that the highest-paid men in the Society were the angle-iron smiths and platers; their weekly wage varied from about £1 6s or £1 7s in one or two yards on the north-east coast, to about £2 4s in the best paid shipyards in the London area. The lowest paid members were the holders-up. Their wages varied from as low as 15s up to about £1 9s in boilershops in the Manchester area. In nearly all parts of the country the normal hours of work were listed as fifty-four per week. Longer hours were, however, worked in some of the shipyards and boilershops on the Clyde and in Dundee.

The membership of the Boilermakers' Society continued to rise throughout the first half of the 1870s. This increase took place during the years of prosperity in 1871–3 and continued even during the years of trade depression in 1874 and 1875.

Robert Knight as General Secretary continued to urge that every effort should be made to settle disputes by negotiation. In the 1872 annual report he said:

> Whenever disputes arise – as they will now and again – it is far better to submit the matter to arbitration and pursue a policy of conciliation than to resort to a strike which is always more or

85

less productive of bad feeling. No one can be more opposed to
strikes than myself, and in this matter the Council are of similar
opinion, believing as they do, that it is far better to send a deputation to the employer to discuss the matter and to endeavour to
bring about a happy termination than to act somewhat hastily
and use extreme measures.

The prosperity of the early 1870s made it easier for members of the
Boilermakers' Society to secure wage increases. Increases were obtained at many firms. In July 1873 the Monthly Report of the
Society commented that 'The money paid for disputes is getting
beautifully less each quarter'. The annual report for 1873 stated
that a large proportion of employers recognised that the Society's
representatives were not agitators but conciliators. The report went
on to say that many strikes were caused by the bad manners of
supercilious employers who, by good luck, had acquired wealth
without the feeling of gentlemen.

HELP TO OTHERS

The policy of conciliation pursued by the leaders of the Boilermakers' Society did not, however, prevent them from showing
sympathy towards and extending practical solidarity to the efforts
of agricultural labourers to organise in trade unions. Frequently the
agricultural labourers were faced with the bitter hostility of employers and the local clergy of the Church of England. Trade union
organisation among agricultural labourers began to take hold in
1871. By the early summer of 1872 a National Agricultural Labourers' Union had been formed on a national basis under the leadership of Joseph Arch. Nearly £200 was given to the new union by
the Boilermakers' Society. In 1873 trade union organisation spread
rapidly among farm workers, mainly, however, in the South of
England. By the end of 1873 it was estimated that the National
Agricultural Labourers' Union had over a thousand branches and
a membership of more than 100,000. A weekly journal supporting
the union was selling more than 30,000 copies each issue.

This strengthening of the National Agricultural Labourers' Union
was, however, short-lived. When trade conditions turned for the
worse many of the farmers launched a bitter attack upon labourers
who were members of the union, and demanded wage reductions.

86

Thousands of agricultural labourers were locked out and were reduced to conditions of extreme poverty. In the spring of 1874 the
Boilermakers' Society took a ballot on a proposed shilling per member levy to assist the agricultural labourers. By a more than ten
to one majority, 6,937 to 613, the Society's members voted in
favour of the levy. This was a magnificent example of trade union
solidarity. Considerable sums to assist the agricultural labourers
were also voted by a number of other trade unions. Nevertheless,
despite this help the agricultural labourers were defeated.

The Boilermakers' Society also gave strong support to the efforts
of Mr Plimsoll, the Member of Parliament for Derby, to improve
the standard of seaworthiness in British ships. Mr Plimsoll addressed a mass meeting of more than 3,000 people in a public hall
in Liverpool in April 1873. The chairman of the meeting was Robert
Knight, the General Secretary of the Boilermakers' Society. Mr
Plimsoll explained that he was seeking to obtain a more effective
method of surveying vessels during their construction, and to improve the standard of repair of vessels. He hoped also to arrange
for the inspection of vessels and to stop the dangerous practice of
sending vessels to sea heavily overladen. The Boilermakers' Society
made a donation of £250 to assist the campaign of Mr Plimsoll
and arranged also for a voluntary collection to be made among
members. In 1873 a further £250 was granted on a ballot vote of
the members. The majority in favour of the donation was 6,684 to
1,203. No doubt many members of the Boilermakers' Society were
moved to support this campaign by their deeply felt concern for
the safety of seamen. At the same time they were aware that an
improvement in the standard of seaworthiness of British ships
would help to create new work for shipbuilding and ship-repair
workers.

CONSTITUTIONAL CHANGES

The prosperity of the early 1870s encouraged the Society to elect
full-time district delegates on the north-east coast, on the Mersey
and in London. Proposals were also advanced for a uniform rate of
payment for members of district committees. The existing payments varied widely between one district and another. The Executive Council suggested that a uniform rate of 5d per hour should

be introduced. This was supported on a ballot vote of the membership by 6,930 to 495. Towards the end of 1873 it was decided to increase the weekly wage of district delegates to £2 12s. This decision was made on a ballot vote of the membership; 2,481 votes were cast for a payment of £2 12s; 1,199 for £2 16s; 2,647 for £3; and 2,838 against any increase at all. The Executive Council decided in the light of these figures that a wage of £2 12s would be acceptable to the majority.

Early in 1874 the Executive Council proposed that there should be a change in the method of amending the rules. Delegate meetings, they said, were not satisfactory. The delegates were drawn from only a minority of branches and the other branches had very little opportunity to express an opinion on the issues before the Society. The Executive Council proposed, therefore, that a General Council should be established and that each member of the General Council should be elected by branches grouped together for this purpose. They further proposed that the General Council should meet once every two years, or whenever summoned by the Executive Council. It was suggested also that a meeting of the General Council should be summoned whenever requested by at least twenty branches of the Society. The General Council, it was proposed, should discuss and determine all matters referred to it by the Executive Council and should consider all proposals for amendments to rules. Any proposed amendments which they approved were then to be submitted to a vote of the membership. This proposal of the Executive Council for the election of a General Council was approved by the Society by 5,828 votes to 1,868.

The first General Council was elected in the spring of 1874. Early in the summer it met and proposed a number of changes in the rules. It proposed that members of the Executive Council and of district committees should receive a payment of 6d per hour for their services. It suggested that branches should be able to decide for themselves whether or not to accept caulkers into membership of the Society. Where, however, they were admitted it was insisted that they should remain as caulkers and should not work in other trades. It was suggested that the four-weekly membership subscription to the Society should be 4s. There were proposals also to improve a number of the provident benefits. A new rule was proposed which, in effect, gave recognition to the existence of shop stewards and to their importance in the structure of the Society. The rule said that, where shop stewards were appointed and where they subsequently lost their jobs because of activity on behalf of the Society, the Executive Council should have power to provide them with benefit. It was suggested also that the rule relating to Trade Protection Members should be amended. It was urged that persons over forty years of age should be admitted as Trade Protection Members on payment of an entrance fee of 10s and a monthly contribution of 2s. Trade Protection Members were to be eligible for dispute benefit. For the first time branches were to be entitled to admit Trade Protection Members into their meetings according to their own discretion. These proposals for amendments to rules were placed before the Society by ballot vote and all were accepted.

DEPRESSION

In the summer of 1874 trade began to turn for the worse. The period of peaceful collaboration between employers and employed, in which all to some extent had shared the benefits of prosperity, was also coming to an end. In Stockton more than thirty members of the Boilermakers' Society were locked out at the boiler shop of Blair and Company. This was the first lock-out for a number of years which affected the Society's members.

During 1872 and 1873 in the period of prosperity the Society had managed to gain membership at Blair and Company, despite the hostility of the firm. For many years previously the management had refused to employ any members of the Boilermakers' Society. By the end of 1873 about 80 per cent of the boilermakers employed by the firm were members of the Society. When, however, trade turned downwards in the summer of 1874 the management locked out all men who had joined the union. The lock-out dragged on through the summer and eventually the Society was left with no alternative but to find jobs elsewhere for most of the men involved. The firm succeeded in breaking trade union organisation among their workers. In October 1874, as trade worsened, the employers on the Clyde passed to the offensive. They issued a circular to their member firms stating that, in their opinion, the time had arrived when an effort should be made to retrieve 'the position lost in

1871 and secure either an increase in the hours of labour or a decrease of wages or both'. The Clyde employers were well aware that they had one tremendous advantage: the majority of the boilermakers on the Clyde were not members of the Boilermakers' Society. The individual Clyde employers were not slow to follow the lead given to them. In November the district secretary of the Boilermakers' Society reported that there were strikes in seven yards on the Clyde. The men on strike were, however, mainly joiners and blacksmiths. Unfortunately, the men employed in the trades covered by the Boilermakers' Society were mainly non-unionists.

The pressure for wage reductions, which started on the Clyde, soon extended to other areas. Notices of wage reductions were posted up outside shipyards and boilershops on the Tyne, the Wear and the Tees. At Hull more than 600 members of the Society withdrew their labour in protest against large pay reductions ordered by the employers. There was a strike also in the Liverpool area, and the district delegate for Liverpool and Birkenhead complained in his report that riveters were doing plating work for riveters' wages. So serious was the attack on the wages of boilermakers in most parts of Britain that the monthly report of the Executive Council for December 1874 asked whether it 'would not be better to submit to a small reduction in those districts where trade is depressed . . . so as to allow the masters to secure work and give employment to all our members'.

The attack of the employers on the wages of the workers continued in 1875. The reports of the district delegates and district secretaries spoke of wage reductions in many yards and workshops. The district secretary for the Tees said that reductions 'spread like an epidemic to the Tyne, Wear, Tees and the Humber'.

The strike at Liverpool finally ended with defeat for the union. At Hull the strike was brought to an end by the men accepting a reduction of 5 per cent in their wages. On the Tyne more than 800 members withdrew their labour to resist a reduction of 10 per cent on day wages and 15 per cent on piece-work prices. In some areas – for example, at Barrow – the Society was able successfully to resist demands by the employers for wage reductions.

In the first three months of 1875 the Society paid out more money in dispute benefit than in the preceding seven years. The Executive

Council said that members had resorted to strike action as a necessary evil in order to avoid greater calamity. They asked, however, 'might not the same ends be accomplished at times without resorting to strikes if our members used a little more discretion, and to this question we are compelled to answer in the affirmative, as our members are too impetuous and rush headlong into difficulties . . .'

TRADE UNION FEDERATION

To meet the attacks of the employers, active members in the engineering and shipbuilding unions urged that some kind of trade union federation should be established in the engineering and shipbuilding industries. Four unions with a total membership of 76,000 – the Amalgamated Society of Engineers, the Ironfounders, the Steam Engine Makers and the Boilermakers – participated in preliminary discussions for the formation of a Federation. Each Society in these discussions, it was stressed, was to retain its individuality but there could be concerted action when the common interests of the unions were affected.

During the period of the 1875 TUC held in January, a number of unions, including the Ironworkers, the Carpenters and the Boilermakers, held a meeting to consider the formation of a federation of unions for the purpose of creating a central fund to be used to support any constituent organisation in an important trade struggle. The societies which participated did not commit themselves to form such a federation, but a committee was elected to draw up a report on the proposal. Nothing, however, came of it, and in February a further conference was held of delegates from the ASE, the Ironfounders, the Steam Engine Makers and the Boilermakers, at which it was decided to set up a central reserve fund to help the unions resist any attack from the employers. A declaration was adopted for submission to the members of the four societies. It drew attention to the efforts of the employers to increase the length of the working day and said that there were good grounds for believing that, unless immediate steps were taken to oppose such attempts, the Employers' Federation would endeavour to carry out their desires upon a national scale. The proposal for the creation of a central reserve fund and for a Federation of Engineering Trades was submitted to the membership of the Boiler-

91

makers' Society and was approved by 8,869 votes to 1,408. Unfortunately, no immediate steps were taken to establish the Federation, although the fault evidently did not rest with the Boilermakers' Society. The Executive Council, and Robert Knight in particular, were strongly in favour of the principle of trade unity.

It was not until almost a year later that more definite proposals were formulated for the establishment of a trade federation. These were then submitted to the members of the Society, together with a strong recommendation for approval from the Executive Council. Nevertheless, this time the majority in favour of the proposed federation was comparatively narrow. The number of votes cast in favour was 5,876, and the number against was 4,371. Opposition to the principle of federation had also become stronger in a number of other unions. Eventually, in view of this opposition, it was agreed that no useful purpose would be served by pursuing the principle of federation. This was undoubtedly a setback for trade union unity in the engineering and shipbuilding industries. The question of federation was not raised again for a number of years. During a period of depression many members of craft unions were concerned mainly to conserve the financial reserves of their organisations. They were reluctant to pool resources with, or even to be drawn into a trade dispute alongside, a poorer union. This did not make for trade union unity.

Robert Knight and his colleagues, however, never lost sight of the advantages to be gained from trade union co-operation among craftsmen in the shipbuilding and engineering industries. The Boilermakers' Society remained a firm supporter of trade union federation. Moreover, the Boilermakers' Society was now playing a leading part in the wider trade union movement. In 1875 the General Secretary of the Society, Robert Knight, was elected to the Parliamentary Committee of the TUC. He was third in the voting. Following his election he was appointed to the chair of the Parliamentary Committee. This was a tribute to his very considerable ability.

UNEMPLOYMENT AND WAGE REDUCTIONS

Trade did not improve in 1875 and the employers' attack on wages continued. Resistance to this attack was widespread. In Dundee the boilermakers were able to defeat a proposal to reduce wages, but only after they had been on strike for about two months. The July issue of the monthly report contained a strong attack on members who rush 'headlong into a strike'. It urged that every effort should be made to settle disputes by peaceful means. The report went on 'there cannot be a greater mistake than to suppose that we should be always acting as antagonists to our employers; it is to our best interest to work on peaceful terms with them, and by our actions prove that it is also to their interest to employ Society men'.

In November it was reported that a 5 per cent reduction in piece-work prices had been accepted on the Tyne. In December the Executive Council reported that the month had been one of continuing conflict between members and their employers. Members were on strike at Dumbarton, Middlesbrough, Port Glasgow, Paisley, Ebbw Vale and Stockton.

During 1875 the Society paid out more than £16,600 in unemployment benefit to members. This was more than the total paid out during the previous seven years. The amount paid out in dispute benefit in 1875 was £4,660, considerably more than during the preceding eight years.

Chapter 8

A Period of Trial and Suffering

The second half of the 1870s was a period of great difficulty for the Boilermakers' Society. Trade was slack and grew steadily worse towards the end of the decade. In 1879 there was more unemployment among the Society's members than in any previous year since the formation in 1834. At one period in 1879 more than 3,500 of the total membership of about 17,400 were drawing either unemployment or dispute benefit from the Society. In the year 1879 the Society paid out no less than £32,000 in unemployment benefit alone.

A NEW ATTACK

Indications that a new attack on wages and hours of labour was to take place came early in 1876. There were strikes in a number of towns against wage reductions. One of the longest was in Dumbarton. The employer, Archibald McMillan of Dumbarton dockyard, reduced the wages of his workers at the end of 1875. The men protested but to no avail. They then took strike action. The firm replied towards the end of January 1876 by circulating a letter to all other employers on the Clyde, giving the names of the men on strike and urging other employers not to employ them. In March 1876 the General Secretary of the Boilermakers' Society wrote an extremely conciliatory letter to Archibald McMillan stating that he hoped that it would be possible to open negotiations for a settlement. A stern reply was received to the effect that when the strikers had had enough they would probably ask the firm to settle the dispute on its own terms. The firm said 'We will let them know our decision.' The Executive Council of the Boilermakers' Society justifiably described the employer as 'nothing less than a blustering, bullying, dogmatic tyrant'. If the men submitted to him, said the Executive Council, they would be treated as abject slaves. The strike was eventually concluded in July 1876. The terms were not favourable to the boilermakers, but they were not so severe as originally proposed by the firm. Unfortunately, the strike had been weakened by the decision of a number of carpenters to undertake riveting. The boilermakers themselves remained as solid at the end of the strike as they were at the beginning.

Despite the partial defeat of the Boilermakers' Society in the Dumbarton dispute the solidarity which had been displayed did much to strengthen the influence of the Society throughout the Clyde area. The result was a significant expansion in membership. Within a few months the Clyde was to become a main battle-ground in the national struggle of the Boilermakers' Society to resist the lengthening of the working-week and a reduction in wages, for in the summer of 1876 it became known that the employers in shipbuilding, engineering and ironfounding were to make a determined attempt to lengthen the working-week. Soon afterwards, notices for a lengthening of the working-day were posted in Barrow, Belfast and Ebbw Vale in South Wales. The boilermakers decided to resist. The dispute at Ebbw Vale was particularly important. After a prolonged strike the employers eventually withdrew their notice to increase the length of the working-day.

MORE CENTRAL CONTROL

An indirect effect of the trade depression was that the authority of the Executive Council in relation to the members and the district committees was strengthened. This arose from the need to conserve the funds of the Society. The Executive Council found it essential to control strictly the Society's expenditure and to maintain and, indeed, to increase its authority in relation to disputes which might involve the spending of money.

In the summer of 1876, following a difference of view between the Executive Council and one of the district committees, the members voted by a substantial majority against district committees having the right under any circumstances to issue circulars outside their own district. A few weeks later a sharp difference arose between the district delegate for the Tyne and Wear and the Executive Council, regarding the conduct of a dispute at Sunderland. The dispute concerned piece-work prices and the Executive Council took the view that the members were not being reasonable in the negotiations. They instructed the members to return to work for a period of one month at the prices previously paid for various jobs. In the meanwhile they were to elect a committee to negotiate on the prices in dispute. If they were unable to reach agreement with the employer the dispute was to be settled by an arbitrator. The members did not accept the instruction of the Executive Council and a bitter controversy developed. The EC argued that under the rules they were responsible for all monies paid to the Society, and all branch trustees were accountable to the EC for money in their possession. Money ought not, therefore, to be spent at local level in support of a strike contrary to the instructions of the Executive Council. The matter was put to a ballot of the members and, somewhat to the discomfiture of the EC, the view of the EC was upheld by only a narrow majority. The voting was 5,642 to 4,771. The surprisingly large vote against the EC was not motivated by a desire to undermine its authority, but by sympathy with the point of view of the members engaged in strike action. There was some feeling in many areas that the Executive Council, though technically in the right in their interpretation of the rules, had dealt harshly with the members on strike. The controversy dragged on through the winter of 1876–7 and finally the Executive Council, under threat of their own resignation, called for the dismissal of the Tyne and Wear district delegate. This was approved on a ballot vote by 5,532 to 2,266. There was, however, so much ill-feeling on the issue that the EC decided to submit the issue to an arbitrator. The arbitration award was published in April 1877 and came down firmly on the side of the EC. The district delegate and the Sunderland District Committee then resigned from office. The significance of this bitter controversy was that, irrespective of the merits of the particular strike, the authority of the Executive Council had in the ultimate been upheld.

7. No. 10 Engine, built by Hackworth in 1837 or 1839 and intended for mineral traffic

8. The first metal railway bridge in England, dating from 1823

STRUGGLES ON THE CLYDE

In the meanwhile in February 1877, following the strengthening of the Society's membership on the Clyde as a result of the dispute at Dumbarton dockyard, the Society had put in a claim for a 10 per cent increase in wages for its members employed in Clyde shipyards. Shortly afterwards the carpenters put in a claim for an increase of 15 per cent. The employers turned down these claims and decided on a lock-out. It appears from the records of the time that the action of the employers was directed at the outset mainly against the carpenters. At the beginning of the dispute the Boilermakers' Society had about 300 members locked out from a total number of about 1,300 in Greenock, Port Glasgow, Govan, Partick and Renfrew. Some of the other branches on the Clyde were hardly affected at all. Many of the employers did not lock out their boilermakers in the early stages of the dispute. Nevertheless, whatever might have been the main direction of the employers' action at the outset, it soon became apparent that the purpose of at least some of them was to smash trade unionism on the Clyde. As the Executive Council of the Boilermakers' Society said at the time, they were aiming to reduce the men to a state of serfdom. The past history of the Clyde employers, added the Executive Council, was one of tyranny and despotism.

The dispute on the Clyde was a prolonged one. The members of the Society throughout Britain voted by a majority of substantially more than two to one for the introduction of a weekly levy of 3d per member to assist their locked-out fellow members. In the middle of the dispute the members also voted heavily in favour of the election of an additional district delegate for the Clyde. Towards the end of September discussions were opened between the employers and the Society for a settlement of the dispute. The meeting was abortive because of the insistence of the employers that discussions should first take place on the rules of the Society, and the efforts of the district delegates to extend membership among eligible workers in Clyde shipyards and engineering workshops. The employers refused also to agree to the participation of Robert Knight, the General Secretary of the Society, in the negotiations. In October they extended the lock-out and more than 1,000 members of the Boilermakers' Society became directly involved in the dispute.

Further attempts were made to start discussions but the employers were still insistent that the rules and trade practices of the Society should be the first item for negotiation.

In November – by which time it was clear that the Society's members were not going to capitulate – further discussions took place and this time a settlement was reached. The employers insisted, however, that no full-time official of the Boilermakers' Society should participate in the negotiations. They sought also to persuade the lay representatives of the Society that it would be in the interest of all concerned if the Clyde boilermakers left the Boilermakers' Society and formed a Scottish organisation, which, it was indicated, would enjoy the approval of the employers. The lay representatives of the Society rejected this proposal and indicated that they had every intention of remaining loyal to the Society. The terms of settlement were that the wages question should be deferred for further consideration after an interval of six months, and that, on returning to work, none of the workmen would be victimised. These terms certainly did not represent a victory for the Society but, on the other hand, the dispute had shown that the employers could not destroy the existence of the Boilermakers' Society on the Clyde. The main dispute on the Clyde had lasted for thirty-three weeks and had cost the Society more than £13,000.

Subsequently, six firms on the Clyde renounced the agreement which had been signed in their name and refused to take back any men who remained members of the Society. The dispute was, therefore, continued in these six yards, and eventually five of the employers withdrew from the position which they had taken. Messrs Caird and Company of Greenock remained the one employer who refused to employ any members of the Boilermakers' Society.

Unfortunately, the return to work at the end of 1877 coincided with a worsening of trade. Despite the agreement made at the conclusion of the dispute, a number of employers insisted on reductions in piece-work prices. In the early summer of 1878 the publication of the annual report of the Iron Trade Employers' Association showed the trend of thinking among organised employers. It suggested that advantage should be taken of the depressed condition of trade to reduce wages, enforce piece-work, lengthen the hours of labour and, where possible, dismiss all foremen who were members of trade unions.

98

At the end of the interval of six months, when wages were due again to be considered on the Clyde, the initiative had passed from the union to the employers. Trade everywhere was in a depressed condition. The employers requested that hours of work should be increased from fifty-one to fifty-four per week and that wages should be reduced. The Society rejected these demands and argued strongly against a worsening of conditions. The employers then dropped their claim for a lengthening of hours, but insisted on a general wage reduction of $7\frac{1}{2}$ per cent. The Society decided to resist this demand, though a number of other trades accepted it. The boilermakers fought the employers single handed, and a strike was called and lasted until February 1879. During the weeks of strike action the trade depression grew even deeper. The employers were in no mood to make any concessions at all in their demands for wage cuts. Eventually the strike was concluded by the Society accepting the employers' terms.

So many men were now unemployed that those who were fortunate enough to have jobs found themselves in too weak a position to resist further attacks from the employers. Not only were wages reduced in accordance with the terms of the agreement, but gradually, from yard to yard and workshop to workshop, the hours of work were also increased from fifty-one to fifty-four. By the end of 1879 the fifty-four-hour week had once again been introduced throughout Scotland.

The successful attack of the employers on the Clyde on wages and hours of work was the first of many that now took place in different parts of Britain. In one district after another wages were reduced. Stoppages of work took place in a number of centres, but there were hardly any boilermakers employed anywhere who did not suffer wage reductions. The issue was not whether there should be a reduction, but rather by how much should wages be reduced. In some cases the resistance of the members of the Boilermakers' Society ensured that the reductions were less than they otherwise would have been.

WAGE CUTS EVERYWHERE

Because of the heavy unemployment among members, and the number of members who were engaged in strike action against wage reductions, including strikes in London, Manchester, on the Tees and other centres, the Society decided by ballot to reduce benefits and to increase contributions. The full-time officials also agreed voluntarily to accept a cut in wages and the members decided by ballot vote to reduce the number of full-time officials. The services of district delegates were ended in Staffordshire and London, and the number of district delegates on the north-east coast and in Scotland was reduced from two each to one each.

In his annual report Robert Knight, the General Secretary, said that the year 1879 had been a period of trial and suffering. Misery, want and desolation had stalked throughout the land. Thousands of operatives, he said, were reduced to the brink of starvation by the want of employment.

> The streets of our towns and cities were crowded with multitudes of willing toilers unable to find a market for their labour. Commerce was paralysed and stagnant; trade dull and profitless. In the mercantile world disaster and collapse followed each other in rapid succession; capital although cheap could find no remunerative outlets for the spirit of speculation was checked.

Chapter 9

Prosperity and Slump

At long last, at the very end of the 1870s, the depression began to lift. Trade showed signs of expanding. The north-east coast was now the main centre of strength of the Boilermakers' Society and ship-building was to grow rapidly on the Wear and the Tyne. In the spring of 1880 as the result of a ballot vote of the membership the head office of the Society was moved to Newcastle.

The new prosperity continued for approximately three years. During this period the membership grew from about 17,500 at the beginning of 1880 to nearly 30,000 at the peak level in 1883. The accumulated financial reserves grew even more rapidly. At the end of 1879 they were less than £10,000 but by the end of 1883 they had reached over £108,000.

PROSPERITY

This strengthening of the Society's financial position owed much to the prudence of the leadership. With the revival of trade the Executive Council, prompted by the General Secretary, Robert Knight, was determined that steps should be taken to improve the Society's finances. The General Council met in the summer of 1880 and proposed that the weekly contribution of 1s 3d should be continued for a further twelve months. At the same time it suggested that unemployment benefit should be paid to members who were out of work, without it being necessary for them to travel from their home town. On a ballot vote the membership rejected the proposal that weekly contributions should continue at 1s 3d. There was strong

101

pressure for them to be reduced to 1s 1d per week. The Executive Council, on the other hand, was well aware of the danger for the future of reducing subscriptions during a period of prosperity. Nevertheless, on a ballot vote it was decided by 2,015 votes to 748 to reduce subscriptions to 1s 1d per week. Approximately one year later the Southampton branch issued an appeal to the Society to vote in favour of an increase of 1d per week in contributions from 1s 1d to 1s 2d. They argued strongly that members should build up reserve funds of the Society during a period of prosperity. The appeal was, however, rejected by 2,248 votes to 1,784. The Executive Council regretted that the members had not accepted 'the very sensible advice given them' by the Southampton branch.

The year 1882 was an extremely prosperous one. In his annual report Robert Knight said that the prosperity had been beyond 'our highest expectations. There has been work in abundance at remunerative rates . . .' During the year new ships were launched with a gross displacement of nearly 1,200,000 tons. For the first time more than 100,000 tons were of ships built in steel instead of iron. Wood as a material for shipbuilding had now been almost completely abandoned. By February 1882 there was so much work available for members of the Society that it was decided to suspend the payment of unemployment benefit to members under fifty years of age. One firm alone, Messrs Leslie & Company of Hebburn, were prepared to employ an additional 200 members of the Society. Platers were in demand on all main shipbuilding estuaries, and it was reported that three new shipbuilding yards – all requiring labour – were to be opened at Sunderland. The Executive Council reported that there were at least 600 vacancies which had been notified to them.

With the coming of prosperity new demands were made for increases in wages. One of the first areas to put in a claim was the Clyde. It met with a curt reply. Trade conditions were, however, on the side of the workers. Wage increases ranging from about $2\frac{1}{2}$ per cent to 15 per cent were secured at shipyards throughout Scotland. A few weeks later the new wages movement spread to the north-east coast. Wage increases were secured in the summer of 1880 in all the main yards on the Tyne and the Wear.

ADVICE TO THE MEMBERSHIP

In his annual report for 1881 Robert Knight pointed out that the wages of workers on the Tyne had increased by amounts of up to 7s to 8s per week. In shipbuilding the earnings of piece-workers had increased by even larger amounts. Piece-work prices, said Robert Knight, had been increased by from 10 per cent to 30 per cent, and in some rare cases by as much as 100 per cent. He thought it a fair assumption from the information which he had received that the weekly wages of members in shipbuilding had increased by at least 10 per cent. Robert Knight then went on in his annual report to give what he described as friendly advice to the membership.

> While fully alive to the advantages derived from good wages, it is possible to venture too far in making unreasonable demands on employers. This, I know, has been the case in some districts on some occasions that have come under my notice. This I must pronounce a mistake. Under pressure, an employer will concede our requests until a certain point is reached. That point is where his profits from business are converted into loss. At this stage self-preservation prompts him to resist. If the members persist in making excessive demands that are much above other districts, they only harass their employers, and either force them into liquidation or otherwise out of the trade . . . Therefore, for any workman to insist upon excessive demands when trade is prosperous, and by this action handicapping their employers unfairly with other competitors in the trade, is an unwise policy, suicidal and must react upon the authors to their own suffering and loss.

In March 1882 the Executive Council reported that further wage increases had been secured on the Wear and in the Liverpool district. At the same time they warned against pushing the employers too far on wage demands. If strikes were to be avoided, said the Executive Council, members should be moderate in their demands, steady and attentive to their work and should faithfully fulfil all contracts in a satisfactory manner. The Executive Council stated that it had been considerably annoyed of late by a number of petty and unnecessary disputes in various shipyards. A caution was issued to all members against the holding of shop meetings at which decisions were made to withhold labour. Such meetings, it was

103

pointed out, were illegal, unconstitutional and contrary to the rules of the Society. All resolutions passed at such meetings were not binding on members. All business, to be legal, said the EC, must be transacted at duly-convened lodge meetings and in no other manner.

Towards the end of 1882 Mr Robert Knight, when speaking at the annual meeting of an employers' organisation, the North of England Boilermakers' and Iron Shipbuilders' Society, stated that the men were getting good pay at the time and he thought they ought to be content with the present state of things. He felt that it was desirable that the men individually should save their money. He emphasised that the Boilermakers' Society had tried to raise the moral standard of its members as well as to raise their wages. Mr Knight advocated long-term agreements for wages. He suggested that in yards or firms where a demand for increased wages was thought to be justifiable, adequate notice should be given to the employers to enable them to consider the course which they should pursue in giving estimates for work to customers. A sudden demand for a wage increase could, if conceded, deprive the employer of his fair profit. Not surprisingly Mr Knight's observations on wages received the approval of the employers who were present at the meeting. Shortly afterwards a letter was received by the Society from the head of the then largest shipbuilding firm in the world, Messrs Palmer & Company of Jarrow, stating that Mr Knight should be thanked for the frank and outspoken manner in which he had expressed his views.

A WARNING

In the spring of 1883 the Executive Council issued a warning against shop stewards exceeding their powers under the rules. In some firms, it was pointed out, stewards had fixed piece-work prices, declared certain jobs to be black and had urged members to go on strike. The rules, said the Executive Council, did not empower any shop steward to act in such a manner. When differences arose in a shop affecting piece-work prices or conditions the members, if unable to settle it at shop or yard level, were to inform the branch secretary and seek the assistance of the district delegate.

In September 1883 the Executive Council again found it necessary to warn members against taking precipitate strike action. They said that when work was plentiful members who took such action considered that they could do as they liked; ignore the instructions of the Executive Council; set at defiance the advice of their district delegate; make unreasonable demands on their employers; and strike whenever they liked. The members who acted in this way, said the EC, were quite wrong. They were acting in a manner opposed to the Society's rules. The EC emphasised that the rules gave to the EC alone the authority to authorise strike action. It warned that in future it might implement the power invested in it to fine any member who violated the instructions of the Executive Council.

ANOTHER DEPRESSION

This warning had hardly been published when signs began to appear that the period of prosperity was coming to an end. In the closing months of 1883 the demand for labour began to disappear. On every hand there were indications of a decline in trade. Employers began to insist on wage reductions. In the opening weeks of 1884 these were enforced in many areas. There were strikes in many Scottish yards, but at best they secured only a reduction in the demands of the employers. On the north-east coast a reduction of 10 per cent was accepted after prolonged negotiations.

Throughout 1884 wage reductions were reported every single month. In some yards on the Clyde eight separate wage reductions took place in no more than a twelve-month period. There were repeated strikes, particularly in Scotland, but they were of little avail. Falling trade deepened into a depression. By the autumn of 1884 platers at a number of Clyde yards were offering to undercut each other in order to secure work. Unemployment throughout the Society rose to about $23\frac{1}{2}$ per cent of the membership. The proportion of those unemployed in shipbuilding was much higher. Fortunately, in many of the locomotive, bridge, boiler and structural shops trade was still reasonable.

In his annual report for 1884 Robert Knight stated that one of the great desires of his life was that there should be the adjustment of all labour disputes without strikes and lock-outs. He suggested that a solution could be found if all the shipbuilding employers of the United Kingdom formed one employers' organisation. It would then be possible, he suggested, for representatives of the employers and the union to meet and to draw up price lists which could be adjusted from time to time by negotiations. In the autumn of 1884 the Society sent two representatives on a mission to France to ascertain whether work was available for members of the Society who might be prepared to emigrate. The delegates visited Calais, Le Havre, Rouen, St Nazaire, Nantes, La Rochelle and Bordeaux, but reported that the opportunities for work for British boilermakers were very limited.

The depression continued throughout 1885 and 1886. Unemployment rose to nearly 27 per cent of the Society's membership in 1885, and 28 per cent in 1886. By the end of 1886 the membership of the Society was reduced to 25,340 from its peak of nearly 30,000 in 1883. The funds were reduced from their high point of £108,000 to less than £22,000. Wage reductions continued in every area and by 1886 wages were lower in many shipyards than they had been for more than twenty years. In the north-east, wages were reduced mainly by negotiation, but finally in February 1886 there was a strike when the employers requested a further substantial reduction. There had already been three reductions in less than two years. The Executive Council stated that during the earlier years of prosperity the members on the north-east coast had not used their strength to force up wages as high as they could have done, in the hope that the employers would deal with them sympathetically when there was a depression. The EC reported that their hopes had not been realised and that the full strength of the employers was now being used to crush the men to the lowest possible level. This dispute on the north-east coast eventually involved about 8,000 members. It was finally settled with wage reductions ranging from $2\frac{1}{2}$ per cent to 8 per cent. Rather surprisingly, the action of the men on the north-east coast in striking against the demand for a further reduction in wages was criticised subsequently by the Executive Council of the Society. They revealed that they had advised the members to accept further wage reductions. They said 'many years of experience have taught us that it must be a very exceptional case if a strike does any good; we have more faith in argument with employers than in strikes'.

With widespread wage reductions and heavy unemployment among the Society's members there was pressure from some branches for a reduction in the wages of the full-time officials. In the late summer

106

of 1886 the officials themselves volunteered to accept a 10 per cent reduction in their wages.

POLITICAL LESSONS?

The depression did not appear to bring any sharp political lessons to the leadership of the Boilermakers' Society. They protested against the ruthlessness of the employers but were inclined to take the view that the proper remedy was to promote better relations between workers and employers, so that in times of prosperity wages were not pushed too high and in times of depression employers could be persuaded not to attack workers' conditions so strongly. Mr Robert Knight in his annual report for 1885 did, at least, say that there was something radically wrong with the distribution of wealth in Britain and he urged that there should be a reduction in the hours of labour. In his annual report the following year he protested against the amount of resources being used throughout Europe for military purposes. He said that the war-like attitude which was present in Europe was a great hindrance to human progress. Nevertheless, despite these protests, there was nothing in the publications of the Boilermakers' Society during 1885 and 1886 which suggested that there should be any kind of challenge to the existing social system. Propaganda for socialism had still not penetrated the ranks of the Boilermakers' Society. It was, perhaps, indicative of the views of the active members that at the end of the meeting of the General Council held in 1885 the chairman was presented with eleven volumes of the works of Disraeli, the Conservative leader.

The one political measure which excited the interest of the Boilermakers' Society in this period was the passing of the Employers' Liability Act in 1880. Employers were made responsible for insuring workmen against the risks of their occupation. This change in the law, said the Executive Council of the Boilermakers' Society, was absolutely necessary to give to working men the protection which they so much required but which up to that time they had not possessed. Unfortunately, employers were still allowed to persuade their workers to contract out of the provisions of the Act. The Boilermakers' Society strongly urged all members not to contract out. They said that members should retain for themselves, their

107

wives and their families the benefit which the Act conferred. The Executive Council also proposed that a special fund should be created from a levy of 1d per quarter to meet legal expenses which might arise in connection with the operation of the new Act.

ORGANISATION

The prosperity of the early 1880s enabled the Boilermakers' Society to strengthen its organisational structure. In 1880 it was decided to elect an assistant secretary for the head office of the Society. In the following year the Tees District Committee applied for the re-appointment of a district delegate. They recalled in their appeal that they had previously had a delegate but that it had been decided to discontinue his services in 1879 when trade was depressed. This request was put to the membership and by the narrowest of majorities, 1,334 to 1,321, it was approved. Requests for additional delegates were also received from the Clyde and the London area. The Clyde asked for a second delegate and London for a delegate of their own. Both requests were granted.

The Society was also steadily building 100 per cent membership in yards and boiler-shops. One of the arguments used against the Society's members when seeking to establish a closed shop was that each workman should be free to decide for himself whether he should join a trade union. The Executive Council addressed itself to this question in a statement which they issued in the summer of 1880. They said that it could be questioned whether this theory of absolute freedom was one that could be fairly or wisely applied in all circumstances. The conduct of each workman affected not only his own prospects but also the position and prospects of others. All citizens were compelled in certain matters to subordinate their personal tastes and wishes to the general good of the public. Were not trade unionists justified, asked the Executive Council, in endeavouring to use a degree of compulsion to induce others to join them in work not pursued for selfish ends but having for its objective the common advantage of the workmen in the trade to which they belonged? The Executive Council pointed out that when a non-unionist took a job in a union yard or workshop he enjoyed the benefits which had been established by the Society's members. He, therefore, owed a debt to the Society's members. If he declined to admit his indebtedness, the Society's members had an undoubted right to refuse to recognise him and to insist that he should secure such work as he could find elsewhere.

ELIGIBILITY FOR MEMBERSHIP

In 1881 by a fairly narrow majority the Society decided on a ballot vote to accept into membership a number of shipbuilding workers at Dumbarton and Sunderland who were now working on metal plates, but who originally had been trained as shipwrights. These men had worked for a number of years in metal and they gave an undertaking that they would not return as wooden shipwrights. Even so, the narrow majority secured for their admission to the Society was an indication of the widespread and strong suspicion entertained by iron and steel shipbuilders towards wooden ship-wrights. An attempt to secure the admission of a small society of smiths employed in the shipbuilding yards of the Wear was, however, defeated. Some of those who at the time opposed the admission of the smiths later acknowledged that they had been mistaken in their campaign.

An important decision was taken early in 1882 to admit holders-up into membership of the Society. The voting in favour was 2,713 to 872. This substantial majority was secured largely as a result of a vigorous campaign in favour of admission conducted by the Executive Council. A statement issued by the EC said that platers and riveters were dependent upon the holders-up; the one could not work without the other. Furthermore, the interests of the riveters was directly parallel to the interests of the holders-up. When riveters received a wage increase so too did the holders-up, but so long as they were not in the Society they made no contribution to the Society's funds. Thirdly, said the EC, the Society had no control over the holders-up so long as they remained outside the scope of membership. The Society could not, therefore, control their actions nor arrange the terms upon which they worked. Although the Executive Council strongly recommended the admission of holders-up to membership of the Society they equally insisted that they would always have to observe stringent conditions of membership. They would have to remain as holders-up; they were not to receive any unemployment or superannuation benefit; and they

109

were not to have a voice or vote in any branch meetings unless the question under discussion immediately affected their interests.

THE 'CORNER SYSTEM'

Relations with one other group of shipyard workers were particularly embittered. These were the platers' helpers employed on the north-east coast. In that area, particularly on the Wear, what was known as the 'corner system' was in operation. Under this system helpers were employed on piece-work. They received so much money for every plate or 'corner' which they handled. This system led to extremely bad relations between the platers and their helpers. The platers complained that they had no control over the helpers. The labourers, they said, had become masters of the situation. The Boilermakers' Society decided to take energetic action to bring the 'corner system' to an end. They sought to open discussions with representatives of the platers' helpers on the north-east coast, with a view to changing the system. They offered to support a claim for the labourers to receive a minimum of time-and-a-half payment if they would agree to go on day-work instead of piece-work. The platers' helpers did not agree with the suggestions of the Society and the Society then decided that new labourers should be recruited for the yards. Because of the pressure they were able to exert they were supported for the most part by the local employers. The dispute became very bitter and there was considerable disorder, including violent assaults in Sunderland. Something like 700 men were recruited from other areas to replace the labourers who had been dismissed.

A number of other trade unions gave financial assistance to the dismissed platers' helpers. The Boilermakers' Society complained of this assistance and said that the Society had done everything possible to resolve the dispute by negotiation, but their members were determined that the pernicious 'corner system' should come to an end. The Boilermakers' Society said that they acknowledged the right of the labourers to refuse to work with members of the Society but, equally, if the labourers took this attitude they could not complain if the Society were then prepared to work with labourers recruited from elsewhere. This unfortunate struggle between the skilled men and the labourers resulted inevitably in the defeat of the labourers. The labourers had been badly advised to insist on retaining the 'corner system' to the point where the skilled men refused any longer to work with them. On the other hand, such a tragic division between skilled workers and labourers could do nothing to promote the long-term interests of all workers in the shipbuilding industry.

NEW MOVES

In about the year 1880 the Society was informed of efforts being made to establish a trade union for boilermakers in the United States. A gift of £20 was sent to assist these efforts. Two years later the Society learnt in a letter received from the United States that the American union now had twenty branches and a membership of 2,740. Following an application for a wage increase in the New York area, a strike had taken place and the employers had sought to import 'blackleg' labour from Britain. The American boilermakers' union notified the British Boilermakers' Society of the strike and the Society was able to prevent any men being sent from Britain.

In the opening months of 1883 the Society recruited a number of draughtsmen in the yards on the north-east coast. The Executive Council was sympathetic to this extension of the scope of membership and suggested that more draughtsmen – and head draughtsmen in particular – should be recruited and accepted as honorary members. They pointed out that yard managers were often recruited from among head draughtsmen and it would be helpful to the Society if in the future a growing proportion of yard managers was recruited from among men who felt a loyalty to the Boilermakers' Society. This recommendation was put to the membership. It was, however, defeated on a ballot vote by 1,506 to 664.

In 1884, despite the steadily worsening condition of trade, the members voted in favour of another delegate being elected for the Tyne and the Wear. As trade grew worse, however, any further ambitions for expansion were thwarted. By 1886 the Society was already beginning to debate whether it could retain its existing staff of full-time officials. Only by the narrowest margin was it decided to retain the second district delegate for the Clyde. Further expansion had to await a revival in trade.

Chapter 10

A Time of Change

Trade began to improve in 1887. The percentage of members unemployed fell from 28 per cent in 1886 to $21\frac{1}{2}$ per cent in 1887. During the period of the depression there had been a substantial decline in the funds of the Society; in four years no less than £170,000 had been paid out in unemployment benefit. In a number of branches, for example those in Sunderland, far more had been paid out in unemployment benefit than had been received in members' contributions.

Trade continued to improve in 1888 and the average rate of unemployment dropped to less than 8 per cent of the membership. There was now general pressure for wage increases, particularly in all the shipbuilding areas. After the wage slashing of the previous four years, claims for increases were put forward in nearly every yard. Stoppages of work in support of wage claims began to occur frequently. One strike in Harland & Wolff, Belfast, involved over 5,000 workers. Wage increases were secured. By an almost unanimous vote the membership balloted in favour of the payment of a levy to support the Belfast strikers. Another successful dispute was on the Mersey where approximately 600 members were involved in strike action.

PROSPERITY

The year 1889 was described as one of the most prosperous in the Society's history. The average rate of unemployment was only $2\frac{1}{2}$ per cent. Wages continued to rise and stoppages of work in support of wage claims were frequent. A fair number of the most skilled mem-

112

bers of the Society were now receiving wages of £2 per week. This put them among the very highest paid of manual workers. The new prosperity brought also new demands for a reduction of working hours. In his annual report for 1889 Robert Knight, General Secretary, expressed support for a reduction in working hours, but opposed the suggestion that it should be achieved by Parliament passing an Eight Hours Bill. He said:

> We should then be handing over our liberties and our right to regulate our own hours of labour and the fixing of our own wages to Parliament who, on the whole, lean more towards the capitalist class than to the workers. If you once acknowledge their right to pass the Eight Hours Bill you also acknowledge their right to increase the hours of labour and regulate our wages as well. We should be taking a long step backward.

The campaign for an Eight Hours Bill was being conducted by the early socialists in the trade union movement. Some of them were members of the Social Democratic Federation. In 1886 Tom Mann, an active member of the ASE and a socialist, published a pamphlet calling for a compulsory limit of eight hours on the working-day. He put forward this proposal not as a legislative alternative to trade unionism but as a supplement to aggressive trade union action.

Whilst the prosperity lasted the Executive Council of the Society suggested that a special levy of 10s per member should be introduced to help to build up the reserves of the Society. This money, they pointed out, might be needed when trade turned for the worse. This proposal was put to the membership and was accepted on a ballot vote by 12,860 to 9,738. Despite the willingness of the majority of members to pay a levy, the normal contributions to the Society had been reduced in June 1888. The contributions were reduced from 1s 6d per week to 1s 3d per week for members who were 'in compliance'. Members who were not 'in compliance' were required to pay 1s 6d per week.

CLYDE DISPUTE

Trade began to slacken towards the end of 1890 and by 1891 a number of employers gave notice of wage reductions. This led to a major dispute on the Clyde. The Society's national officials negotiated a smaller reduction than the amount at first demanded by the employers, but this was rejected by the Clydeside members. Against the advice of the Executive Council thousands of members withdrew their labour. The unofficial strike continued for six weeks. At the end the workers returned on lower wages. The Clyde dispute caused a bitter controversy between some of the Scottish branches and the Executive Council. A majority of the Scottish branches expressed support for a statement condemning the Executive Council. The Council in reply vigorously defended their role and argued that it was better to accept a negotiated wage reduction than to precipitate a dispute which would inevitably result in suffering and defeat. The attitude of the Executive Council in the Clyde dispute reflected the strong personal views of Robert Knight. He expounded his point of view in his annual report for 1891. He said that until very recently all differences between boilermakers and shipbuilding employers on the Clyde had been settled by the barbarous method of strike action. The Boilermakers' Society had not been recognised by the employers. This had now changed, and Robert Knight felt sure that experience would teach the Clyde members that differences of a serious nature could 'better be settled between the employers' associations and ours than by the system previously adopted'. Robert Knight went on to say that there was so much in common between the employers and the unions that everything possible should be done to avoid the unnecessary expenditure of the union's capital, especially when the union found that the employers were anxious to deal fairly with their workers. Robert Knight said that it was a great mistake to regard capital and labour as irreconcilable enemies.

ROBERT KNIGHT

The most significant administrative change in the Boilermakers' Society during the period of prosperity between 1887 and 1890 was the decision to build a new permanent headquarters. This was approved by a ballot of the members, who then decided that the new offices should be situated in Newcastle. The new offices, known as Lifton House, were opened on 22 September 1890. More than 7,000 members of the Society, with banners, emblems and a dozen bands, marched through the city of Newcastle to celebrate the occasion.

Shortly after the opening of the new headquarters Robert Knight was re-elected unopposed as General Secretary of the Society. In June 1891 his salary was increased. The increase was endorsed by the membership by 11,360 votes to 7,458. The increase amounted to ½d per member per year. The membership of the Society at that time was about 37,000. The increase was equivalent, therefore, to about 30s per week.

Robert Knight was now at the height of his power. The Executive Council was not a nationally representative body but was elected locally from the lodges in the Tyne district. It consisted of lay members. Lodges took it in turn to nominate one of the seven members of which the EC was composed. Real control in the Society was exercised by the General Secretary and the network of full-time district delegates. There was no annual conference, the General Council was only a very occasional affair, and there was very little controversy in the monthly journal. Even the tradition of submitting issues to a ballot vote of the membership observed the form rather than the content of democracy. There was little if any opportunity for the exchange of views between active members in one part of the country and another. Moreover, the authority which now resided in the office of General Secretary was reinforced from another direction. The members of the Boilermakers' Society were subject to severe fluctuations in trade, particularly in shipbuilding. When trade was good the members of the Society were well paid by normal working-class standards; when trade was depressed thousands of them were unemployed and looked to the Society for financial assistance. It was natural, therefore, that to many members the role of the General Secretary was primarily that of a financial guardian. Collective bargaining could be conducted locally and the boilermakers could depend on their own strength in shipyard or workshop, but it was the specific function of the national office to build up and conserve the funds and distribute them fairly when assistance was needed. It was in this respect that Robert Knight's particular talents made him such an effective office-holder. He was efficient, thorough, sober, honest, intelligent and thoroughly dedicated to the interest of the Boilermakers' Society.

In his book *Industrial Democracy*, Sidney Webb said of the Boilermakers' Society at this time and of its General Secretary.

The efficiency and influence of this remarkable union is, no doubt, largely due to the advantageous strategic position which has resulted from the extraordinary expansion of iron shipbuilding. It is interesting, however, to notice what a perfect example it affords of a constitution retaining all the features of the crudest democracy, but becoming, in actual practice, a bureaucracy in which effective popular control has sunk to a minimum . . . But although the executive committee, the branch meeting and the referendum occupy the main body of the Society's rules, the whole policy has long been directed and the whole administration conducted exclusively by an informal cabinet of permanent officials which is unknown to the printed constitution. Twenty years ago the society had the good fortune to elect as general secretary, Mr Robert Knight, a man of remarkable ability and strength of character, who has remained the permanent premier of this little kingdom . . . Mr Knight's unquestioned superiority in trade union statesmanship, together with the invariable support of the executive committee, have enabled him to construct, out of the nominally independent district delegates a virtual cabinet, alternately serving as councillors on high issues of policy and as ministers carrying out in their own spheres that which they have in council decided. From the written constitution of the society, we should suppose that it was from the evening meetings of the little Newcastle committee of working platers and riveters that emanated all those national treaties and elaborate collective bargains with the associated employers that have excited the admiration of economic students. But its unrepresentative character, the short term of service of its members and the practical rotation of office make it impossible for the constantly shifting executive committee to exercise any effective influence over even the ordinary routine business of so large a society. The complicated negotiations involved in national agreements are absolutely beyond its grasp. What actually happens is that, in any high issue of policy, Mr Knight summons his district delegates to meet him in council at London or Manchester, to concert, and even to conduct, with him the weighty negotiations which the Newcastle executive

116

formally endorses. And although the actual administration of the benefits is conducted by the branch committees, the absolute centralisation of funds and the supreme disciplinary power vested in the executive committee make that committee, or rather the general secretary, as dominant in matters of finance as in trade policy. The only real opportunity for an effective expression of the popular will comes to be the submission of questions to the aggregate vote of the branches in mass meeting assembled. It is needless to point out that a referendum of this kind, submitted through the official circular in whatsoever terms the general secretary may choose, and backed by the influence of the permanent staff in every district, comes to be only a way of impressing the official view on the whole body of members . . .

In the case of the Boilermakers, government by an informal cabinet of salaried officials has, up to the present time, been highly successful. It is, however, obvious that a less competent statesman than Mr Knight would find great difficulty in welding into a united cabinet a body of district officers separately responsible to the whole society, and nominally subject only to their several district committees. Under these circumstances any personal friction or disloyalty might easily paralyse the whole trade policy, upon which the prosperity of the society depends. Moreover, though under Mr Knight's upright and able government the lack of any supervising authority has not been felt, it cannot but be regarded as a defect that the constitution provides no practical control over a corrupt, negligent, or incompetent general secretary. The only persons in the position to criticise effectually the administration of the society are the salaried officials themselves, who would naturally be indisposed to risk their offices by appealing, against their official superior, to the uncertain arbitrament of an aggregate vote. Finally, this constitution, with all its parade of democratic form, secures in reality to the ordinary plater or riveter little if any active participation in the central administration of his trade union; no real opportunity is given to him for expressing his opinion; and no call is made upon his intelligence for the formation of any opinion whatsoever. In short, the Boilermakers, so long as they remained content with this form of government, secured efficient administration at the expense of losing all the educative influences and political safeguards of democracy.

117

Sidney Webb wrote that at that time Robert Knight and his 'informal cabinet' were absolutely supreme in the affairs of the Boilermakers' Society. There was a good deal of justification for this judgement, but even then there were rumblings from below about this personal concentration of power. These rumblings of democracy were to grow and be reinforced by the example of the new trade unionism which from 1888 onwards, often under the influence of socialists and militants, began to organise among the semi-skilled and unskilled workers. Long before Robert Knight put down the reins of office in 1899 there were signs of democratic change inside the Boilermakers' Society.

COLLECTIVE ORGANISATION

The period of prosperity at the end of the 80s also saw a significant strengthening of collective organisation both among employers and unions. A Clyde Employers' Association was formed in 1889, and shortly afterwards a meeting was held in Carlisle of shipbuilding employers from all parts of the United Kingdom, for the purpose of forming a national federation. The rules of the proposed employers' federation indicated some hostility towards trade union organisation among workpeople. Robert Knight commented in his annual report that he did not object to the formation of a national federation if it had no hostile intentions towards the workmen's unions. If it were the employers' aim to adjust all labour difficulties by peaceful means, as had been done in recent years by employers on the north-east coast, then the federation would at all times receive the support of the Boilermakers' Society. Robert Knight emphasised that the formation of this new employers' federation should cause the unions engaged in the shipbuilding and engineering industries to draw closer together. He was able to report that preliminary moves towards such a trade union federation had already taken place.

The proposal for a trade union federation in shipbuilding and engineering was again put to a ballot vote of the membership in the spring of 1890. The members voted overwhelmingly in favour of the proposal. The voting was 19,464 to 484. The Federation of Engineering and Shipbuilding Trades was formed at a meeting in Manchester on 16 December 1890. Robert Knight had acted as convener of the meeting and occupied the chair. Thirteen unions were represented at the meeting. The engineers indicated that they were not able to join at that stage, and two unions of carpenters also remained outside the Federation. The objects of the Federation were defined in the rules as 'to maintain the right of combination of labour by trade unionism, by mutually supporting any of the societies within the Federation after individual contact by employers or bodies of employers; to use every legitimate means to abolish the character note system; to promote arbitration or conciliation in trade disputes; and the elevation of labour in general'.

In 1892 a small Clydeside union of holders-up decided to transfer themselves to the Boilermakers' Society. This brought about 1,000 members into the parent body. This transfer of engagements, as it would now be called, removed what had been a local cause of friction.

THE DOCK STRIKE

Though the Boilermakers' Society took a leading part in bringing about trade union co-operation in the engineering and shipbuilding industries, the support which it was prepared to give for the extension of trade union organisation among unskilled workers in other industries was less enthusiastic. In 1889, for example, in the middle of an extremely prosperous period, the Society gave only £20 to assist the London dockers in what was to become one of the most famous industrial disputes in British history. The monthly report of the Society for January 1890 commented that the year 1889 had been a most eventful one for trade unionism and that large numbers were now classed as trade unionists who probably had never thought of it before. It was equally uncertain whether they would exist as trade unionists a year hence. The monthly report went on, in effect, to say that this kind of upsurge had been seen before. In circumstances of prosperity certain groups of workers formed an organisation, took strike action and 'with equal promptitude issued printed appeals to bona fide trade societies to help them by contributions to their strike fund'. Sometimes, and not long afterwards, when further requests were made, the same workers were not able to fight a losing battle and they lost faith in trade unionism. The moment adversity showed itself, said the Executive Council, their unionism vanished. The Executive Council drew a distinction

119

between bona fide societies and the many unskilled labourers' societies that had recently sprung into existence. Clearly, the Executive Council of the Boilermakers' Society at that time – and Robert Knight personally – had failed to grasp the historic significance of the extension of trade union organisation to groups of unskilled workers. This development was to have a lasting and growing importance for the British trade union and labour movement.

In contrast to this almost reluctant support for the London dockers was the support given by the Society to Australian workers who were involved in a dispute. On a ballot vote, and by an overwhelming majority, the members agreed to a levy to provide £500 to be sent to Australia. In the outcome this money was not needed, but the levy was used to help members of the Boilermakers' Society involved in disputes in Britain.

ANOTHER DEPRESSION

By 1893 there was yet another depression. The rate of unemployment among members of the Society rose to about 16 per cent. The employers demanded wage cuts and, as usual, the Clyde employers were to the forefront in making these demands. During the winter of 1892–3 no less than three separate wage cuts were imposed in Glasgow and the surrounding area. The January 1893 monthly report said 'The hundreds of pinched and hungry faces have told a tale of suffering and privation which no optimism could minimise or conceal'. In 1894 no less than £48,000 was paid out in unemployment benefit to members. Despite these adverse conditions the Society fought and eventually won a long battle for higher wages for boilermakers employed in a number of steel works in South Wales. The centre of the dispute was at Dowlais where the men were receiving no more than from 2s 4d to 2s 9d per day in wages. A strike began at the Ebbw Vale steel works in January 1892. It was later extended to other steel works. For more than fourteen months the steel employers bitterly resisted any settlement for an improvement in wages. Finally in May 1893 the Society issued notices to the effect that their members everywhere would refuse to 'work, use or manipulate any iron or steel plates or angles manufactured by the Dowlais Company'. They further gave notice that ship-repairing members would not carry out repairs on any ship carrying iron ore to Britain destined for use by the Dowlais Company. In reply to this act of solidarity the Shipping Federation attempted to persuade their member firms to take counter action against members of the Boilermakers' Society. This failed, and within two months the steel companies agreed to negotiate with the Society. This resulted in wage increases from between 20 per cent and 33 per cent. Solidarity had brought victory.

PROCEDURE AGREEMENT

One important consequence of the demand of the employers for successive wage reductions in 1893 and 1894 was the signing of a new negotiating procedure agreement between the Society and the Tyne, Wear, Tees and Hartlepool shipbuilding employers. The agreement was signed in July 1894. It stipulated that there was to be no general alteration in wages until after six calendar months had elapsed from the date of the last alteration, and that no single alteration was to be of more than 5 per cent. The agreement also outlined a procedure for the settlement of disputes at yard level. It said that work should proceed without interruption pending a settlement. Standing committees consisting of three employers and three of the Society's members were established for each of the rivers. The function of the standing committees was to consider local disputes. This agreement was submitted to a ballot vote of the entire membership and was endorsed by 15,950 votes to 11,840. Of the members directly affected by the agreement, however, a majority voted against it. This led to a long and heated debate in the Society, and, some six months after the agreement had been endorsed, the Executive Council found it necessary to issue a long statement defending itself against the many criticisms made by active members of the north-east coast. Some of this criticism was directed against the authority of the General Secretary. Demands were voiced for constitutional changes to curtail the power of the General Secretary.

Through this period of depression the General Secretary continued to urge restraint, thrift and temperance upon the members. 'We have more to fear from the brewer and the bookmaker' he said in his 1894 annual report 'than from any combination of capitalists of whom we have ever heard'. Nevertheless, Robert Knight condemned the widespread unemployment of the time. The industrial worker, he said, had a precarious existence. Without luxuries and with only few comforts, he lived, he added, in constant dread of those recurrent epidemics of trade that bring idleness, sorrow and suffering to his heart and home. 'It is a terrible commentary upon, and indictment against, the present social system under which we live and labour, that men, capable and willing to work, are doomed to walk beneath the shadows of starvation in a land teeming with wealth.'

APPRENTICES

In 1893 agreements were made regulating apprenticeship in boiler shops and shipyards. The general principles of the agreements were that there should be a five year period of apprenticeship; that apprentices should be indentured; that they should not belong to the Society whilst apprenticed except for benefit purposes; and that there should be no more than two apprentices to every seven journeymen. This latter condition did not, however, apply to boiler shops. This agreement was the outcome of efforts made by the Society to control unilaterally the employment of apprentices. Apprentice cards had been issued by the Society and an instruction had been given that no one was to be admitted to membership of the Society who had not held one of these cards. The cards were issued only on the basis of one apprentice to every five journeymen. The employers strongly objected to this unilateral act of the Society and eventually the Society agreed to withdraw the apprentice cards on condition that further negotiations took place for the regulation of apprenticeships. These negotiations led to the agreement of 1893.

WIDER ACTIVITIES

Despite the earlier tardiness of the Society in supporting the dockers in their historic strike in London in 1889, it was the boilermakers who helped to save Hull dockers from defeat in a strike in 1893. The support given by the boilermakers was a magnificent act of solidarity. The Executive Council first made a donation of £20, but then took a ballot among the membership to ascertain their views on the imposition of a levy. Nearly 16,000 members voted for a 6d levy and nearly 7,000 members for a 3d levy. The result

122

was that the Society gave about £800 to the dockers. The letter of thanks received by the Society for this donation said, 'Your cheque this morning saved us from an ignominious defeat.'

A note in the monthly report of the Society on the dockers' dispute at Hull gave some advice to the strikers. It was to the effect that they ought not to enter into a dispute if they were not prepared for it financially. The monthly report said that it was criminal for any body of men deliberately to throw up their employment and leave themselves and their families without support unless there was adequate provision to help to maintain them during the period of a dispute.

In 1893 Robert Knight, the General Secretary of the Society, was offered a job at a salary of £400 per annum in the new Labour Department. He declined the appointment. Despite the growing internal uneasiness about the power wielded by Robert Knight, there was no doubt that he was deeply devoted to the progress and welfare of the Society. He was immensely proud of the fact that during his period as General Secretary the membership had risen from 7,000 to more than 28,000.

Towards the end of 1893 a member of the Society was put on trial on a charge of libelling Robert Knight. According to newspaper reports published at the time, the case was brought at the instigation of the Public Prosecutor. The member was found guilty and was sentenced to four months' imprisonment.

Robert Knight was influential in persuading the Society to invest £10,000 in preference shares of Sir William Armstrong, Mitchell & Company, the owners of the giant Elswick Works at Newcastle. Many members of the Boilermakers' Society were employed at the Elswick Works. The shares appreciated in value and, not surprisingly, by 1896 the monthly report was expressing pleasure at what it could claim had been a good investment. Funds of the Society were also invested in the shares of a number of railway companies. But despite this excursion into big business, a very strict control was still maintained over expenditure at the head office of the Society. In the autumn of 1894 members were asked to vote upon a request from the Executive Council that the pay of a 20-year-old clerical assistant in the office should be increased. The statement from the Executive Committee said that it was a discreditable thing for the Society to keep the wages of a young clerical assistant at a standard to which the word 'sweating' could be applied. Despite the strength of this appeal, the members voted by only a narrow majority in favour of a wage increase. The majority in favour of the increase was 11,843 to 9,891. By a rather larger majority 8,383 to 5,840 they also agreed to the employment of a boy messenger in the office.

AGREEMENTS

At the beginning of 1894 the Society concluded an important agreement with the Ship Repairers' Association for special payments for members of the Society engaged on the repair of oil ships. Ever since 1891 the Society had been conducting a running battle with ship-repairers to obtain supplementary allowances for members working on oil ships. The battle was fought yard by yard. Towards the end of 1893 the Ship Repairers' Association, which represented the leading firms on all the main estuaries, invited the Society to meet them to discuss wages paid to members working on oil tankers. In the negotiations the Society emphasised that members working on oil ships were facing special hazards. Explosions had frequently occurred. Eventually agreement was reached under which platers were to receive 15s per day, riveters 12s 6d per day and holders-up 10s per day. The employers also agreed that, before men were put to work on a specified list of jobs on oil tankers, an expert's certificate should be obtained daily to the effect that the tanks were safe. This certificate was to be posted in a conspicuous place.

The developing practice of the Society in signing agreements with individual employers and employers' associations about negotiating procedure, wages, apprenticeship and other matters led the Executive Council to emphasise the importance of electing representatives of the members at workshop and shipyard level. Members were informed that shop stewards should be appointed in all shops where six or more members were employed.

In the autumn of 1894 the Society decided that, as it had now concluded a number of written agreements with employers and employers' associations, it should arrange to have them printed and circulated to branches. This was done, and copies were also distributed to a number of other trade unions. In acknowledging receipt of the new handbook of agreements the Amalgamated Society of

Engineers said that the agreements were proof of the efficacy of the conciliatory policy consistently carried out by the Boilermakers' Society in preference to ill considered strikes and violent methods.

CONFLICT IN THE TUC

This adherence of the Society to a policy of conciliation and narrow concern with occupational matters led to a serious conflict with new trends in the TUC. Immediately after the 1894 Congress of the TUC held at Norwich a report from the Boilermakers' representatives appeared in the monthly report of the Society, stating that to call the Congress a trade union conference was a misnomer. In the view of the Society's representatives the Congress had become an annual gathering of socialists, 'whose dreamy ideas find vent in strongly worded resolutions which we cannot endorse'. Many of the resolutions, said the boilermakers' representatives, were political and demanded that the power of the State should be used so as to supersede the necessity of personal or combined exertion on the part of workers for their mutual benefit or protection. The report from the representatives concluded by stating that they differed fundamentally and utterly with all such proposals. Collectivism, they said, could never take the place of individualism.

At the 1894 TUC there had been a number of controversies between the socialists, led by Keir Hardie, Tom Mann and others, and the older leaders of the trade union movement, including Robert Knight. These controversies centred on demands for legislation for an eight hour day, for the nationalisation of the land, mines, minerals and royalty rents, and for the election of a new secretary of the Parliamentary Committee.

Following the publication of the critical report of the proceedings of the TUC from the representatives of the Boilermakers' Society, a number of letters of protest against the TUC were received from branches. One of these from the South Shields No. 2 branch contained a resolution stating that the TUC had ceased to be of any value to the Boilermakers' Society. It urged that a vote should be taken as to whether the Society should continue to send representatives to the TUC. The Executive Council decided to submit this resolution to a ballot vote of the members and appended to their request an analysis of the representation from various unions

125

at the last TUC. This analysis showed that there were fewer delegates from the main skilled trades than from unions organising gas-
workers, dockers and general labourers, miners and textile workers.
The Executive Council also published a letter which they had
received from the Parliamentary Committee of the TUC, drawing
attention to a resolution passed by the Congress stating that, in the
event of any blacklegging by one union against another, an aggrieved
society could report the circumstances to the Parliamentary Committee who could then appoint three of their number to act as
arbitrators. The Executive Council of the Boilermakers' Society
deplored this step taken by the TUC and suggested that the great
majority of the members of the Parliamentary Committee had no
knowledge of the skilled trades. They concluded their criticism of
this TUC initiative by pointing out that if the Society were to
disaffiliate it would result in a saving of at least £60 per year.

This criticism of the TUC, to which the Executive Council gave
its support, was, in fact, part of the rearguard campaign being
fought by Robert Knight and the older generation of craft union
leaders against the new unionists and socialists. It found some
reflection inside the Boilermakers' Society, not so much in political
controversy as in the demand for more democracy and for a tougher
official policy towards the employers. Robert Knight was still very
influential but the movement of dissent was gathering strength.

The result on the vote of affiliation to the TUC was announced
towards the end of 1894. It showed a majority of 5,163 in favour of
disaffiliation. The voting was 14,241 to 9,078. The significance of
this result was not that it supported disaffiliation, as favoured by
Robert Knight and the EC so that they could put pressure on the
TUC, but that it revealed an important division of opinion within
the Society. An energetic campaign against the socialists was conducted by the 'old guard' leadership of the TUC, including Robert
Knight. They planned to reassert their authority at the 1895 Congress. Their plans went well, and it was soon clear that the ballot
vote of the Boilermakers' Society to disaffiliate was intended by
Robert Knight to strengthen his hand in these TUC counter moves
rather than as a declaration of intent to dissociate the Boilermakers'
Society from the rest of the trade union movement. By the summer
of 1895 a ballot vote of the Society had returned an overwhelming
majority in favour of representation at the TUC. This was now

favoured by the EC. In the same ballot it was also decided that two delegates should attend the Congress from each electoral district.

The 'old guard' leadership succeeded in no uncertain fashion in reasserting their domination at the 1895 Congress. The struggle for power centred on the standing orders, and the report of the Boilermakers' representatives drew attention to the fight that had taken place. Under the new standing orders accepted by Congress no person was allowed to attend as a delegate 'unless he is actually working at his trade at the time of appointment or is a permanent paid working official of his trade union'. The effect was to exclude, among others, Keir Hardie, the most prominent of the socialists. Another important change made by the Congress was that representation should not be accepted except from trade unions.

The Boilermakers' representatives pointed out in their report to the membership that the first change aimed at excluding 'bogus labour representatives and men who have no immediate interest in and are not in direct touch with those whom they are supposed to represent'. The second change precluded trades councils from sending delegates to the Congress. It was in the trades councils that 'new' unionists and socialists were particularly influential. Professor B. C. Roberts in his history of *The Trades Union Congress 1868 to 1921*, says 'the pendulum had, indeed, swung back a long way from the days when the new unionists, flushed with their victories, imagined they had revolutionised the Trades Union Congress'.

The Boilermakers' representatives in their report said that they had no hesitation in giving an affirmative answer to the question whether Congress could be used in any way to further and advance the special and direct interests of the Boilermakers' Society. The new approval of the TUC by the Boilermakers' Society also found expression in a ballot vote conducted in the following year to appoint the General Secretary as a permanent delegate to the annual Congress of the TUC. The voting in favour was 16,463 with 3,385 against.

Chapter 11

Democracy Asserts Itself

The growing feeling that more democratic control should be exercised within the Society and that the power of the General Secretary should be curtailed led to an important constitutional change in 1895. The Society decided that the Executive Council of lay members drawn from one particular locality near to the head office should be replaced by a full-time Executive Council consisting of representatives elected from various districts. The new Executive Council was thus elected on a district basis by all members of the Society and not only by those working near to the head office. This decision to replace a locally elected lay Executive Council by a full-time, nationally elected Executive Council evoked strong opposition from Robert Knight. It all started towards the end of 1894 when, in accordance with the rules, a vote was taken of the Society's members as to whether the General Council should be called together to revise the rules. The existing rules stipulated that such a vote should be taken every five years. The members voted by 14,048 to 2,237 in favour of convening the General Council.

A FULL-TIME EC

When the General Council met in 1895, by far the most controversial of its proposals was that the lay Executive Council should be replaced by a full-time Executive Council. It soon became clear that this was vigorously opposed not only by the existing lay Executive Council but also by the General Secretary. Nevertheless, the proposal was carried. In the monthly report of August 1895 a very strong attack was made on it. The article in the monthly report argued,

128

first, that there was not sufficient work at the head office of the Society to employ seven permanent Executive Council members. Secondly, it expressed disapproval of the division of the Society into seven electoral districts for the purpose of EC elections. It said that this would create a dangerous disunity. Each Executive Councillor would in future regard himself as the representative of a division instead of a representative of the whole Society. The third ground of opposition was that it would add substantially to the expenses of the Society. Shortly afterwards a majority of the members of the General Council circulated a document to the branches answering the attack made in the monthly report upon their proposal. One part of this circular caused extremely bad feeling. It said that the new permanent Executive Council would strip the General Secretary of the autocratic power he had wielded for too long. Subsequently, however, it was revealed that a number of members of the General Council had appended their signature to a draft which did not contain this offending paragraph. Apparently it was inserted afterwards. The leading figure in the publication of the General Council's circular was one of the youngest members of the Council, D. C. Cummings of London. His role in the revolt from below helped to secure his election shortly afterwards as district delegate for Yorkshire. Four years later he was to be elected General Secretary. The Executive Council issued a further vigorous reply to the circular from the majority of the General Council. They condemned the attack made on the General Secretary. The controversy continued to be ventilated in the columns of the monthly report.

The new rules proposed by the General Council had to be submitted to a ballot vote of the members. The monthly report appealed for branches to submit their returns and made it very clear in which direction the sympathies of the Executive Council and General Secretary lay. Strangely, however, no voting results were published in the monthly report. Nevertheless, it was clear that the proposed change had been approved by the membership. The existing Executive Council and Robert Knight had to accede to the wishes of the membership, and the new full-time Executive Council of seven members was subsequently elected from seven electoral districts. Some impression of the feelings of Robert Knight on this change was conveyed in the monthly report of January 1897, the month in which the new full-time Executive Council assumed office. He said that each year saw a thinning of the number of personal friends and acquaintances. Nevertheless, work had to be carried on in obedience to principle and with untiring energy and unselfish aims. His mood was reflected in his phrase 'like a clock worn out by beating time the wheels of wearied life at last stand still.' He concluded by stating that the Society was being handed to the keeping of successors: 'it is the most perfect organisation the world has ever seen.'

Despite the strong current in the Society to curtail the powers of the General Secretary, Robert Knight was re-elected unopposed in 1896. His unopposed re-election followed twenty-five years of service as General Secretary. When he was first elected, the Society had ninety-four branches, 7,000 members and very little money. After twenty-five years he could claim that the Society had 257 branches, about 40,000 members and £154,000 as accumulated capital. In the following year a donation of £600 was made to Robert Knight 'as a mark of admiration and esteem for his noble and sterling qualities as organiser, trade union leader and diplomatist in the prevention and settlement of industrial conflicts, and in commemoration of his silver jubilee of office'. The money was subscribed by members of the Society and by employers.

In the second half of the 1890s there was prosperity in the ship-building and engineering industries. The membership grew to more than 47,000 and the funds to more than £290,000. Between 1895 and 1897 wage increases were secured in nearly all districts. A conciliation agreement was also concluded with the employers, covering firms on the north-east coast. Under the agreement, standing committees, consisting of three employers' representatives and three boilermakers' representatives, were appointed for each of the main rivers on the north-east coast. Any disputes about piece-work prices or other matters not resolved in the yard or workshop where they arose could then be referred to one of these standing committees.

THE EIGHT HOUR DAY

In the early part of 1897 a committee was formed in London, consisting of representatives of various engineering trades, to press for a reduction in hours and the establishment of an eight hour working

130

day. This committee was known as the Eight Hours Committee and
included representatives of the local boilermakers. By May a number
of London firms had conceded a shorter working week and had
introduced a forty-eight-hour week. In the meanwhile, however,
largely on the initiative of employers on the north-east coast, an
employers' federation of engineering associations had been formed.
By the early summer of 1897 the new Employers' Federation represented many of the principal employers in the main industrial centres
of Britain. London employers, however, remained outside. The
demand for a shorter working week, centred on the London area,
gave an impetus to the organisation of employers in the London
area. A branch of the Employers' Federation was soon established
in London.

The relationship between the unions and the employers, particularly in London, became more and more hostile. The Employers'
Federation recognised that the demand for a shorter working week
was not one which concerned only London. They countered the
demand by a threat of a lock-out. They said that they would lock
out batches of men, starting from a date in July. This threat was
enforced and more than 25,000 workers were involved in the initial
stages of the dispute. This later rose to more than double that
number. The dispute attracted enormous press publicity and public
attention. The employers sought by every means to recruit blackleg
labour, and the unions received substantial financial assistance not
only from other trade unionists in Britain but also from unions
abroad. In his *The Story of the Engineers* James B. Jeffreys states
that in all about £116,000 was raised by voluntary subscriptions.
The dispute dragged on into the early part of 1898 when eventually,
after protracted negotiations, a settlement was reached. The settlement represented a victory for the employers. The unions were in
serious difficulties because of a shortage of money. The demand
for an eight hour day was withdrawn in exchange for some minor
concessions, and the terms of settlement were approved by something like a two to one majority in a ballot vote in the principal
union, the Amalgamated Society of Engineers.

The terms of settlement imposed on the unions were severe. They
established the principle that the unions should not interfere with
the management of the firms. This assertion of managerial preroga-
tives, which the employers have always sought to interpret in the

131

widest possible manner, has coloured relations between the engineering employers and the unions right down to the present time.

The role of the Boilermakers' Society in the engineering dispute of 1897–8 came in for considerable criticism from the main body of engineering workers. Shortly after the dispute began in the London area the Boilermakers' Society withdrew from it. The policy of the Society was, however, very strongly defended by the Executive Council and by Robert Knight in particular. In his annual report for 1897 he said that the aim of shortening the working week was a very urgent one. During the latter part of 1896 an attempt had been made by the engineering unions to arrange a national conference with the employers to discuss a claim for reduced hours of work. Unfortunately, this had not proved possible to arrange. Shortly afterwards, according to Robert Knight, the members of the ASE in the London area, without consulting other unions, made a demand on the London employers for an eight hour day. In Robert Knight's view the engineers in London ought not to have taken this initiative. It would have been better to confine the initiative to shipbuilding. According to Robert Knight, 'the concession could have been obtained from the shipbuilders with much less difficulty than the engineering firms.'

The Boilermakers' Society had agreed that two of their members from the London District Committee should represent the Society on the London Eight Hours Committee, but they had also made it clear that the Society's representatives were not empowered to authorise any action other than peaceful negotiations. When it appeared likely that the dispute might result in a stoppage of work, the Boilermakers' Society wrote to the Amalgamated Society of Engineers to suggest that a conference should be held between the various unions before any final decisions were taken. The ASE did not agree to this suggestion. A ballot vote was then taken among members of the Boilermakers' Society as to whether the claim should be pursued nationally by the unions in co-operation or whether it should be pursued first in the London area. The result of the ballot was an overwhelming majority in favour of the first of these two alternatives. The voting was 25,433 to 3,403. In the light of this result the Boilermakers' Society withdrew their support from the movement for an eight hour working day in London.

Robert Knight came under particularly strong criticism because of this decision of the Boilermakers' Society. A statement was then issued by the Shipbuilding and Engineering Federation, excluding the ASE, regretting the repeated attacks made on Robert Knight, who was not only the General Secretary of the Boilermakers' Society but also the President of the Federation.

In September 1897 the Engineering and Shipbuilding Federation, representing the unions other than the ASE, wrote to the ASE again suggesting that a joint conference should be held. This suggestion, however, was again rejected by the ASE. The Boilermakers' Society, now having withdrawn from the dispute, predicted that no satisfactory settlement would emerge from the dispute.

In the 1898 annual report Robert Knight returned to the subject of the engineering dispute. He said that more than 9,000 members of the Boilermakers' Society had been involved in the dispute because of the employers' lock-out and it had taken considerable time before the majority of them could secure employment. After these bitter experiences his advice was 'to keep steadily to the straight and safe path of conciliation'.

Although relations between the Society and the ASE were now very strained, the boilermakers continued to give support to workers involved in disputes in other industries. In the early months of 1897 a 6d levy was introduced to provide financial assistance to quarrymen in Wales. The voting in favour of a 6d levy was roughly ten to one throughout the Society. £200 was also sent to assist Hamburg dockers.

RELATIONS WITH OTHER UNIONS

At the end of 1896 the Society was faced with a threatened lock-out of all its members on the north-east coast. The threat arose from a dispute between caulkers, members of the Society at Walker yard, and members of the independent Drillers' Society. A demarcation dispute was referred to arbitration and an award was given in favour of the drillers. The caulkers then refused to accept the award. They were not supported by the Executive Council of the Society, and eventually a ballot vote of the whole membership was taken as to whether the caulkers should be instructed to return to work. The employers had threatened to lock out all members of the Boilermakers' Society on the north-east coast. The ballot resulted in a majority in favour of such an instruction being given. The voting was 6,297 to 935.

Later in the year a number of local unions of drillers and the National Society of Drillers applied for admission to the Boilermakers' Society. The National Society of Drillers claimed over 2,000 members and there were some hundreds of other drillers in local organisations. When the question was put to a ballot the members of the Boilermakers' Society voted heavily against the admission of drillers. The voting was 24,173 against to 6,349 for admission.

The Society's members took a more sympathetic attitude towards the application for admission of sheet iron workers, centred mainly on the Clyde. The sheet iron workers were employed on the fabrication of ventilators, hoods, cowls, tanks and other fittings in which light plates were used. The Executive Council of the Boilermakers' Society pointed out that this was a growing section of the industry and that it would be to the advantage of the Society if the sheet iron workers were admitted. On a ballot vote the members voted by 14,190 to 11,031 in favour of their admission. It was, however, made clear that the sheet iron workers would form a section of the Boilermakers' Society and be confined to their own special class of work.

In 1898 the Society also took over a small organisation of boilermakers in London, whose members were mostly employed at the Thames Iron Works & Shipbuilding Company Limited. Under an agreement made in October 1897 the members of this small London union were admitted to membership of the Boilermakers' Society, and this was later confirmed in a ballot vote by 15,835 to 12,324. A small local society on the Wear was also admitted to the Boilermakers' Society as a branch. This, however, was strongly resisted by the employers of the men concerned.

Relations with the Associated Shipwrights' Society also improved sufficiently for a demarcation agreement to be concluded in November 1897. The agreement stipulated that, in the event of a demarcation dispute, the job or jobs concerned should be suspended and an effort be made to resolve the dispute at shipyard level. If this proved unsuccessful, the dispute should then be referred to a joint committee consisting of five representatives from each of the two unions. The secretary of the employers' association was also to be notified.

134

If the joint committee was unable to resolve the dispute, then the issue was to be referred to a board of referees. The agreement insisted that work – other than the job in dispute – should go on without interruption. The parties to this agreement included not only the Shipwrights' Society and the Boilermakers' Society but also the Smiths' Society. The agreement applied to all shipyards on the Tyne and the Blyth.

The movement towards closer working between trade unions in the 1890s was also reflected in the desire of unions representing unskilled workers to affiliate to the Federation of Engineering and Shipbuilding Trades. In 1894 the Federation had voted by 22,410 to 17,908 against the admission of societies representing unskilled workers. A majority of the small organisations, however, were more favourable towards the proposal. Finally it was decided that the unions should consult their members about it first. Members were asked whether they favoured the admission of unskilled workers into the Federation, and secondly, whether the question of affiliation should be decided on the basis of one vote for each society or by aggregating the votes of the membership of the various societies. The issue was put to a ballot vote in the Boilermakers' Society and resulted in a majority of more than two to one against the admission of unskilled workers. The voting was 11,632 to 5,229. The Boilermakers' Society also voted overwhelmingly in favour of the proposition that the issue should be decided by aggregating the votes of the various societies. The voting on this question was 15,238 to 972. Clearly this method of determining the issue gave a bigger voice to the larger trade unions. The unions of unskilled workers remained outside the Federation.

The same attitude of exclusiveness was expressed shortly afterwards in a vote of the Society on a proposal, supported by the Executive Council, that there should be a reduction in the entrance fee payable by applicants for membership. The Executive Council asked for this reduction in entrance fee as a temporary measure in order to assist recruitment efforts in areas where the degree of organisation was not as high at is could be. This included Staffordshire, Lincolnshire and parts of Yorkshire. Despite this appeal by the Executive Council, the request was rejected by a three to two majority.

The movement for closer working between unions also led to a proposal for the formation of a general federation of trade unions. This proposal was worked out at a special conference held early in 1899. The main idea behind it was that the new federation, which was to cover numerous trades and industries, should be able to provide financial assistance to any one group of unions involved in a dispute with their employers. It was emphasised in the proposed constitution, nevertheless, that the purpose of the federation would be to promote industrial peace and to prevent strikes or lock-outs. There were to be two scales of contributions and two scales of benefit. The intention apparently was to provide a financial formula which would meet the needs of both the unions of craftsmen and the unions of unskilled workers. The Boilermakers' Society participated in the meetings for the drawing up of this proposal but both the General Secretary, Robert Knight, and the Executive Council were critical of the suggested scheme. They felt that the rates of contribution were inadequate to sustain the suggested rates of benefit, and they were also doubtful as to whether the new federation would infringe the autonomy of the affiliated organisations. The Boilermakers' Society was also satisfied that its interests were covered by the Federation of Engineering and Shipbuilding Trades. They did not see the need for a new federated organisation. When the proposals were put to a ballot vote of the membership they were heavily defeated. The voting was 28,901 against the proposed scheme and 2,666 in favour.

The proposal for a general federation of trade unions was very much a consequence of the engineering dispute of 1897–8 and of the generally recognised need for unions to render assistance to each other. The committee to examine the proposals for a new federation was set up by the TUC, and Robert Knight acted as its chairman. The special conference to consider the proposal for a new federation was also convened by the TUC. In the outcome, most of the stronger unions took much the same attitude as the Boilermakers' Society. They were doubtful of the financial soundness of the proposed new federation and they were apprehensive as to whether it would infringe their autonomy. Nevertheless, the General Federation of Trade Unions was established with an affiliated membership at the outset of forty-four societies, with a membership of nearly 350,000, representing one quarter of the total number of workers organised in TUC affiliated unions. It was a very loose collection of organisations, most of them financially weaker than the strong craft unions. Almost from the beginning it developed into a mutual insurance society to meet the needs of a number of smaller unions. It has remained in existence to this day.

A HISTORIC LEGAL CASE

In the second half of the 1890s the Boilermakers' Society was involved in a case which made legal history and had a very important bearing on the evolution of trade union rights in Britain. It all started in the Glengall Company works in London. Two men, Flood and Taylor, both shipwrights, were engaged to work on a vessel called the *Sam Weller*. Most of the men employed by this company were members of the Boilermakers' Society, and there was strong feeling against Flood and Taylor because it was felt that they were taking work which should have been given to boilermakers. The members of the Boilermakers' Society got in touch with the London district delegate, Mr Allen, and he in turn saw the managing director of the company. He advised the managing director that if Flood and Taylor were continued in employment it was likely that the members of the Boilermakers' Society would walk off the job. The managing director then dismissed Flood and Taylor. A claim for damages by Flood was brought against Allen, against the chairman of the Executive Council of the Boilermakers' Society, and against the General Secretary. The case was heard before Mr Justice Kennedy and a jury. Mr Justice Kennedy held that no case of conspiracy, coercion or intimidation had been established and he therefore dismissed the claim against the chairman of the Executive Council and the General Secretary. However, he put two questions to the jury: 'Did Allen maliciously induce the Company to discharge the plaintiffs?', and 'Did Allen maliciously induce the Company not to engage the plaintiffs?' The jury replied in the affirmative to both these questions and damages against Allen were awarded. The trial took place in February 1895 and judgement was given in the following month. The Boilermakers' Society decided to appeal, but in the Court of Appeal the decision of the court of first instance was upheld. It was then decided to make a further appeal to the House of Lords. The hearing before the House of Lords was extended over a very long period. It was first argued before the

137

House of Lords towards the end of 1895 but, because of differences of opinion among the Lords, it was announced that the appeal was to be reheard in the presence of certain of Her Majesty's Judges. Eventually the Law Lords by a majority of six to three reversed the decision of the lower courts and entered judgement for Allen.

The decision in the case of Allen *v*. Flood was widely welcomed by liberal opinion. The *London Chronicle* said that the judgement of the House of Lords rested on broad principles of common freedom. The chief of these principles was that 'a man's right not to work is in law a right of precisely the same nature and entitled to just the same protection as a man's right to work.' In the labour market both sides should be free to buy and sell labour on whatever terms they liked and each side should be free to arrange to act collectively. The *Manchester Guardian* said that it would hardly be possible to exaggerate the importance of the issues raised by the case of Allen *v*. Flood. The district delegate of the Boilermakers' Society had exercised his own right to protect the interests of his members. A worker had a right to exercise an option with regard to the persons in whose society he agreed to work.

RESIGNATION OF ROBERT KNIGHT

In January 1899 Robert Knight submitted his resignation as General Secretary of the Society. He explained that he was now sixty-five years of age and he was no exception to the rule that advanced years brought infirmity. He recalled that he had started his working life as an apprentice when he was twelve years of age and had worked at the trade for more than twenty-five years. He had held the position of General Secretary for nearly twenty-eight years, making a total of fifty-three years of labour. In his letter of resignation he said that he could not possibly describe his feelings. His life had been bound up so much with the Boilermakers' Society that to sever his official connection meant a wrench that no one but himself could understand. He went on to emphasise that the Boilermakers' Society was not built for the sole purpose of increasing wages and shortening the hours of labour. Its purpose was also to increase the confidence of men in each other. Its purpose, too, was to foster independence among working men and to promote industrial peace. Mr Knight paid tribute to his colleagues in the Society and expressed gratitude for the kindness which he had received at the hands of employers. The Executive Council submitted the letter of resignation to the branches and numerous requests were received to retain in some way or other the services of Robert Knight. As a result of this correspondence the Executive Council decided to submit to the membership a proposal to retain Robert Knight as a consulting secretary. The result of the vote, although showing a small majority in favour, nevertheless revealed a large body of opposition. The voting was 17,041 for the proposition and 15,830 against. The Executive Council explained that some of the opposition had come from members who took the view that the General Secretary had now earned a retirement and that he ought not to be burdened with further duties. Others who opposed the proposition felt that the new General Secretary, whoever he might be, would be inhibited if Robert Knight was still acting as a consulting secretary.

The members were also asked to vote on the amount to be paid to Robert Knight in his new position as consulting secretary. Three alternative figures were offered, £3 10s, £3 and £2 10s per week. The members decided in favour of the largest of these three figures. 10,325 votes were cast for £3 10s per week, 3,683 for £3 per week and 3,770 for £2 10s per week.

A NEW GENERAL SECRETARY

Three candidates were nominated for the election of a new General Secretary. All were district delegates. They were Mr F. A. Fox of South Wales, Mr J. Connolly of Scotland and Mr D. Cummings of Yorkshire. None of them in his letter of application published to the membership promised any significant change in the policy or conduct of affairs of the Society. Mr Fox said that he would support a peaceful and conciliatory policy, whether in relation to employers or other trades. Mr Connolly said that he would strive to oppose aggression and to adjust the interests of the members with the least possible disturbance to the *status quo*. Mr Cummings said that as the days went by it was more and more realised that there was great advantage in settling differences without resorting to the old method of strike action. Strikes, he said, were the last resort of well-organised men and need scarcely ever be undertaken. Mr Cummings did, however, say in his letter of application that he was in

139

favour of space being provided in the monthly journal for ventilating the opinions of members of the Society.

The first ballot placed Mr Fox well ahead of his two rivals. Mr Fox received 17,057 votes, Mr Connolly 9,689 and Mr Cummings 8,806. Nevertheless, Mr Fox had not secured an absolute majority and it was necessary, therefore, to conduct a further ballot between the two candidates with the largest votes. No sooner had this been decided than a telegram was received from Mr Fox stating that he had decided to withdraw from the contest. This threw the Society into consternation. It was later learnt that Mr Fox had accepted the secretaryship of an employers' organisation, the South Wales Federation of Ship-repairers. In the circumstances the Executive Council decided to hold a ballot between Mr Connolly and Mr Cummings for the vacancy. It was a very closely contested election and resulted in a victory for Mr Cummings. The voting was 18,389 to 17,830. Mr Connolly subsequently protested against the decision of the Executive Council to conduct a ballot between himself and Mr Cummings. He argued that when Mr Fox had withdrawn from the final ballot he, Mr Connolly, should have been declared the successful candidate. He also asked for a scrutiny of the votes. This was then submitted to the membership by the Executive Council but was turned down.

In the meanwhile Mr Fox, who almost certainly would have been elected General Secretary if he had not withdrawn, explained his action to a mass meeting of members in South Wales. A report in the journal said that he delivered a spirited address for about an hour and that several members spoke warmly in favour of his action. A resolution was then carried unaminously, tendering thanks to Mr Fox for his able and effective service in the past and expressing the view that his action in accepting the office of secretary of the South Wales Federation of Ship-repairers was 'perfectly honest, straightforward and thoroughly consistent with his principles as a trade unionist'. The resolution went on to say that the members believed that his taking this new post would deepen and strengthen the good feeling which existed between 'master and man'.

The new General Secretary, Dave Cummings, was born in Greenwich in December 1861. He left school in 1875 and became an apprentice at Rennie's shipbuilding yard. When he was nineteen he joined the Boilermakers' Society, and at the age of twenty-one he was elected a branch official. Shortly afterwards he represented the Society on the London Trades Council and was then elected to the Executive Committee of the London Trades Council. In 1895 he was elected district delegate of the Society for the Yorkshire district. He had thus been a full-time official for slightly more than four years when he was elected General Secretary.

LABOUR REPRESENTATION

In 1899, in the final year of office of Robert Knight, the Boilermakers' Society supported the historic resolution of the Trades Union Congress inviting the co-operation of socialist, co-operative and trade union organisations to devise ways and means for securing the return of Labour Members to the next Parliament. The resolution was carried at the TUC by the relatively narrow majority of 546,000 to 434,000. It was supported by the new unions which had grown rapidly in the 1890s and by a number of craft unions which were becoming increasingly impatient at the impossibility of securing legislation favourable to their trade interests from an unsympathetic House of Commons. The resolution was opposed principally by the miners' unions and the cotton textile unions. These unions, because of the concentration of their membership in a limited number of areas, were able to act as an effective pressure group on local Conservative and Liberal Members. The miners, too, had been able to secure the election of a number of representatives standing under the banner of Liberal-Labour.

The decision of the TUC to convene a conference of representatives favourable to the principle of independent labour representation was the result of a number of parallel developments. In the 1890s there had been a number of court decisions which endangered trade union rights. This underlined the importance of securing the election of more Members of Parliament sympathetic to trade union aims. Secondly, the Conservative Government of the time had shown itself very indifferent to a number of proposals affecting the trade interest of trade union members. Thus the Boilermakers' Society, for example, had shown a special interest in promoting a fair wage resolution through the House of Commons. The last fair wages resolution was in 1891 but it was regarded as unsatisfactory in a number of respects. The Society was also interested to secure

141

Parliamentary approval for the registration and inspection of boilers. This was felt to be necessary to protect workmen required to work on boilers.

The third development contributing to the TUC decision of 1899 was the consistent propaganda and activity conducted by socialists in and out of the trade union movement in favour of the principle of independent labour representation. By this time some of the earlier personal controversies had died down and the arguments advanced by the socialists were gaining ground among trade union members.

In their report of the 1899 Plymouth Congress the representatives of the Boilermakers' Society expressed their sympathy with the decision of the Congress to convene a labour representation conference and said that it was only by the carrying out of the idea embodied in the resolution that it would be possible to get the reforms agreed upon by Congress carried into practical effect. The labour representation conference was convened for February 1900. The Executive Council recommended that the Society should be represented and decided to submit their recommendation to a ballot vote of the membership. It was rejected by 6,880 to 3,157. The majority of the Society's members were not yet persuaded of the need for independent labour representation.

In the closing years of the century the Boilermakers' Society reaffirmed its long tradition of solidarity with other workers engaged in industrial disputes. In 1898 a majority of 29,968 to 1,036 voted in favour of a levy of 3d per member to assist South Wales miners who were engaged in a dispute with their employers. In the following year an even bigger majority, 31,690 to 1,719, voted to send £200 to assist Danish workers who had been locked out by their employers. A grant of £20 was also sent to textile workers in Austria who were engaged in an industrial dispute.

Chapter 12

Trade Union Rights and Labour Representation

Between 1900 and 1906 the trade union movement was confronted with new legal problems. The period started with a House of Lords judgement in 1900 which took away from the trade union movement rights which they had believed they possessed ever since the trade union reform legislation of the 1870s. The first reaction of the unions to this attack on their legal rights was somewhat hesitant. Some leaders quickly grasped the real significance of the judgement but others remained doubtful and a few were inclined to welcome it. As time went by, pressure for new legal protection for trade unionism grew, and by 1902 and 1903 a campaign was beginning to be mounted for a new Trade Disputes Bill to protect union activities. The campaign developed and more and more unions gave support to the principle of independent political action. Considerable sympathy was also evoked from influential sections of Liberal opinion. Eventually in 1906, after the election of a new Liberal Government with a sweeping majority, a Trade Disputes Bill was introduced which gave the unions the protection they desired.

THE TAFF VALE JUDGEMENT

The Taff Vale judgement was the outcome of a legal case which started with a strike of railwaymen employed by the Taff Vale Railway Company in South Wales. The strike was called irregularly by the West of England organiser of the Amalgamated Society of Railway Servants, who had already established a reputation for himself as a militant. The General Secretary of the Amalgamated Society, Richard Bell. opposed giving official recognition to the strike but he was overruled by his Executive, even though they expressed their disagreement with the manner in which the strike had been started. The company brought in blacklegs and, in addition, decided to try to break the strike by legal action. The legal case started in the late summer of 1900 and dragged on through various stages until July 1901, when the House of Lords decided that the company could proceed with a claim for damages against the union for having conspired to induce workers to break their contracts of employment and also for having conspired to interfere with the traffic of the company by picketing. The claim for damages was eventually settled in the Company's favour and the total costs to the union, including the damages and the expenses of litigation, amounted to more than £40,000.

The Taff Vale judgement was not an isolated and accidental phenomenon which changed the course of trade union history. In the 1890s there had been a significant growth in trade union strength, and towards the end of the century employers began to look towards the courts to redress the changing balance of strength in the labour market. Not all court decisions went the way desired by employers. The judgement in the case of Allen *versus* Flood, for example, referred to in the last chapter, was regarded as a victory for the unions and was taken at the time to have upheld the right of workers to decide not to work with persons whom they regarded as objectionable because they were not members of a particular trade union. On the other hand, there was a number of other legal decisions in the final years of the nineteenth century which indicated that the courts were lending a sympathetic ear to claims for the curtailment of trade union strength.

It will be recalled that the members of the Boilermakers' Society had rejected on a branch vote the recommendation of their Executive Council that the Society should send representatives to the labour representation congress convened for February 1900. By the end of the year, however, there were indications of a new awareness of the need to protect trade union rights by political action. In February 1901, well before the judgement of the House of Lords in the Taff Vale case, a pamphlet from the TUC was distributed to members, drawing attention to the implications of the earlier stages of the Taff Vale legal action, particularly in relation to picketing.

At the 1901 Congress of the TUC the delegation of the Boilermakers' Society supported a resolution urging trade unions to affiliate to the Labour Representation Committee. At the same Congress the Parliamentary Committee submitted several recommendations dealing with the House of Lords' decision in the Taff Vale case. The unions were concerned to protect the right to picket and to protect their funds in industrial disputes.

LABOUR REPRESENTATION

Despite the decision of the membership not to support the labour representation congress, the Executive Council decided – in the new situation following the Taff Vale case – that representatives should be sent to a meeting convened by the Labour Representation Committee. The report of the boilermakers' representatives stated that they approved of the objects of the Labour Representation Committee and recommended that the members should be asked to vote on whether they wanted direct representation in the House of Commons. The representatives urged that, if they voted in favour, a further vote should be taken for and against affiliation to the Labour Representation Committee.

In his annual report for 1901, the General Secretary, D. C. Cummings, said that the Taff Vale judgement, together with other recent legal decisions, had considerably altered the legal standing of trade unions. He hinted at his misgivings in relation to the conduct of the Taff Vale dispute by the railway union. 'Many of us,' he said, 'no doubt believe that mistakes have been made and maybe a want of tact displayed.' Nevertheless, he concluded, the time for recrimination was past and it was necessary for all to work together to restore the rights which had been lost.

In December 1901, the Executive Council issued a strong appeal to the membership to vote in favour of political representation, affiliation to the Labour Representation Committee, and the introduction of a levy of threepence per year for purposes of securing political representation. The appeal referred to the need to alter the law following the Taff Vale judgement to 'ensure the safety of the funds we have for long years been building up for relief in sickness, old age and accident, death and want of work'. The appeal also referred to the need for a Boiler Registration and Inspection Bill. The Executive Council pointed out that Parliament did not sit throughout the year and that, in the event of a Boilermakers' sponsored candidate being elected, it would be possible during the long vacation for him to do special organising work for the Society in isolated parts of Great Britain and Ireland. The EC regarded it as 'absolutely impossible' for the position of General Secretary and Member of Parliament to be combined, but the dual position of MP and special organiser could, they argued, be carried out with benefit to all concerned. The appeal to the membership concluded by asking all members to discuss and vote upon the EC proposal 'without political feeling or dissension'. The question at issue, said the EC, was the direct representation of the interest of boilermakers, combined with 'the giving of a helping hand to all such legislation as will be beneficial to trade unionists and workers generally'.

The appeal of the Executive Council met with a resounding response from the membership. The proposal for political representation was carried by 25,581 votes to 6,995. In the following month there was a similarly large majority in favour of affiliation to the Labour Representation Committee. The voting for affiliation was 26,478 with 8,905 against. Before the vote was taken on affiliation to the LRC, the constitution of the committee was put to the membership. It included the following important statement of principle:

1 That the Committee was in favour of working-class opinion being represented in the House of Commons by men sympathetic with the aims and demands of the Labour movement, whose candidatures were promoted by one or other of the affiliated societies.
2 That the Committee was in favour of establishing a distinct Labour group in Parliament with its own Whips. This group would be ready to co-operate with any party which for the time being might be engaged in promoting legislation of direct interests to labour.

Immediately after the vote of the membership on political representation the Executive Council and the full-time district delegates met to consider who should be put forward as a parliamentary candidate. A number of officials who were suggested as candidates declined to stand, including the General Secretary, Mr Cummings, and the retired General Secretary, Mr Knight. Mr Knight, who was not present at the meeting, wrote to decline nomination because of his age. He was then approaching seventy. Mr Cummings declined on the grounds that it was impossible for one man to be both General Secretary and a Member of Parliament. Eventually it was decided to suggest three full-time district delegates as nominees. It was agreed to submit the nominations to a ballot vote and also to ask members whether a salary of £325 per year or £350 per year should be paid. The three district delegates nominated were Mr James Conley, Mr John Hill and Mr J. H. Jose. In a subsequent vote of the membership Mr Conley, one of the full-time district delegates on the Clyde, came top of the poll. The members decided that in the event of his election to Parliament he should be paid a salary of £325 per year.

James Conley, who thus became the first member of the Boiler-makers' panel of parliamentary candidates, was a native of the north-east. He started work in the shipbuilding industry at the age of eleven. After completing his apprenticeship he worked for fifteen years at John Redhead & Company, South Shields, and was then elected as a full-time district delegate for the Clyde. Mr Conley described himself as a Liberal, 'but unpledged to party measures'. He also declared himself a staunch supporter of Irish Home Rule.

THE CAMPAIGN DEVELOPS

In September 1902 a number of the Glasgow branches of the Society played a prominent part in a united trade union demonstration held in Glasgow to protest against the Taff Vale judgement and to call for better housing for Glasgow's workers. More than 30,000 trade unionists participated, representing some fifty separate unions. The Glasgow 1, 2, 4 and 5 branches marched behind a pipe band and the new banner of the No. 1 branch. This banner, said to be the most colourful in Glasgow, had been painted by a member of the Boilermakers' Society. A banner representing the Govan branches was also in the demonstration. The boilermakers' contingent displayed sets of tools and models lent by the Clydebank branch. A flute band also marched with the boilermakers' contingent.

The award of substantial damages against the Amalgamated Society of Railway Servants in 1902 did much to bring home to trade unionists the real danger in which they were now placed. The

147

January 1903 issue of the Boilermakers' journal carried a full length article outlining the background to the Taff Vale judgement and calling on members to right their wrongs through the use of the ballot box. Nevertheless, the article was by no means clear as to the kind of legal changes wanted by the unions. It spoke of excesses committed by pickets, which all right-thinking men condemned, and of breaches of contract by workers who had not given proper notice. For these illegalities, the article said, the individuals concerned should be made to suffer. It went on to deny that there was anything in the Taff Vale case to connect the unions with an alleged conspiracy.

In March 1903, the TUC, together with the Labour Representation Committee, published a Trade Disputes Bill which they hoped would gain acceptance as a Private Member's Bill. The terms of the Bill sought to legalise peaceful picketing, to amend the law of conspiracy, and to protect trade unions against claims for damages. It was put forward by a Labour Member but was rejected by 258 votes to 228. Among those who voted for the Bill were Mr Asquith, Mr Churchill and Mr Lloyd George. In defeating the Private Member's Bill, the Government decided to set up a Royal Commission on Trade Disputes and Trade Combinations. The Boilermakers' Society was invited to give evidence to the Commission but the Society declined on the grounds that the composition of the Commission, though it included Sidney Webb, excluded representatives of organised labour. In the spring of 1904 the TUC prepared another draft Trade Disputes Bill. This time the Second Reading was carried by a majority of thirty-nine. The majority was made up of the Liberals, the Irish Nationalists, and thirty-one Conservatives. The Bill did not, however, survive further parliamentary stages. Yet another attempt was made in 1905 to secure the passage of a Trades Disputes Bill. Again, it was carried on Second Reading but did not survive the Committee stage.

Meanwhile, inside the Boilermakers' Society, some dissatisfaction had been expressed with the Liberal views of James Conley, the elected member of the Boilermakers' parliamentary panel. Several branches requested that there should be a ballot vote as to whether Mr Conley should be regarded as a Labour candidate. In reply to these requests the General Secretary stated that Mr Conley was a trade union candidate and he did not think that members should concern themselves with whether he was a Conservative, a Liberal, a Home Ruler, a Socialist or anything else. The boilermakers' leadership was still in the Liberal-Labour tradition and they suggested, even within the wider movement, that in some circumstances Labour candidates should co-operate with Liberals or Conservatives.

The issue of the Boilermakers' journal which carried the report of branch criticism of Mr Conley's Liberal views also carried an article entitled, 'Should Trade Unions Incorporate?' by the distinguished American labour lawyer, Clarence Darrow. It was written in a very forthright style and condemned as impudent and presumptuous the demand made by employers for the incorporation of trade unions. Darrow said that if unions ever consented to become corporate bodies they would be constantly in the courts.

Early in 1903 James Conley was adopted as Labour candidate for Wednesbury. The adoption meeting was held in Darlaston Town Hall which was filled to capacity. In his adoption speech Mr Conley said that he had been a Liberal all his life but he intended to stand solely as a Labour candidate. He was not prepared to accept certain conditions stipulated by the Liberals even if they were prepared to adopt him as a Liberal candidate. He was not, however, to remain prospective Labour candidate for Wednesbury for very long. By the late summer it was reported that there were divisions among the trade unionists and Labour supporters in the Wednesbury constituency. The result was that Conley decided not to contest the seat. There is no indication in the available records of the nature of the divisions which existed among trade unionists and Labour supporters in Wednesbury. Possibly some of them were critical of Mr Conley's Liberal views. Shortly afterward Mr Conley was adopted as prospective Labour candidate for the Kirkdale division of Liverpool, and within a matter of weeks another boilermaker was selected as a prospective Labour candidate for Parliament. He was John Hill, another full-time district delegate, who was selected to fight the Govan division of Glasgow. John Hill was not put forward officially by the Boilermakers' Society but was asked to become prospective Labour candidate by the Govan Labour Representation Committee. The Executive Council of the Boilermakers' Society agreed to meet half the election expenses of Mr Hill, subject to the consent of the membership. This vote was taken in the spring of 1904 and the proposal was supported by an overwhelming majority.

The vote was 32,141 in favour of giving financial assistance for John Hill's candidature and 4,807 against. By a very similar majority the membership also agreed to pay an additional penny levy to the Labour Representation Committee. The effect of this was to increase the levy from threepence to fourpence per member per year.

The campaign for new trade union legislation was now gathering strength. The TUC wrote to all Members of Parliament to enquire as to their attitude to a new Trade Disputes Bill. Trade unionists were urged to vote only for candidates who supported new legislation. In 1905 a series of articles was published in the Boilermakers' journal, outlining the need for independent Labour representation in Parliament. Attention was drawn to the support given to the social-democrats in Germany. In the 1903 election to the Reichstag over three million votes were cast for social-democrat candidates and eighty-one social-democrat members were elected.

On 19 August 1905, the Boilermakers' Society organised a demonstration in Manchester in support of Labour representation. Between 600 and 700 members participated. They marched behind a band and with banners flying to Belle Vue Gardens. The chairman of the meeting said that the Taff Vale decision had put trade unionists back into oppression and any man who voted for a parliamentary candidate who was not pledged to the cause of labour was an enemy to himself.

With the approach of a General Election, the TUC stepped up its campaign for new legislation to protect trade union activities. Towards the end of October 1905 the TUC sent a letter to all affiliated unions saying that the time was now favourable for a vigorous campaign throughout the country in favour of trade union legislation. This campaign was also linked with a demand for Government action to reduce unemployment. Unemployment had been at a high level ever since 1902. In 1903 and 1904 no less than 15 per cent of the members of the Boilermakers' Society were unemployed.

Following the 1905 Congress of the TUC, Mr D. C. Cummings, the Boilermakers' General Secretary, was elected Chairman of the Parliamentary Committee of the TUC. One of his first tasks was to lead a deputation to the Prime Minister, Sir Henry Campbell-Bannerman, and the Lord Chancellor, urging them to introduce new legislation to protect trade union activities.

THE 1906 GENERAL ELECTION

When the date of the General Election was announced the TUC issued an election manifesto. It urged trade unionists to vote for all Labour candidates and for all candidates who were pledged to support trade union law reform, opposition to tariffs (taxes on food), and support for the extension of the social services. The proposals put forward by the TUC were as follows:

Support for a new Trade Disputes Bill.
The amendment of the Compensation Act, so as to give compensation to all workers in every trade from the date of the accident.
The amendment of the Truck Act to prevent stoppages of any description from wages.
The amendment of the Unemployed Act so that employment could be found at trade union rates for those unable to obtain work.
The abolition of enforced Chinese labour in South Africa.
The establishment of a State Pension Fund at sixty years of age.
An extension of the Housing of the Working Classes Act.
The returning officer's fees to be a charge on the national Exchequer.
Adult suffrage.
The establishment of an eight hour working day.

The Conservative Government had resigned towards the end of 1905, primarily because of a split in Conservative ranks over the issue of tariff reform. The Government had been replaced by one led by Sir Henry Campbell-Bannerman. The General Election was called for early in the new year and resulted in a sweeping victory for the Liberals. They had a majority of 220 over the Conservatives and 84 over all other parties. Even more significantly, the General Election resulted in the return of a substantial number of Labour representatives. The February issue of the Boilermakers' journal listed thirty Labour members elected under the direct auspices of the Labour Representation Committee. In addition, there were twelve others who were elected on the sponsorship of miners' organisations. There were then a further twelve trade unionists who ran under various auspices. The total number of trade unionists was thus fifty-four. To that number the journal added the names of a

151

number of other members who were known to have strong Labour sympathies. The conclusion of the journal was that there was now a force 'of at least 70, who can be relied upon to stand together for Labour in almost any emergency'.

Neither James Conley nor John Hill was elected. At Kirkdale, James Conley failed by the narrow margin of 592 votes. He polled 3,157 votes against his Conservative opponent 3,749. His opponent was a shipowner. At Govan, John Hill had to face both Conservative and Liberal opponents. The voting was as follows:

Conservative	5,224
Liberal	5,096
Hill (Labour)	4,212

A new Trade Disputes Bill was introduced shortly after the General Election. It spent the rest of the year proceeding through its various parliamentary stages. Its journey was not smooth. Some members of the Government were known to be out of sympathy with the demand of the unions for full protection. They were reinforced by the published conclusions of the Royal Commission on Trade Disputes and Trade Combinations. The majority report, which included the signature of Sidney Webb, held that the Taff Vale judgement had involved no new principle and was not inconsistent with the legislation of 1871. The report was condemned by the Boilermakers' General Secretary. He said that it was not satisfactory and that it had been answered by the General Election.

The pressure for new legislation continued throughout 1906 and Liberal MPs were constantly reminded of the pledges which many of them had made during the election campaign. Eventually, by the end of the year, the new Bill found its way on to the Statute Book.

Though the campaign for trade union law reform certainly helped to defeat the Conservatives in the 1906 General Election, the Liberal victory and the striking advance made by Labour owed much to public discontent with rising prices and unemployment. The swing in the Conservative Party towards a policy of tariffs also alienated working-class opinion, which feared that the inevitable result would be higher food prices.

THE STATE OF TRADE

The century opened in prosperity. The Boilermakers' annual report for 1900 recorded that the output of the British shipbuilding industry was approximately twice as much as that of the rest of the world put together. Nevertheless, the report spoke of competition from foreign shipyards. It pointed out that in the U.S.A., in particular, new methods had been developed and new equipment was being employed. The report said that 'the use of electricity in shipbuilding yards, the employment of pneumatic tools and the services of cranes and derricks in handling heavy materials at every stage have revolutionised shipmaking methods in the United States to such an extent that the best shipyards in America are even better equipped than those of Europe'.

There were the first signs of a decline in trade in the summer of 1900 but wages were still at a relatively high level. On the Mersey it was recorded that angle-ironsmiths were receiving 44s for a basic week, platers 42s, riveters from 32s to 38s, and holders-up from 25s 6d to 32s. There were very few disputes, and in the whole of 1900 the Society paid out only £34 in dispute pay. A sum of £54,000 was added to reserves. Prosperity continued in 1901, and with it there was record output in shipbuilding. U.K. output exceeded 1,800,000 tons, in comparison with 870,000 tons for the rest of the world. In 1901 the output of the north-east-coast shipyards, including those on the Tyne, Wear, Tees and at Hartlepool, exceeded the output of the rest of the world, excluding other British shipyards.

Despite the prosperity of the British shipbuilding industry, *The Times* launched a strong attack on the alleged restrictive practices of the Boilermakers' Society. In its issue of the 18 November 1901 it wrote 'what with the waste of time by these autocrats of the British shipbuilding yards, and what with the restrictions imposed on their output when they are at work, it is not surprising to find that long delays sometimes occur in the execution of orders'. The Boilermakers' Society gave as good as it received. *The Times,* said the Boilermakers' journal, was either gullible and unsophisticated or vicious enough to let anything appear that sought to injure those with whom it disagreed. The journal had no difficulty in pointing to the success of the British shipbuilding industry in competition with foreign yards. It concluded by suggesting that the real reason

153

for the attack launched by *The Times* was to be found elsewhere. *The Times* had been urging the Government to make war in South Africa but had found that the war had not gone as easily as it anticipated. The drain on resources was bringing about a depression and *The Times*, said the journal, was now turning to attack others to cover up its own iniquities.

This prediction of a forthcoming depression was soon to be confirmed. Throughout 1902 unemployment increased. By the end of the year more than 6,000 members of the Society were out of work. There were wage reductions by agreement on the north-east coast, on the Clyde, and later in the year at Belfast. With rising unemployment the Society was plagued by a succession of demarcation disputes with other unions. In 1904 trade continued to decline. Further wage reductions took place in almost all areas. On the north-east coast, wages were reduced both at the beginning of 1904 and again towards the end of 1904. Although in 1905 trade began to revive, it was not until the end of the year that some part of the wage reductions on the north-east coast was regained. Throughout 1906 movements for wage increases developed in different parts of Britain and for the most part were successful. On the Clyde there was an eight week strike which was not settled until 1907. A marked feature of the strike was the solidarity of the boilermakers. It was reported that there was not a single blackleg in any yard on the river. The Executive Council recommended a return to work before a settlement was reached and this evoked considerable opposition. It was, nevertheless, adopted after a series of mass meetings. The members returned to work unitedly. Wage increases were secured shortly afterwards. There was also a major dispute affecting the Society's members on the Tees and at Hartlepool. It lasted for ten weeks and concerned piece-work prices. The employers sought a reduction in prices because of the introduction of new machinery. Eventually, a compromise settlement was reached.

NEGOTIATIONS

The main achievement in negotiations in 1906 was the conclusion of an agreement for the payment of wages on the Clyde at weekly instead of fortnightly intervals. The fortnightly payment of wages had been a source of grievance for many years. As long ago as

154

1895 members of the Boilermakers' Society had succeeded in persuading the Govan Trades Council to form a committee of representatives from various shipbuilding unions to campaign for the weekly payment of wages. Repeated attempts were made to persuade the employers to discuss the issue but it was not until after a ballot vote had been taken in favour of strike action that the employers agreed to enter into negotiations. As a result of these negotiations it was agreed, towards the end of 1898, that a weekly system of payment should be introduced for a trial period of twelve months. At the end of the period, however, the employers reverted to fortnightly payment. There was some disunity among the trade unions and no action was taken. A new movement began to develop among the rank and file but by then trade was declining and conditions were no longer favourable for the prosecution of the claim. When trade revived in 1906 the unions again pressed the claim vigorously and eventually the Clyde employers agreed to introduce the weekly payment of wages. The great disadvantage of the fortnightly system was that many of the workers found it necessary in the second week to go to credit-shops and pawnbrokers to obtain credit or money to buy the necessities of life. Thousands of shipbuilding workers were regularly in debt and under the credit-shop system found themselves paying higher prices for food.

The question of the limitation of the number of apprentices in shipyards continued to be a source of friction between shipbuilding employers and the Boilermakers' Society. The limitation on the number of apprentices to be employed, stipulated in the agreement of 1893, had always been regarded unfavourably by the employers. The agreement lasted for six years and the employers then requested that it should be modified. No decision was reached and the agreement was allowed to lapse. Some shipbuilding employers then increased the number of apprentices in their yard and there were immediate protests from the Boilermakers' Society. Prolonged negotiations took place and eventually in 1901 a proposed draft agreement was submitted to the membership. There were two main points of contention. The first concerned the ages between which an apprenticeship should begin and the second concerned the limitation on the number of apprentices. On a ballot vote of the membership the draft was defeated by 18,968 votes to 14,787, despite a recommendation in favour of it from the Executive

Council. The Executive Council, deeply disturbed at the result, undertook an explanatory campaign to emphasise the importance of accepting the proposed draft. At the conclusion of this campaign another vote was taken and this time the membership accepted the draft by 25,080 to 12,213. The agreement stipulated that apprenticeship should commence not earlier than sixteen years of age nor later than nineteen years of age. Members of the Society had originally wanted an upper age limit of eighteen years. The draft also contained a clause stating that the employers were opposed to any limitation in the number of apprentices but that it was not their intention 'to overstock yards with apprentices'. The draft stated that any complaints from the Boilermakers' Society about the number of apprentices employed could be submitted through the secretaries of the Shipbuilding Employers' Federation. The new agreement was signed on 18 December 1901, but a few months afterwards, the Boilermakers' Society complained that an unduly high proportion of apprentices were employed at Messrs Ramage & Ferguson's yard, Leith. Despite lengthy negotiations and exchange of correspondence no agreement could be reached. The Shipbuilding Employers' Federation took the view that Messrs Ramage & Ferguson were employing fewer journeymen than usual because of a severe depression in trade. The Federation said that they did not regard it as the intention of the agreement that action should be taken with regard to any particular yard or district. The agreement, in their view, referred to the general average of apprentices employed in shipbuilding. This interpretation was totally unacceptable to the Boilermakers' Society. The depressed state of the trade, however, made it difficult for any effective action to be taken. Finally, when trade improved in 1906 the Executive Council, following consultation with representatives of the Society from shipyard areas, resolved that in all cases where there was just cause of complaint about the employment of excessive numbers of apprentices, the members, in the event of the employers refusing to take action, should be permitted to cease work. This, said the Executive Council, was essential in order to insist upon the observance of the agreement. This decision of the Executive Council undoubtedly had effect. It was taken at a time when there was new prosperity in the industry. Pressure in a number of shipyards was sufficient to bring about some improvement in the ratio of apprentices to journeymen.

THE SOCIETY'S DEVELOPMENT

After the expansion of membership in the final decade of the nineteenth century a number of unions suffered a decline in the opening years of the twentieth century. This decline affected mainly the unions catering for unskilled workers. The membership of the Boilermakers' Society, however, remained remarkably stable. At the end of 1900 the number of members was 47,670. At the end of 1905 it had increased slightly to 49,630. There was a more rapid increase in the prosperous year of 1906 and by December the membership stood at approximately 52,000.

A meeting of the General Council of the Society held in June and July 1900 decided to amend the rules of membership. First-class members were required to pay a subscription of 3s per fortnight. Persons who had not served five years at the trade before the age of twenty-three, but who had worked five years successively at some department of the trade before the age of thirty and providing that they were not older than forty, were eligible for second-class membership. Their subscription was 1s 2d per week. They were entitled to a lower scale of benefits. Persons who were older than forty years of age and were working at any branch of the trade were eligible for third-class membership. The subscription was 1s 2d per fortnight but the benefits were restricted. After the introduction of the new rules in April 1901, it was found that there were approximately 36,000 first-class members, 6,700 second-class members and 3,600 third-class members.

The meeting of the General Council in 1900 also proposed that the office of consulting secretary held by the retired General Secretary, Robert Knight, should be abolished. It will be recalled that there had been considerable opposition to the establishment of this post at the time that Mr Cummings was elected as the new General Secretary. This recommendation was put forward by the General Council without consultation with Robert Knight. When he learnt of it he asked for an interview. He then found, according to his own version of the events, that he was being asked to continue certain duties but without the formal title of consulting secretary. He asked that a retirement sum should be given to him to replace the salary which he had received as consulting secretary. The General Council recommended that as an alternative to a weekly retirement allow-

157

ance a sum equal to one shilling per member should be given as a lump sum to Robert Knight. This sum, they suggested, should be taken from the general fund of the Society. This proposition was heavily defeated on ballot vote by 23,493 votes to 12,295. There was now a good deal of ill-feeling in the Society about the financial provision for Robert Knight and the Executive Council were in favour of deferring further consultation with the membership until feeling had subsided. Members of the General Council were, however, anxious to settle the issue and requested that the membership should be asked to vote on a proposal that Robert Knight should be given a retirement allowance of either £3 10s, £3 or £2 10s per week. An appeal from Robert Knight for the largest of these three amounts was published in the monthly journal. The result of the voting was as follows:

For £3 10s per week	19,308
For £3 per week	1,792
For £2 10s per week	13,811

In the summer of 1902, Mr Cummings was re-elected unopposed as General Secretary of the Society. Immediately after his election Mr Cummings asked for an increase of salary of £1 per week. This increase would have brought his salary up to the level paid to his predecessor, Robert Knight. Unfortunately for Mr Cummings his appeal was put to the membership at a time when trade was declining. It was turned down by 18,224 votes to 17,046. He appealed for a further vote to be taken, on the grounds that the branches had voted proportionately to their total membership and that this result had contradicted the individual vote at branch meetings. It was decided to take an individual ballot vote, but this decision also caused a good deal of controversy in the Society. It resulted in the highest ballot vote in the history of the Society. By a very narrow margin of thirty-two votes the General Secretary's application for a salary increase was carried. The voting was 3,489 to 3,457. A number of branches did not submit their returns in time and if their votes had been included the majority for the salary increase would have been even smaller. In view of the strong feeling aroused by the decision to take an individual ballot, Mr Cummings indicated that he would accept only a half of the proposed increase, namely 10s, and that he would leave the further increase until trade revived. By accepting only a half of the proposed increase Mr Cummings did much to placate the feeling that had been aroused by the salary application and the taking of a re-vote on the proposition. When he came up for re-election in 1905 he was again unopposed.

DRILLERS AGAIN REJECTED

Despite the wishes of the Executive Council the membership continued to oppose the admission of drillers to the Society. In June 1900, the London & District United Society of Drillers renewed the application, last made in 1897, to be accepted into membership as a section of the Boilermakers' Society. They pointed out that this would give to the Society the advantage of having under its own control another important group of workers in the shipbuilding industry. They also pointed out that a society of drillers in Newcastle was contemplating joining the Shipwrights' Society. The London drillers emphasised that they would prefer to join the Boilermakers' Society. The Executive Council responded favourably to the application and strongly urged the membership of the Boilermakers' Society to accept it. With the drillers in their ranks, they said in a statement published to the membership, the Boilermakers' Society would include every branch of the trade from driller to angle-smith. This would strengthen the Society in its relations with the employers and would bring harmony among an increased number of shipbuilding workers. The proposition of the Executive Council was that the drillers should be admitted into the Boilermakers' Society as a separate section. Despite this strong appeal, the application was overwhelmingly rejected by the membership. The voting was 24,953 against admission and 8,918 in favour of admission. In 1902 the issue of the admission of drillers was again raised. On the north-east coast many of the drillers were members of the Shipwrights' Society. In other areas they were in membership of the Carpenters' Union. It was known that a number of districts of the Boilermakers' Society had accepted drillers into membership and the Executive Council asked that this position should be maintained. The view of the EC was that drillers had a closer affinity to boilermakers than to either shipwrights or carpenters. A vote was taken at the November 1902 branch meetings but again the majority against admission was overwhelming. The voting was 6,413 against

159

admission and 1,948 for. However, the Executive Council was not to be deterred, and again raised the issue some three years later. Once again the voting was overwhelmingly against the admission of drillers. This time the proposal was rejected by 5,924 votes to 1,235. The members did, however, vote by 4,618 to 2,270 to organise workers in Government dockyards. Many of the boilermaking trades in the dockyard had traditionally been organised by the Shipwrights' Society. The Executive Council welcomed the decision and said that it was one that should have been taken many years previously.

In August 1904, the Society celebrated the seventieth anniversary of its formation. It was arranged that the General Secretary should publish a historical survey of the Society. This came out in a handsomely produced volume in 1905. It provided a brief sketch of the history of the Society and dealt at length with many of the prominent officials in the Society's history. There were very few who were still alive who remembered the formative years of the Society, though in 1901 the journal recorded that one member, a Mr Thomas Hudson of Liverpool No. 7 branch, had served as branch secretary for more than fifty years. At that time he had already been a member of the Society for fifty-nine years. A testimonial fund was raised to mark the occasion.

SOLIDARITY

The Boilermakers' Society continued to maintain its tradition of giving support to workers in other countries who were engaged in struggles for their rights. In December 1899 an appeal was received from the American Brotherhood of Boilermakers for assistance in a strike at the shipbuilding firm of William Cramp & Sons, Philadelphia. The strike was for a nine hour working day, which had already been established in other shipbuilding firms. William Cramp & Sons dismissed nearly 300 men belonging to the Brotherhood of Boilermakers, the Brotherhood of Blacksmiths, the Ships' Joiners Association and the International Association of Machinists. The strike began on 1 September 1899. The Executive Council of the Boilermakers' Society recommended that a levy of sixpence per member should be paid to assist the American boilermakers. This was approved on a ballot vote by the enormous majority of 30,335 to 697. The sixpenny levy realised a total sum of £950, of which

£200 was sent immediately to the United States. It was then learned that there were internal problems in the American Brotherhood of Boilermakers concerning the conduct of the strike. The strike was concluded and no further money was sent from Britain.

Almost a year later an appeal was received from locked-out lace-workers in the French port of Calais. The appeal said that workers in the lace industry in the Calais area were working twelve hours a day and thousands of women and children were employed on night work. The lace-employers were seeking to evade a new French law abolishing night work for women and children. The appeal said that approximately 14,000 lace workers were being locked out by their employers. One interesting feature of the appeal was that it reminded British trade unionists that during the last national engineering lock-out the lace-makers of Calais had levied themselves to assist British workers and had raised approximately 15s 2d per head for this purpose. The Executive Council of the Boilermakers' Society sent an immediate donation of £20, the maximum allowed by rule, and also sent £200 from the fund originally raised to assist the American boilermakers. The donation of £200 was approved on a ballot vote of the membership by 31,104 votes to 1,685.

An appeal was also received to assist a strike of 2,000 London lightermen. An initial donation of £20 was made and then a further donation of £100 was sent from the fund raised to assist the American boilermakers. This too was approved on a ballot vote by 33,390 votes to 610.

The Boilermakers' Society also displayed an interest in labour problems in South Africa after the conclusion of the Boer War. An article in the December 1902 monthly report explained that there was an acute shortage of African labour in the South African mines. (The word African was not used. It was explained that all native labourers, as they were called, were known as boys. The term Kaffir was also used to describe them.) The pay of African labourers had been reduced from 50s a month before the war to a new level of only 30s a month. Labour was recruited by labour agents who, it said, were often irresponsible and had never been scrupulous as to the methods they adopted to bring new labour to the mines. The African labourers were housed in huts and were supplied with two rations of mealies a day. The mealies, the article said, did not cost more than sixpence per day per worker. The article continued: 'but in South Africa it would seem that the measure of payment is not the value of the work but the colour of the skin of the man who does it.' The article concluded by stating that, in view of the shortage of African labour, the mining companies were agitating for the introduction of Chinese labour.

A number of branches of the Boilermakers' Society were formed in South Africa immediately following the Boer War. By the end of 1903 the Society had branches in Durban, Johannesburg, Uitenhage, Capetown, East London, Pretoria and Bloemfontein. Indeed, of the seven new branches opened by the Society in 1903 four were in South Africa.

In 1904 the British Government's decision to permit the introduction of Chinese labour into the South African colony excited a good deal of opposition from boilermakers' branches. The full parliamentary division list on the vote for and against Chinese labour was published in the monthly report. Those who voted for the introduction of Chinese labour were listed as having voted for slavery and a wage of 6s 3d per week. The monthly report said that those who had voted against the introduction of Chinese labour had 'voted against yellow slave labour and in favour of those dearly bought colonies being peopled with a white working population with freedom to organise into trade unions and have a voice in their own destiny'. There was, unfortunately, more than a hint of racialism mixed up with the legitimate trade union objection to the introduction of cheap labour. The introduction of Chinese labour in South Africa was also roundly condemned by the General Secretary, D. C. Cummings, in his annual report. His condemnation too carried a hint of racialism. He referred to 'highbred financiers of unpronounceable names', presumably referring to the numerous Jewish interests in the ownership of the South African mines. Mr Cummings said that the British workers had a right to expect that the great army of unemployed would have been relieved by the Government giving easy facilities for emigration to South Africa. An unjust war had been waged, he said, because the war had been fought in the interests of rich capitalists with interests in South Africa. The sacrifice of the British people had been repaid by the introduction of cheap serf Chinese labour.

Much nearer home the Boilermakers' Society gave support to slate quarrymen engaged in a long dispute in North Wales. The

162

quarries were in the monopoly ownership of Lord Penrhyn. The dispute lasted for more than two years and as a result more than 1,400 quarrymen left to work in the coalfield of South Wales and elsewhere. Six hundred remained and were without work. Financial assistance was rendered by the trade union movement, including the Boilermakers' Society, but eventually it was decided to launch a co-partnership quarry project in North Wales. The Boilermakers' Society agreed to invest £300 in the co-partnership project. This was endorsed by the membership in a ballot by 16,617 votes to 332.

In 1902 the General Secretary was invited to participate in an official commission to visit the United States and look at American industry. It was agreed that he should accept the invitation. After his visit he wrote a number of articles in the monthly report outlining his impressions. He explained that in a number of boiler-shops and shipyards extensive use was made of pneumatic tools. He did not think, however, that the American shipbuilding industry would be able to compete with the British industry. Wages varied widely from one area to another. He found some skilled workers earning as much as 25s per day; elsewhere similarly skilled workers were receiving less than half this amount. Hours of labour were much the same as in Britain. He noted that housing conditions also varied enormously. In some cities housing accommodation was available to skilled workers at a higher standard than was normal in Britain. In other industrial areas the housing standards for unskilled workers were very poor indeed.

In January 1905 the first shots were fired in the Russian Revolution. Workers participating in a demonstration in St Petersburg were fired upon by the army and police. The Labour Representation Committee appealed to unions for subscriptions to assist those who had suffered from the massacre. The appeal spoke of the tyrannical barbarities of the Czarist Government and said that unless aid was forthcoming immediately there was a danger that brutal military force might be successful in crushing the movement for constitutional liberty and the right of combination. Hundreds of liberty loving Russians, the appeal said, had already been killed and hundreds were doomed to dungeons in Siberia. The Executive Council of the Boilermakers' Society immediately gave a sum of £20 to the appeal and invited branches to express their views on whether a further donation should be made. According to the monthly report, 'an

163

exceedingly large number of our branches' passed resolutions in favour of sending further aid. The initial donation of £20 was then made up to £100.

CHANGES

The General Council of the Society met in the summer of 1905. It proposed that the Society should join the General Federation of Trade Unions, which by now had established itself on a firm footing as an organisation through which affiliated unions could render financial support to each other in disputes. On a ballot vote the membership accepted this recommendation by 4,990 to 1,693, but rejected both of two alternative methods of paying the levy to the Federation. The Executive Council pointed out that this left them in an impossible position. They therefore requested that a further vote should be taken as to whether the levy should be taken from the general fund or whether it should be collected separately from each member every quarter. On this second ballot only a minority of branches bothered to return their figures to the Head Office. The Executive Council said that they were not prepared to accept such a result and they therefore insisted upon a third ballot vote being taken. This time by a majority of 4,225 to 2,770 the members decided against a separate collection every quarter. The Executive Council accepted this decision as meaning that the levy should be taken from the general fund of the Society.

In the autumn of 1905 the Society lost through retirement its longest serving full-time official. He was Mr Matt Smith, the district delegate for Merseyside. He started work in 1854 in Bradford and joined the Society at the age of twenty. Two years later he became secretary of Birkenhead No. 1 branch and he was afterwards elected to the Executive Council. He was elected district delegate in September 1874 and was re-elected to that office on fourteen occasions. A proposal that a levy of 3d per member should be paid as a donation to Matt Smith was defeated on a ballot vote by 4,014 to 2,712. A few weeks later, however, it was agreed by 5,295 votes against 3,585 that Matt Smith should receive a donation made up of a levy of 2d on every member.

The November 1902 issue of the monthly report carried a short article about the newly formed Ruskin College, Oxford. The college, it said, had been founded so as to bring some of the exceptional advantages of Oxford within the reach of working men. It went on, 'it is not intended that a man should rise out of his class to swell the already overcrowded professional classes. The aim of the institution is that each man by raising himself may help to raise through influence or precept the whole class to which he belongs.' The article outlined the subjects taught at the college and explained that each student was expected to work two hours a day at cooking and cleaning; thus by mutual help the cost of residence was kept at a low level. Some two years later, by the narrow margin of 20,135 to 17,162 votes, the membership decided against giving a grant to Ruskin College. The following year Ruskin College offered a free scholarship to the Boilermakers' Society to send one of the Society's members for a year's residence and tuition. Mr F. W. Morrice of Bristol was the selected candidate. Shortly afterwards he was joined by another member of the Boilermakers' Society, William Waterton, who for a number of years had been secretary of the Newcastle No. 1 branch.

THE TUC

The president of the 1906 TUC was the General Secretary of the Boilermakers' Society, Mr D. C. Cummings. In his presidential address he referred to the very significant advance made by Labour in the recent General Election. He said that it was cause for rejoicing among trade unionists. He looked forward to new legislation to give the trade union movement the protection it needed. Mr Cummings referred also to the evil of unemployment. He said that the causes of unemployment were many but they could be traced to the private ownership of land and the use of science and production for the benefit of the few as against the interests of the many. Mr Cummings called for more measures for social security, including housing, pensions and the feeding of children. He called also for proportional representation in Parliamentary elections. He pointed out that under the existing system each Liberal Member of Parliament represented an average of less than 6,500 votes, whereas each Labour Member represented an average of over 9,000 votes and each Social-Democrat represented over 41,800 votes.

It was a fitting tribute that in the year 1906, when new trade union legislation was introduced, the presidential chair of the TUC should have been occupied by a member of the Boilermakers' Society. The Society had played a full part in the campaign for new legislation and for independent working class representation in Parliament. Moreover, in the defence of the occupational interests of its members there was no stronger union in Britain than the Boilermakers' Society. They were truly the aristocrats of organised labour. In his book, *Labouring Men*, Eric Hobsbawm published a table showing that in 1906 a higher proportion of shipyard platers were receiving more than 45s per week than any other group of skilled manual workers for whom records were available.

Chapter 13

The First Seventy Years

There are very few unions that can claim such a proud history as the Boilermakers' Society. For nearly one hundred and forty years it has maintained a continuous and vigorous existence. The Society has faced every kind of vicissitude. There is no other union whose members have been affected by so many booms and slumps. Shipbuilding has always experienced more violent fluctuations in trade than other industries. Relatively small variations in world trade lead shipowners either to accelerate or to defer orders for new ships. This instability has strongly influenced the Society. Its members have fought for higher wages and better conditions when trade was good and have suffered repeated attacks from employers when trade was bad.

SKILLED WORKERS

The traditions of the Society were formed in the last century. They remain with it and influence it to this day. The Society has changed in many ways, not least because of changes in industrial techniques, but there are many aspects of its behaviour which have remained remarkably constant. The policies and actions of the Boilermakers' Society can be understood only against the background of its history.

The boilermakers were among the most skilled of the new mechanics of the Industrial Revolution. They originated, as their occupational title clearly implies, as the makers of boilers, but the skills which they acquired for the craft of boilermaking later found new outlets in the growing industries of iron shipbuilding, loco-

167

motive building and bridge building. In the second half of the nineteenth century the Boilermakers' Society became a union not only of men engaged in the making of boilers but also, and above all, of builders of iron ships. Later still, in the years to be covered by the second volume of this history, even shipbuilding was to be replaced eventually as the principal industry for the employment of members of the Boilermakers' Society. The development of structural steelwork, welding and flame-cutting techniques brought new employment opportunities in the engineering and construction industries.

THE CHARACTERISTICS OF CRAFT UNIONISM

The history of the Boilermakers' Society is more than a study of the history of a single union. It is a study of the development and characteristics of an important sector of the British working class. The craftsmen of the engineering, construction, printing and other main industries have strongly influenced the history of the British labour movement. They have given it both strength and weakness. The particular strength which they have bestowed is the tradition of occupational solidarity. British craftsmen established well organised and properly financed unions, capable of winning for their members some share in the newly created wealth of Victorian England. They developed a system of collective bargaining with employers and accumulated substantial funds in times of prosperity to assist their members when unemployed or when injured at work.

In order to accumulate these funds, to protect them and to distribute them fairly, some of the craft unions developed an efficient central administration. The Boilermakers' Society, under the secretaryship of Robert Knight, was outstanding in this respect. Whatever his other weaknesses, including in his later years his undoubted tendency towards personal dictatorial control, Robert Knight's contribution in developing the organisational structure and protecting the funds of the union give him a special place in the history, not only of the Boilermakers' Society, but also of trade unionism.

In the second half of the last century members of the Boilermakers' Society looked to their general secretary primarily as a guardian of the funds rather than as a leader in national collective

168

bargaining. Nearly all the bargaining was done at workplace or district level and the members themselves were able to influence the course of negotiations without necessarily seeking the guidance of their general secretary. But when they were out of work, injured, or when they came to the age of retirement, the members looked to the Society's administration to provide financial benefits. This was why strong central control of finance was needed. This need tended also to evoke in the general secretary a prime regard for the conservation of the Society's funds. He measured his success – and many members also measured his success – by his ability to resist calls upon the Society's central funds to finance local disputes and, conversely, by his ability to provide money when needed for the Society's provident benefits. To this extent Robert Knight was the product of the circumstances in which the Society then existed. The situation produced the man. His general characteristics fitted the particular organisational and financial needs of the time.

But if the strength of the Boilermakers' Society was its occupational solidarity, its weakness was its craft narrowness. This weakness manifested itself in many ways. The members of the Society were extremely reluctant to extend their organisation to embrace men of closely related occupations, particularly if those occupations called for a rather narrower skill than those of the main boilermaking trades. The Society was also engaged in recurrent disputes with members of other unions about trade demarcation. For many years the Society's relationship with the shipwrights was particularly strained. The shipwrights were often seen as rivals rather than as fellow-workers. The shipwrights were associated with the wooden construction of ships, whereas the boilermakers regarded metal structural work on the new iron ships as their work.

The Boilermakers' Society was also slow to recognise the historic significance of the new unionism which emerged towards the end of the last century with the organisation of dockers and gas workers. This reluctance of the boilermakers was largely attributable to the inherent conservatism of their craft unionism, but it was also given special emphasis because of the hostility shown to the early socialists by Robert Knight. Indeed, the Boilermakers' Society played an important part in the rearguard action of the 'old' unionists against the 'new' unionists in the TUC in the middle eighteen-nineties.

This weakness of the Boilermakers' Society, based on craft

169

exclusiveness, did not go unchallenged from inside the ranks of the Society. Nor indeed was it an unrelieved weakness. There were many occasions when the Society came to the assistance of other workers, both at home and abroad, including not only craftsmen but also semi-skilled and unskilled workers. There was hardly any significant group of British workers engaged in trade union struggle in the second half of the last century who did not receive financial help from the Boilermakers' Society. Moreover, although the Society, particularly in the person of Robert Knight, played an active part in the resistance to the early socialists inside the TUC, it was also one of the early group of unions to associate itself with the Labour Representation Committee and with the formation of the Labour Party. This move towards political action was, however, very definitely seen as an extension of trade union activity and not as an ideological conversion to the need for a new kind of social order. To the Boilermakers' Society in the early years of this century, the case for independent parliamentary labour representation rested on the need to reverse the Taff Vale judgement, to protect the right to picket in industrial disputes and, above all, to protect trade union funds against claims for damages made by employers whose workers took strike action.

The weaknesses of the Boilermakers' Society, important as they were, were not the weaknesses of every member. Every weakness was challenged at some time or another from within the Society. There were always members whose trade union and social vision extended beyond a narrow and exclusive concern for their own craft. On many occasions the challengers were defeated and at times their voice was weak. But with the passage of time events themselves compelled the Society to change its course. For years it appeared that Robert Knight was all-dominant. It is clear, however, that the forces making for change were much stronger than appeared on the surface. In the end the views of Robert Knight, despite his great contribution in many directions, were overtaken by events. The path followed by the Boilermakers' Society and its eventual support for independent labour political action was indicative of a far-reaching and profound change taking place within the trade union movement.

CHANGING ATTITUDES

The history of the Boilermakers' Society provides an illuminating insight into the developing attitude of skilled workers towards trade unionism from the 1830s until the campaign for new legislation to reverse the Taff Vale judgement of the House of Lords. In the formative years of the Society great stress was placed upon the concept of brotherhood among boilermakers. Much of the inspiration for this promotion of brotherhood came from Christianity. Religious nonconformists played a particularly important part in drafting the ceremonies and precepts for the guidance of members. The value and importance of occupational unity was constantly underlined. The prime purpose of the Society was 'to administer to each other's necessities and to relieve each other in sickness and poverty'. The provision of financial benefits for members in need was central to the existence of the organisation. These benefits were designed to assist members who were unemployed, injured at work, or sick, and to provide support for members who reached the age of retirement. It was also characteristic of the Christian inspiration of many of the Society's founders that it was considered important that members who died should be buried respectably and should not 'suffer' a pauper's grave.

There is little, if anything, in the earliest records of the Society to suggest that members regarded their organisation as a collective-bargaining agent. This was to come later. Nevertheless, it came fairly quickly. By the 1840s the rules provided for the payment of dispute benefit, and at the 1845 annual meeting reference was made to a dispute at a boiler shop in Smethwick from which the labour of the Society's members had been withdrawn. From the 1840s onwards the collective bargaining function assumed an increasingly important role in the Society's activities. In 1848 the rules defining the purpose of the union were amended to include the unity of members 'for the support of their trade'. A new class of membership was also created – protective fund members – for men who, because of age or other reason, were not eligible for full membership but whose support, nevertheless, was necessary for what were then called trade purposes.

171

POWER IN THE WORKPLACE

A special feature of the boilermakers' history has always been the power exercised by members in collective bargaining at the workplace. It is a sobering reflection that it was not until the publication of the report of the Royal Commission on Trade Unions and Employers' Associations (the Donovan Report) in 1968 that public attention was focused on an aspect of trade unionism that has always characterised a number of unions of skilled workers. It may well be argued that in the last century there was not in the Boilermakers' Society the same divergence between the formal and the informal system of bargaining as, the Donovan Report suggested, existed in the engineering industry in the middle of the twentieth century. On the other hand, there can be no doubt that on many occasions the rank-and-file membership conducted their bargaining in a manner which left the leadership with very little influence or control except in the one important matter of the payment of dispute benefit. This situation was not dissimilar from that which excited the attention of the Donovan Commission.

Unofficial strikes are no new phenomenon in the Boilermakers' Society. Indeed, what emerges from their history in the last century is that it was much more typical for the members themselves in a shipyard, boiler shop, or even a district, to decide upon strike action than for them to look to the Executive Council for an 'official' strike call. No one at that time described such action as 'unofficial', though the Executive Council frequently cautioned members against taking precipitate action and then finding it necessary to seek the intervention of the Society's officials in order to negotiate a settlement. The concern of the Executive Council was, above all, with the conservation of the Society's funds. When there was no call upon the funds, the wisdom or foolishness of taking strike action was more likely to be judged by the success or failure of the action than by any other consideration. The tradition of workplace autonomy and rank and file democracy in the Boilermakers' Society was extremely strong, providing always that this autonomy did not undermine the right of the Executive Council to control the funds of the Society. If members made a request for financial assistance, the Executive Council regarded it as within their prerogative to pronounce on the action taken by the members.

172

In the final thirty years of the last century – the age of expansion in British iron and steel shipbuilding – many of the major disputes in which boilermakers were engaged began without the prior authorisation of the Executive Council. And this, it should be noted, was the period when Robert Knight, the most authoritarian of general secretaries, was in office. The winning of the nine hour day on the north-east coast in 1871 was, for example, the result of a strike wave initiated by members of the Amalgamated Society of Engineers against the advice of their leaders. Boilermakers joined the strike and it was only later that they were given financial support by the Society. In the meantime substantial sums of money had been contributed by members in other parts of the country.

SHOP STEWARDS

This strike demonstrated the important role of members in ship-yards and boilershops who acted as representatives or stewards. Their part was crucial in the winning of the nine hour day on the north-east coast. In 1874 they were, in effect, recognised in the rules of the Society. The Executive Council were empowered to pay victimisation benefit to stewards dismissed from their employ-ment because of trade union activity.

In the depression of the middle 1870s there were strikes against wage cuts in shipyards on every estuary. These strikes were not called by the Executive Council. The decision to take strike action was made by the members directly affected, though in many cases they appealed successfully to the Executive Council for the pay-ment of dispute benefit. Even so, the Executive Council on more than one occasion during this period suggested that it might have been wiser for members to accept some reduction in pay rather than resist the employers' demands by strike action. The employers themselves were also sometimes reluctant to deal with representatives other than those from their own yards. To negotiate with a full-time official of the Society was seen as a gesture of recognition which might be regarded as a precedent for all future disputes. This reluctance to negotiate with the Society's officials was particularly evident among the Clyde employers. In a dispute in 1877, which lasted for thirty-three weeks, the Clyde employers refused to accept Robert Knight as a negotiator for the boilermakers. Inevitably such an attitude on the part of employers was likely to reinforce the dependence of the Society's members on their workplace democracy and their rank-and-file representatives. In 1882, when the shipbuilding industry was going through one of its periods of boom, the Executive Council complained of petty and unnecessary disputes in a number of yards. Significantly, however, their criticism was that decisions for strike action were being taken at yard meetings and not at branch meetings. It was in this sense that the disputes were described as unconstitutional. The complaint was not that strike action was being taken without the prior approval of the Executive Council.

THE EXECUTIVE COUNCIL AND STRIKE ACTION

The following year the Executive Council returned to the theme of its complaint. This time, however, it insisted that the Executive Council alone had the authority to authorise strike action. It said that in a number of firms shop stewards had exceeded their powers under the rules by urging members to go on strike. When there was a dispute about piece-work prices the proper course, said the Executive Council, was to attempt to settle it peacefully at workplace level. If the attempt was unsuccessful, the branch secretary should be informed and assistance should be sought from the district delegate.

By this time Robert Knight was firmly established as General Secretary – he had held office since 1871 – and there was a growing tendency to exert central control over the affairs of the Society and the industrial activities of its members. It was during this same period of prosperity that Robert Knight, in an address to an employers' organisation in the north of England, stated that the men were receiving good pay and should be content with the existing state of things. In turn, he urged the employers to agree to long-term wage agreements. He disliked the instability of the industry, which he saw was good neither for employer nor workman, but recognised that if greater stability was to be achieved, both sides would have to give up their right to demand immediate changes in wages under threat of coercive action.

Despite Robert Knight's vision of a more stable industry with long-term wage agreements, it proved impossible to prevent sharp

174

struggles between employers and men almost every time the ship-building industry experienced one of its periodic upswings or downturns. Robert Knight might write that it was a mistake to regard capital and labour as enemies, but in the shipbuilding industry the behaviour of employers and workers certainly revealed a conflict of interest.

One of the more serious disputes between a section of the rank and file and the leadership of the Society centred on the Clyde in 1891. With a slackening of trade, the Clyde employers gave notice of wage cuts. The Society's national officials, under instructions from the Executive Council and with the strong support of Robert Knight, negotiated a reduction of an amount lower than that originally demanded by the employers. The Clyde members rejected the agreement and withdrew their labour for a period of six weeks. In the end they returned to work defeated.

The Executive Council and Robert Knight were convinced that they had been right in the circumstances of the industry to agree by negotiation to a wage reduction. Robert Knight spoke of strike action as a barbarous method for settling disputes in industry. He now more than ever held the view that there was sufficient common interest between employers and workers to permit agreements to be reached which would take some account of economic fluctuations but would, in the long term, provide workers with a fair share of the benefits of industrial progress. He saw the achievement of this objective being thwarted by needless militancy among the rank and file.

Some three years later in 1894 it was the turn of members on the north-east coast to run into conflict with the leadership. In 1893 and 1894 successive wage cuts were imposed on members while the industry was going through one of its periodic slumps. In July 1894 a new negotiating procedure agreement was signed by the Society with the Tyne, Wear, Tees and Hartlepool employers. The agreement provided a procedure for the settlement of disputes without stoppages of work, and insisted that general alterations in wages should not be more frequent than at six-monthly intervals. No single alteration was to exceed 5 per cent. The new agreement embodied the philosophy which Robert Knight had been expounding for a number of years. Many active rank-and-file members on the north-east coast, however, saw the agreement in a different light. They had recently suffered a succession of wage cuts. With a partial recovery of trade they regarded the new agreement not as a protection against further cuts but as a brake upon their power to exert pressure for wage increases. The new agreement was endorsed by a four to three majority of the members in a national ballot but was rejected by a majority of members on the north-east coast who were directly affected.

The controversy aroused by this agreement was long and bitter. It was not only the terms of the agreement which were called into question but also the views and the authority of the General Secretary. The rumblings of revolt which eventually forced changes in the Society against the wishes of Robert Knight were now clearly to be heard. Members were urging that the powers of the General Secretary should be curtailed.

THE EIGHT HOUR DISPUTE

After an interval of a further three years – this time in 1897 – the leadership of the Boilermakers' Society was again involved in a bitter controversy because of its opposition to an outbreak of militancy which it regarded as wrong-headed and misdirected. Under the influence of the Executive Council the boilermakers withdrew from the Eight Hours Committee in London which led the campaign for a forty-eight hour week. The employers insisted that the claim for a shorter working week was a national issue and not one for the London area alone. In substance the leadership of the Boilermakers' Society agreed with this view. Moreover, they were confident that it would have been easier in shipbuilding than in London engineering firms to achieve a reduction in hours of work. A further complicating factor was that, according to the Executive Council of the Boilermakers' Society, the Amalgamated Society of Engineers, whose members were in the majority in the London dispute, had shown reluctance and even outright opposition to co-ordinate their plan of campaign with other unions.

The eight hour dispute ended in defeat for the unions. Robert Knight and the Executive Council were able to claim that events had confirmed their warnings about misdirected activity. This did not prevent them from being the target of a great deal of criticism from engineering trade unionists. For a period relations between the Boilermakers' Society and the Amalgamated Society of Engineers reached a level of extreme acrimony.

ROBERT KNIGHT

The contrast, in the period 1870–1900, between the policy of the ledership – and of Robert Knight in particular in his attitude to relations with employers – and the frequent outbreaks of militancy among the membership provides one of the most fascinating aspects of the history of the Boilermakers' Society. Yet it is not a contrast which can be attributed to a fundamental dissimilarity between the views of Robert Knight and those of the members he represented. In many respects Robert Knight embodied what a substantial proportion of the members wanted in their general secretary and his vision of industrial relations was what they too would have preferred. But developments and events sometimes take place independently of what men would *like* to happen. The harsh reality of shipbuilding kept asserting itself. Slump followed boom and in each slump wages would be cut and thousands of men would be thrown out of work. But just as surely another boom would follow the slump and there would be a new opportunity to push up wages under threat of strike action. Despite these fluctuations, shipbuilding was an expanding industry and the standard of living of the workers in the long term was rising. It was thus the industrial expansion of Victorian England which gave Robert Knight and those who thought like him the evidence to justify their belief that, if only greater stability could be achieved, better conditions could be obtained by peaceful negotiations. Strikes and lock-outs were seen as symptoms of the very instability they were seeking to overcome. They had as little sympathy with militancy in industrial relations as they had with the propaganda of the socialists when considering the broad aims of the trade union movement.

When boilermakers were in employment their standard of living was high by the prevailing working class standards of the time. In 1889, a prosperous year, a substantial proportion of the most highly skilled members were receiving more than £2 per week. This was in the same year that London dockers were striking for a rate of pay of 6d an hour. In the provinces many unskilled workers were paid less than London dockers.

PIECE-WORK

In the great period of shipbuilding expansion the boilermakers pushed up their earnings by piece-work. Eventually nearly all of them became piece-workers, yet in the early years of the Society piece-work was prohibited and members' acceptance of piece-work was frequently deplored in official pronouncements.

It was at the 1848 annual meeting of the Society that for the first time there was a long discussion on piece-work. It was unanimously condemned, and branches were urged to do everything possible to abolish it. The Society continued to campaign against it, and in 1856 and 1857 organised an essay competition among members on the evils of piece-work. A selection of the submitted essays was subsequently published. They contained four main arguments against piece-work. In the first place, so it was said, piece-work provided employers with an opportunity to induce men to work harder for an advantage which proved only to be temporary. For a period earnings were higher as a result of piece-work, but when trade became slack the piece-work prices were cut by the employers and the men still had to work with an additional effort to maintain their original day-rate wages. Secondly, piece-work created strife between man and man. The men competed for the better paid jobs. Co-operation and brotherhood were replaced by competition and rivalry. Thirdly, piece-work encouraged shoddy work. It destroyed pride of craftsmanship and the dignity that went with such pride. It replaced this dignity of labour with a money-grubbing immorality. Fourthly, piece-work encouraged men to be irresponsible towards their work and their family responsibilities. If they thought that they could earn sufficient in three days on piece-work, they would fail to turn up to work on the other days and spend the time drinking in public-houses. One of the essayists complained that it was well known that, in the shipbuilding yards on the Mersey where there was piece-work, it was rare during a period of prosperity for a full complement of workers to be present during Monday, Tuesday or Wednesday. Many workers were away from work either drinking or recovering from drunkenness, and it was only on Thursdays, Fridays and Saturdays that there was usually a full turn-out of workers.

One particular form of piece-work which was roundly condemned was the system under which one man accepted a contract for a portion of work and then hired a group of workers to work under his instruction and at a price offered by him. The 'contractor' thus became the agent of the main employer and often tried to exercise tyrannical control over his gang.

Nevertheless, despite all these arguments against piece-work an ever-growing proportion of the membership found themselves employed on it. In the main the employers favoured it. They appreciated the incentive value of a system of payment by results. In an industry in which there were also heavy overhead expenses it paid the employers to provide a generous reward for a rate of labour performance above that normally found with day-wage workers. Furthermore, the employers could offer generous rates when trade was good because they knew that shipowners were pressing for delivery. Between 1885 and 1900 about 70 per cent of the world's shipping was built in British yards. When trade was depressed the employers sought and were usually successful in obtaining cuts in piece-work prices.

From the point of view of the men, piece-work proved not to be so disadvantageous as many active members of the Society had feared. As a system of payment it lent itself to the constant guerrilla warfare that took place in many shipyards. The industry was never really stable, and, in turn, wages were always fluctuating. They were either rising or falling according to whether trade was buoyant or slack, and whether labour was in demand or in surplus. When it was in demand the initiative was with the Society's members; when it was in surplus the initiative was with the employers.

Payment by results also gave to boilermakers, through the strength and vigour of their workplace trade union organisation, the opportunity to ensure that they shared in the benefits of technical progress. When new techniques, tools or equipment were introduced to help labour productivity, piece-work prices were not always reduced proportionately. This was not because the employers were unduly benevolent but because of the resistance of the men. Boilermakers were among the earliest of metal-workers to come to an understanding, by experience, of the possibility of influencing and partially controlling a system of payment by results. One hundred years later, in the engineering industry the effect of workers' influence on payment-by-results systems has become much more widely recognised. A number of firms have sought to introduce measured day-work to replace payment-by-results systems which, they allege, have been eroded so that piece-work earnings rise year by year without any corresponding increase in effort.

By the early 1860s piece-working was so widespread among boilermakers in shipyards that its existence was recognised in the rule-book. The fiction was still maintained that men accepted it only when compelled to do so, but members were now made eligible for dispute benefit when resisting a reduction in piece-work prices.

JOBS IN THE COLONIES

Though the standard of living of boilermakers was high when they were in employment, it must never be overlooked that for many of them work in shipbuilding was rarely stable. They were in and out of work from one year to another.

The expansion of British colonialism created new job opportunities for boilermakers. Most openings were in South Africa, immediately after the Boer War. A number of branches of the Society were opened in that country. After the Boer War the Society was extremely critical of the policies pursued by the British Government which, it suggested, were prompted by a narrow concern for the profits of private industrialists and financiers. It would have been pleasing to record that this criticism reflected a genuine opposition to colonialism and colonial wars on the part of the Society's leaders. Perhaps this was one contributory element – at least among some of the Society's more radical members – but it also has to be said that another important factor was the concern felt by the Society at the proposal to admit Chinese 'coolie' labour into South Africa. The Society wanted skilled jobs to be maintained for Europeans.

A CENTRAL ADMINISTRATION

It has sometimes been held that the formation of the Amalgamated Society of Engineers in 1851 marked the beginning of the new model trade unionism of Victorian England. The hallmark of this new unionism was the existence of a centralised, national, professional administration responsible for the accumulation and distribution of funds, the acquisition of property, and the maintenance of stable organisation. Of course this change did not take place overnight, even in the case of the Amalgamated Society of Engineers. In the new model unions, many of the traditional practices of the earlier local societies, with their direct lay control, their secrecy, and their ritual, were maintained.

The Boilermakers' Society provides in some ways a better subject for study of the development of an efficient centralised system of administration than the Amalgamated Society of Engineers. In the Boilermakers' Society there was no sharp point of departure to coincide with the formation of a new amalgamation. Moreover, among boilermakers the tradition of primitive democracy remained extremely strong, even when the professionalism of the central administration, represented by the person of Robert Knight, was second to none in the entire trade union movement. The Boiler-makers' Society maintained an almost religious belief in the value and validity of rank-and-file referenda. In addition, as pointed out in earlier paragraphs, the members employed in shipbuilding dis-played an unyielding obstinacy in insisting upon their right to take their own decisions about strike action on changes in piece-work prices. The central leadership was never able to bring completely under control the propensity of the membership to decide for them-selves when action was necessary.

This is not to argue that the Boilermakers' Society was always the very epitome of democracy. For a long time during Robert Knight's period of office the forms of democracy – and in particular the referenda – provided to a considerable extent a façade behind which there was authoritarian control exercised by the General Secretary and a number of the district delegates. The real require-ments of democratic trade unionism, including the ventilation, exchange and conflict of views at local, district and national level through regular conferences and a lively journal, were missing. It was only on the narrow workplace, industrial, trade union issues that the bureaucracy was unable to stifle the discussion of the membership. In the end, fortunately, changes were forced on a reluctant leadership.

CONTROL OF THE FUNDS

The emergence of a professional, central administration in the Boilermakers' Society had much more to do with the need to

181

accumulate and safeguard the funds of the Society and to distribute them fairly to members in need than with the creation of a solid front of members for purposes of collective bargaining and industrial struggle with employers. One of the first moves towards centralisation was made in 1842, when provision was made for each branch to submit to the head branch a statement on its membership and financial reserves. Arrangements were then made for the branches with proportionately low outgoings or benefits to send money to branches with high outgoings. The need for this kind of financial equalisation, as it was sometimes called, was underlined when unemployment in 1842 caused a severe drain on the finances of a number of branches.

In the 1840s much of the time at annual meetings of the Society was spent in discussing finance (including rates of contributions), benefits, and arrangements for the equalisation of funds between branches. The existing part-time secretary, John Roberts, who had been elected in 1842, was appointed full-time in 1845. In the same year important decisions were taken to establish branch-protection funds, to re-introduce travelling or tramping benefit to assist unemployed members, and to provide a new important benefit for members totally disabled as a result of an injury at work. Clearly, the appointment for the first time of a full-time General Secretary and the introduction of important changes in benefits was not a coincidence. A full-time General Secretary was seen to be necessary, above all as a financial administrator.

Three years later it was decided that annual delegate meetings need not be held. The view that the main function of the leadership, consisting of the General Secretary and the head branch, was to administer the funds had by now taken a fairly firm hold. Provision was made for referenda on disputed issues but there was little if any conception of the need for democratic discussion on, say, a national policy for collective bargaining or, indeed, for anything else. Delegate meetings could be summoned from time to time, but mainly to discuss contributions, benefits, and rules relating to membership.

One of the first indications of any recognition of the need for a measure of co-ordination for collective bargaining, as distinct from co-ordination for provident purposes, was the decision in 1852, following the amalgamation of small local societies in Scotland and London, to provide for district committees. It was not, however, until some ten years later that the general need for district committees for co-ordination in local collective bargaining was clearly seen. The rules were then changed to empower the Executive Council to draw up district boundaries and to arrange for district elections. Thus the co-ordination of branches for collective bargaining through district committees came later than the national co-ordination of branches for provident purposes.

In the meantime, in 1856 the annual delegate meeting had taken a further important step towards central financial control. A new rule was introduced, which established beyond any possibility of doubt that all money in the possession of branches belonged to the whole Society. The financial control exercised by the Executive Council was strengthened, and it was provided that an Executive Council of seven members was to be elected by a head branch or group of branches to be determined every two years by the entire membership.

The view that delegate conferences of the Society should be concerned primarily with contributions, benefits and rules found further confirmation in a proposal submitted by the Executive Council in 1874. It suggested that the delegate meetings, to which only a minority of branches had been in the habit of sending delegates on the relatively rare occasions when they were convened, should be replaced by a General Council, whose members would be elected by branches grouped together for the purpose. The General Council was to meet at two-yearly intervals, or whenever summoned by the Executive Council. There was no suggestion for motions and amendments to be submitted by branches except in relation to rules. Other matters could, however, be referred to the General Council, but only by the Executive Council. Any proposed rule changes, if supported by the General Council, had then to be submitted to a referendum.

During the period of office of Robert Knight the published annual reports of the Society became extremely informative about funds and benefits. They became a model for the trade union movement, and in Robert Knight's later years they extended to over 500 pages, providing the most detailed information, branch by branch, on the distribution of benefits and the allocation of funds. Robert Knight's standard of management was of the very highest order.

A trade depression in 1876 and the consequent need to conserve the funds of the Society led to a further strengthening of central control over funds, though not without a good deal of bitter feeling being aroused. The immediate issue which gave rise to the controversy was a dispute at Sunderland about piece-work prices. The Executive Council took a different view from that of the membership about the dispute, and insisted that branches should not spend money in support of the dispute. The Sunderland branches strongly objected to this ruling of the Executive Council and challenged the Council to submit it to a referendum. The Executive Council's view was upheld in the subsequent referendum, but by such a narrow majority that the Sunderland membership, the Sunderland District Committee and the district delegate – who sided with the membership against the Executive Council – regarded the vote as a moral victory for themselves. The Executive Council, too, were seriously disconcerted by the reaction of the membership and, in the turbulence created by the controversy, decided that, as the referendum had been inconclusive, the issue should be submitted to an arbitrator. The arbitrator awarded in favour of the Executive Council and, though this in turn led to further bitterness, including the resignation of the District Committee and the district delegate, the principle that there should be firm central control of the funds was upheld.

The opening of new head offices in Newcastle for the Society in 1890 was symbolic of the importance of the central administration. Robert Knight was at the height of his power. He was efficient, financially prudent, sagacious in matters of narrow craft interest to the Society, honest, and generally a very able administrator. His power was virtually unchallenged by a lay Executive Council and by a General Council which met very infrequently. There was no annual conference to discuss wider issues of policy, and the journal was in the nature of a monthly report under the control of the General Secretary. Divergent or dissident views were rarely ventilated. Through the district delegates, who could be summoned to Newcastle just as frequently as the General Secretary and the Executive Council desired, Robert Knight had access to a permanent network of officials whose influence could be exerted in virtually every branch. Finally, by his competence in handling the funds of the Society he not only commanded the support of thousands of members who looked to the Society from time to time for financial assistance but, in addition, he was able to exert leverage on every aspect of the Society's activities.

AN EXPRESSION OF DEMOCRACY

Yet, despite this power wielded by Robert Knight, the revolt from below against authoritarian control continued to gather strength. As already noted, there were intermittent but nevertheless strong challenges from rank-and-file movements in industrial disputes. There was a minority of socialists and members with strong radical views who did not look with favour upon Robert Knight's machinations inside the TUC against the 'new unionists' of the late 1880s and 1890s. There were others who just wanted more popular say in the affairs of the Society, and there were still others who harboured particular personal grievances against Robert Knight. In the end this groundswell of discontent burst through, and in 1895 a majority of members of the General Council were pledged to vote for a full-time Executive Council to replace the existing locally elected lay committee. No one at that time, on either side of the controversy, was in any doubt as to its real significance. The issue was seen as one between the continuation of authoritarian control and the introduction of a new measure of membership participation and effective control over the General Secretary.

Democracy, as it was seen by its advocates, won the day. Robert Knight's wings were clipped. Thus by the end of his period of office not only had the principle of national control and leadership – to which Robert Knight himself had made a great contribution – been firmly established but also provision had been made for the members themselves, through the election of a full-time Executive Council, to participate to a greater extent than hitherto in the exercise of national leadership. Much more still remained to be achieved for trade union democracy, but the change made in the late 1890s was of real significance for the Society.

CRAFT NARROWNESS AND CLASS SOLIDARITY

The history of the Boilermakers' Society in the last century displayed repeated contradictory trends between craft narrowness and class solidarity. The Society's members were quick to grasp the

185

common interest between men who practised the skills of boiler-making, but they were sometimes slow to appreciate that they had common interests with other workers in the same industries. It must be said in fairness, however, that they often displayed a higher standard of solidarity with workers in other industries with whom they did not have to compete for employment.

The most significant and partially successful early attempt at an all-embracing engineering union amalgamation, to cover all mech-anics, took place in 1850–1. It led to the formation of the Amalgamated Society of Engineers. The boilermakers were invited to join in the amalgamation discussions but declined to do so. Their scales of benefits were generous, and members generally were more concerned with financial protection than with co-operation with others in collective bargaining. Nevertheless, the prevailing mood, which prompted discussion about amalgamation, helped to bring two small societies, one in Scotland and one in London, into the United Society. Even though the Society declined the invitation to participate in the engineering amalgamation discussions, there were a number of members and a few branches who were sympathetic towards the idea of an amalgamation. At one stage it was reported that at least two Boilermakers' branches were about to transfer to the new amalgamation, but eventually all remained within the Society.

Relations with the Amalgamated Society of Engineers remained cool for some years after the 1851 amalgamation, and relations with the Shipwrights' Society were very strained. Both the Boiler-makers' Society and the Amalgamated Society of Engineers claimed the right to organise angle-smiths. There were disputes at a number of firms because either members of the Boilermakers' Society or members of the Amalgamated Society of Engineers refused to acknowledge the card of the other union. Relations became so difficult that in 1865 the Boilermakers' Society issued a pamphlet arguing that the responsibility for this inter-union rivalry rested with the Amalgamated Society of Engineers, which, it was said, was pursuing an expansionist policy.

Rivalry between the Boilermakers' Society and the Shipwrights' Society was even more intense. There was a constant struggle between the two organisations over trade demarcation. The Ship-wrights' Society, as a union of craftsmen whose traditional raw

186

material was wood, were fighting a rearguard action against the constant encroachment of metal mechanics, whether boilermakers or fitters. Most of the disputes were inevitably resolved to the advantage of the Boilermakers' Society, because the boilermaking skills were associated with the new techniques of ship construction.

These trade rivalries, though destructive of the unity of shipbuilding workers, were, however, often a favourable factor in recruitment. The claim that only men with boilermaking skills should be employed on iron structural work in shipbuilding served to strengthen the appeal of the Boilermakers' Society. It was a contributory element, for example, in the surge in recruitment in Tyne and Wear shipyards in 1863.

AN ENGINEERING FEDERATION?

The serious trade depression of the mid–1870s and the accompanying wage cuts brought about an important change in the attitude of the Boilermakers' Society towards trade union co-operation in the engineering industry. Hitherto the Society had stood aloof from moves towards further amalgamation. In 1875, however, there was a growing feeling among active members in a number of engineering unions, including the Amalgamated Society of Engineers, the Boilermakers, the Steam Engine Makers and the Ironfounders, that, even if amalgamation was unattainable or undesirable, much greater co-operation, including some form of federation, was necessary. The formation of a federation with a central fund would, so it was argued, enable any one union to resist more strongly an attack from an employer. The other unions would be able to render financial assistance through the central fund of the federation. This concept of an engineering trade union federation was thus derived from the collective bargaining function of trade unionism. The federation was intended to strengthen the workers in their relations with the employers.

It is to the credit of Robert Knight and the Executive Council of the Boilermakers' Society that they saw clearly the need for an engineering federation. They participated in the discussions, supported the proposals which were advanced, and campaigned for them within the Society. In a ballot vote the proposal for the creation of a Federation of Engineering Trades was approved by

187

a large majority. It was not the fault of the Society that the subsequent further discussions ran into difficulty. After another year even the enthusiasm of the Boilermakers' Society was damped by the differences of view between the unions about their proposed financial obligations. When definite proposals were formulated, the number of Boilermakers' members in favour of the suggested federation was much smaller, despite the continuing support of the Executive Council. Opposition had also developed in other unions, and finally the whole proposal was dropped. It was not revived until some few years later.

AN EXCLUSIVE ATTITUDE

After the unsuccessful moves for an engineering federation, the Society continued only very slowly to relax its exclusive attitude towards extending its membership. In 1882 holders-up were admitted to membership, though only on condition that they were not to be eligible for unemployment or superannuation benefit, and were not to be entitled to vote at branch meetings unless the question under discussion immediately affected their interests. The Executive Council, in recommending their admission, pointed out that, whilst they benefited from the Society's activities, they made no contribution to its funds.

In their attitude to platers' helpers the members of the Boilermakers' Society were frequently much less sympathetic. In particular, on the north-east coast they were strongly opposed to the 'corner' system, a form of piece-work for platers' helpers. The Society wanted to end this system because it felt that it tended to take away from platers the control of the pace of work. The Society offered to support the helpers in a claim for a minimum day-wage equivalent to time-and-a-half of their existing basic rate if the helpers would abandon the 'corner' system. The platers' helpers refused, and the Boilermakers' Society then decided that their members on the Wear should not work with helpers who insisted on being paid on the 'corner' system. In effect, this meant that hundreds of helpers had to be dismissed and new labourers recruited to take their place. There was intense bitterness in Sunderland around this dispute and a great deal of suffering among helpers. There were outbreaks of violence when the Boilermakers' Society decided to assist

188

in the recruitment of new labourers, many of them from outside the district. A number of other unions gave financial assistance to the helpers and the whole episode was a tragic chapter in the history of shipbuilding trade unionism.

The Society defeated by ballot an attempt to admit to its ranks a small union of blacksmiths on the Wear, and in 1883 an even more significant decision was taken, when by 1,506 votes to 664 the Society defeated on a ballot vote a recommendation that draughtsmen should be admitted to membership. In fact, before this decision was taken a number of draughtsmen had been recruited on the north-east coast. Some few years later there was an attempt to form a draughtsmen's union on the Tyne, but it collapsed with the victimisation of its active members. After the turn of the century there was another unsuccessful attempt to form a draughtsmen's union, this time on the Clyde, but again the active members were victimised. It was not until 1913 that a draughtsmen's union was successfully launched in John Brown's yard, Clydebank. In its early days it was supported by the Clyde district of the Boilermakers' Society, but it is possible that, if a different decision had been taken on the admission of draughtsmen by the Society in 1883, the whole course of trade union organisation among shipbuilding draughtsmen, and even among engineering draughtsmen, would have been different. The union of draughtsmen formed in John Brown's yard grew eventually to become the Draughtsmen's and Allied Technicians' Association, which is now the technical and supervisory section of the Amalgamated Union of Engineering Workers.

During a period of prosperity in the late 1880s, when claims for wage increases were being pressed in nearly every shipyard, the shipbuilding employers decided to meet together to consider how their collective resistance to union claims could be strengthened. This, in turn, revived discussion in the unions about the formation of a federation of engineering and shipbuilding trades. Again the proposal was strongly favoured by Robert Knight and the Executive Council. It was commended to the membership and was approved by them. This time the efforts to form a federation were successful. Robert Knight was, in fact, the leading spirit in the formation of the Federation of Engineering and Shipbuilding Trades in 1890. This was a great step forward for trade unionism, and the Boilermakers' Society can claim major credit for the initiative which led to its formation. Significantly, the Amalgamated Society of Engineers decided not to join. This disunity had disastrous results some few years later in the eight hour struggle in 1897.

Despite the Society's advocacy of a trade union federation for engineering and shipbuilding, the tradition of craft exclusiveness persisted with but little modification. A small society of holders-up based on the Clyde was accepted into membership in 1892 and a sheet-iron workers' society, also based on the Clyde, was accepted on a ballot vote by a fairly narrow majority a few years later. It was made clear, however, that the sheet iron workers were not to be permitted to undertake boilermakers' work. Small societies were also accepted in London and on the Wear but, as usual, there was a good deal of resistance and reluctance to afford them normal membership. Applications for admission by drillers' societies were consistently rejected, even though the applications were supported by the Executive Council. The majorities against admission were overwhelming, and showed clearly that the Executive Council was well in advance of the membership in its recognition of the need to build an all-embracing union for workers employed on metal structural work in shipbuilding.

Even inside the new Federation of Engineering and Shipbuilding Trades the influence of the Boilermakers' Society was exerted to keep out the unions of unskilled workers. The issue was put to a ballot of the membership, and resulted in a vote of 11,632 to 5,229 for exclusion. Perhaps the real significance of this vote was that there was by now a substantial minority of members who accepted that trade unionism in engineering and shipbuilding, in order to be effective, could not be confined exclusively to craftsmen. But among the majority, craft consciousness was still more pronounced than class consciousness.

SUPPORT FOR OTHER UNIONS

Yet the Boilermakers' Society was never an insular union. Its record of support for other unions, despite occasional lapses, was outstandingly good. Moreover, it played a significant part in the development of the wider trade union and labour movement. It was one of the earliest members of the TUC; its initiative played a major part in the formation of the Federation of Engineering and Shipbuilding Trades; and it was among the first group of craft unions to support the Labour Representation Committee.

As early as 1859–60 the Boilermakers' Society organised a substantial levy to assist London building trade workers involved in a long dispute with their employers. The employers were seeking to destroy trade union organisation among their employees. Five years later the Society, on a branch vote, empowered the Executive Council to make grants to other unions involved in trade disputes. From that time onwards grants were regularly made to other unions, not only in Britain but also abroad. Grants were made at various times to unions in the U.S.A., Australia, Germany, Denmark, Austria and France. Financial support was also given to Russian workers following the defeat of the 1905 revolution. Among the more significant donations made to other British workers – in addition to the levy for the building-trade workers in 1860 – were the levy of 1s per member in 1874 to assist the agricultural workers; a vital donation of £800 to Hull dockers in 1893, which saved them from defeat in a dispute with their employers; and a levy to assist South Wales miners in a dispute in 1898.

In common with a number of other well established trade societies, the Boilermakers' Society regarded with some caution what has since come to be regarded as the founding congress of the TUC in 1868. The congress was representative mainly of trades councils, except London and Glasgow. The 1871 Congress was the first which was really representative of the trade union movement, and delegates from the Boilermakers' Society were present. Some five years earlier, in 1866, the Society had participated in the largely abortive United Kingdom Alliance of Organised Trades. The Society can certainly claim to have participated in the formative stages of a British national trade union centre. It was also closely associated with the setting up of the General Federation of Trade Unions, though in the outcome the proposals for the constitution of the Federation did not commend themselves to the Society. The idea of a federation, through which financial assistance could be rendered to a union or unions in dispute, came to be much more widely supported as a result of the defeat of the engineering unions in the 1897 eight hours' dispute. Robert Knight acted as the chairman of the TUC committee to examine the idea of a trade union financial federation, but when the proposals were worked out he felt that they were unsound and that, in addition, the existence of a federation with a measure of financial control in major disputes might undermine the autonomy of the Society. He carried the Executive Council with him in this expression of opposition and their views were subsequently confirmed overwhelmingly in a ballot vote of the Society. Some six years later, however, in 1905, well after the retirement of Robert Knight, opinion had changed sufficiently in the Society for the General Council to recommend affiliation to the Federation. This was confirmed by a vote of the membership, but, illogically, two suggested alternative methods for paying the affiliation fee were rejected. In the end it was decided that the fee should be taken from the general funds.

The most likely explanation of the change in attitude of the Society towards affiliation to the GFTU is that, in 1899, the Society was still strongly influenced by the views of Robert Knight on the 1897 engineering dispute and on the strict financial standards by which he measured any proposal for a trade union federation. But by 1905 the Society felt the influence of a new set of circumstances and series of events. The experience of the Taff Vale dispute underlined the need for trade union solidarity, and the new leaders of the Boilermakers' Society were less inclined to assess every proposal for trade union change in strict financial terms. Significantly, the General Federation of Trade Unions was not destined to play any major role in later disputes affecting the Society.

The action of the Society in sending financial aid to the victims of police repression in the unsuccessful 1905 Russian Revolution was probably the first significant example in the Society's history of international solidarity on a directly political issue. It is worthy of record that the gesture of the Executive Council in sending money was supported by the branches and that a large number of them urged that more should be forwarded. Altogether the Society sent £100 to the victims of Tsarist oppression.

POLITICAL ACTION

The manner in which the Boilermakers' Society came to be among the earliest trade union supporters of the Labour Party affords an illuminating example of the important influence of the struggle for

192

trade union rights and the very limited influence of socialist ideo-
logy. The Society took up political action because it saw the
campaign for new legislation on trade disputes as an extension of
its trade union activity. It did not – certainly in the years covered
by this volume – participate in a deep and thoroughgoing theoretical
discussion about a new social order. Its politics were *trade union*
politics rather than *labour* politics. Even less were they *socialist*
politics.

From its earliest days the Society had been concerned with the
legality of its activities. It could not be otherwise. The year of its
formation was the year of the Tolpuddle Martyrs, when men were
transported to Australia for, in effect, joining a union. The early
branch ritual of the Society was designed to protect members against
informers, spies and *agents provocateurs*. Hence the secret signs
and words to gain admission to a meeting and the election of outside doorkeepers and inspectors, whose job was to examine every
person in the branch room to ensure that all were members.

Among the early active members of the Society were a number
of Chartists, one of whom, John Roach, participated in drawing
up the first rule-book. The Chartists were the first politically active
members of the Society. It is not true, therefore, as is sometimes
said, that politics only came much later in the Society's history.
Indeed, it is nearer the truth to say that it was 'pure and simple'
trade unionism that came later, though in the early formative years
there was no formal provision for the discussion of political matters.
There is now no way of finding out to what extent the majority of
members of the Boilermakers' Society in its very earliest years
sympathised with or participated in the Chartist movement. But
that a number of active and early members were Chartists is
established beyond all doubt.

After the decline of the Chartist movement and until the passing
of the trade union legislation of the 1870s, the main concern of the
Society in relation to politics and the law was to ensure that trade
union funds could be protected against misappropriation; that members should not be sent to prison for breach of employment contracts; and that the liability of employers for injuries sustained by
workmen in the course of their employment should be firmly established. There were strong practical reasons for each of these areas
of interest.

It had aways been doubtful in the early years of trade unionism whether trade unions could by legal process recover money stolen by voluntary officials. Nevertheless, there were occasions when successful legal action had been taken. In 1865, however, the decision of Bradford magistrates not to uphold a claim by the Society to recover £25 stolen by the Bradford branch treasurer confirmed that trade union funds were not necessarily protected by the Friendly Societies Act, 1855. The decision of the magistrates was upheld on appeal. In the following year a number of boiler-makers on Tees-side were sent to prison for breach of employment contracts arising out of a trade dispute. Thousands of workers in other industries had suffered similar penalties under the then existing law of master and servant. To change the law was of urgent importance to the union.

The demand for legal protection for injured workers was as long-standing as the trade union movement itself. This was always, and has remained, an issue of vital interest to the unions, both indus-trially and politically. There were frequent references in the publications of the Boilermakers' Society to the need for proper financial protection for injured workers, long before the movement took shape for independent labour representation in Parliament. One of the first major campaigns conducted officially by the Society to influence forthcoming legislation took place in the late 1860s, following the publication of the report of the Royal Commission set up to investigate trade unionism. The Society, together with other unions, opposed the recommendations of the Majority Report and supported those of the Minority Report which, in brief, called for the legal recognition of unions and protection for their funds, without imposing any new conditions upon them. Members of the Boilermakers' Society were urged by their Executive Council to make representations to their Members of Parliament. The trade union campaign had some effect, and the eventual legislation was, in important respects, helpful.

The campaign in the late 1860s for new legislation more sympathetic to trade unionism brought the Society for the first time into formal support for the principle of independent labour representation. In 1871 the Society gave support to the Labour Representation League. In the following four years vigorous activity was conducted to influence Members of Parliament to introduce legislation for the recognition of trade union rights.

Only a few years before the celebrated Taff Vale case the decision of the House of Lords in favour of boilermakers in the Allen *versus* Flood case was widely interpreted as a victory for trade unionism. It appeared to confirm that trade unionists had the right not to work with men who did not belong to their organisation. For a time it strengthened the claims of those who argued that the existing state of the law was satisfactory to the unions and that changes were unnecessary. Their optimism was to prove short-lived and unjustified.

DECLINE – AND A NEW AWAKENING

After this period of political participation, political interest and activity declined. This decline coincided with the great expansion of shipbuilding and the growth in influence of Robert Knight. Even in the periods of acute economic depression no real political lessons were drawn. Poverty and unemployment were deplored, but no support was expressed for thoroughgoing changes in the social order. Robert Knight was an opponent of the socialists in the TUC and disliked any suggestion that hours of work might be reduced by legislation. He opposed the socialist agitation for an Eight Hours Bill and argued that workers should rely on their unions for improvements, and not look to Parliament to achieve results which ought to be obtained through collective bargaining. In Robert Knight's view the real enemies of the workers were not the capitalists of manufacturing industry but the brewers and the publicans.

So strongly did Robert Knight and the then leadership of the Society oppose the early socialists that they carried through a campaign to denigrate the TUC, which they felt had come partially under the influence of the socialists. They succeeded at one point in securing a majority in a vote of the Society in favour of disaffiliation from the TUC, though the size of the minority vote in favour of continued affiliation probably surprised them. This, however, was essentially part of a counteraction to the socialists, and, when the 'old guard' leaders in the TUC re-established their firm grip, the suggestion to disaffiliate was dropped.

This was, however, the period of challenge and change inside the

195

Boilermakers' Society. By 1899 there was sufficient strength of feeling in favour of political representation to ensure that the vote of the Society was cast at the TUC in favour of the historic resolution calling for a conference of organisations to secure the return of Labour Members of Parliament. This resolution was carried at the TUC by a narrow majority. The Executive Council recommended that the Society should be represented at the subsequent Labour Representation Conference but this recommendation was rejected by a more than two-to-one majority on a ballot of the membership. The result of the ballot showed clearly that the Society was still divided on the subject of political action and that, despite the internal changes which had taken place in the Society, a substantial majority of members saw no adequate reason to favour independent labour representation in Parliament. Nevertheless, rank and file opinion within the Society was to change fairly rapidly, assisted by the political sympathies of many active members and the majority of the new leadership. A TUC pamphlet on the Taff Vale case was widely distributed among the membership and the Executive Council did not fail to point out the need for political action to reverse the wrongs done by legal judgements.

At the 1901 TUC the Boilermakers' delegation supported a resolution urging unions to affiliate to the Labour Representation Committee, and the Executive Council of the Society decided to send representatives to a conference convened by the Labour Representation Committee. In the new situation following Taff Vale, and in response to a strong appeal from the Executive Council and the new General Secretary, D. C. Cummings, the membership voted overwhelmingly, with a more than three-to-one majority, in favour of political representation and affiliation to the Labour Representation Committee. Opinion among the rank and file had swung decisively in favour of political action, thanks to the effect of the Taff Vale case and the vigorous response of the Society's leadership.

In the next four years political interest among the Society's membership reached a new high level. Branches in every part of Britain participated in campaigns, deputations, meetings and demonstrations in favour of trade union law reform. Candidates were chosen to fight under Labour's banner at the General Election. The Society was now set firm on a course which recognised the

196

fundamental indivisibility of the labour and trade union movements. This change in the Society was a fitting culmination of the first seventy years of its history. From being a pioneer in craft organisation, based on considerations of mutual help, the Society had taken a significant part in the development of a mass labour movement.

Appendix One

The Ritual of the Boilermakers' Society 1857

The ritual of the Boilermakers' Society for the opening and closing of meetings and for the admission of members is almost as old as the Society itself. With very few amendments it has remained unchanged over the years and is still used to this day. The language of the ritual and some of the sentiments which it expresses may be somewhat out of place in the contemporary scene, yet the ritual continues to express the mood of brotherhood and idealism which has inspired active members of the Society for over 139 years. For this reason the Society has been reluctant to change the ritual. The text is issued as a private small booklet within the Society. As far as is known the text, set out below, has never previously been published in a form available to anyone outside the membership of the Society.

THE RITUAL OF THE BOILERMAKERS' SOCIETY

ADDRESS AT THE
OPENING OF THE MEETING
OF
EACH BRANCH OR COMMITTEE

Worthy Officers and Brothers,
  We are now assembled together to transact the business of our Society; I hope, therefore, you will deal fair and impartially in any case that may be brought before you in honour to yourselves and to the credit of the Society you belong to.
Worthy Brothers, I declare this branch duly opened.

INSTRUCTIONS
in reference to the
PROPOSITION OF CANDIDATES
wishing to be admitted into
THE AMALGAMATED SOCIETY OF BOILERMAKERS, SHIPWRIGHTS, BLACKSMITHS AND STRUCTURAL WORKERS

AFTER a candidate has been proposed and seconded he must be admitted to the branch meeting and asked the following questions:

What is your name?
How old are you?
What branch of the trade do you follow?
How long have you followed the same?

The above questions having been answered, the President should ask if any member present has any further question to ask the candidate. All such questions must be addressed to the President.

The candidate having answered all the questions should be requested to leave the room.

The candidate having left the room, the proposition that he be admitted should then be discussed, and if carried by a majority of the members voting, it shall become the duty of the President to see that the candidate is on that same evening supplied with a copy of the rules.

One month must elapse between the night of a candidate's proposition being accepted and his admission, in order to allow enquiry to be made as to the truth of the candidate's replies to the above questions.

THE INITIATION CEREMONY

RESPECTED FRIEND – You are now about to enter The Amalgamated Society of Boilermakers, Shipwrights, Blacksmiths and Structural Workers to participate in its privileges and share its responsibilities; you will be expected to conform to all our laws and usages, to cultivate a kind of brotherly feeling amongst our members. Their cause must be your cause, their good your good, their troubles your troubles, and all past indifference transformed into a profound sympathy, and all prejudice into a sacred devotion for the elevation of the Order you are about to enter; and if these precepts are carried out in your everyday life you will at all times receive the approbation of your fellow members, and the shield of the Society will be raised to protect you in time of need.

200

WILL YOU PLEASE ANSWER THE FOLLOWING QUESTIONS?

What is your name?

Have you had a copy of the rules?

Are you willing to conform to our rules and regulations? Is it of your free will and at your own desire that you are brought here to become a member of this Society?

THESE QUESTIONS HAVING BEEN SATISFACTORILY ANSWERED, THE PRESIDENT SHALL ADDRESS THE CANDIDATE AS FOLLOWS:

BROTHER – You are now admitted a member amongst us and will therefore be required to conform to our rules so far as you have promised before this assembly of your fellow-men. You will also be expected to conform to the laws of this country and not to do that to another which you would not have done to yourself.

We are united not to set class against class but to teach one another that all are brothers. Our greatest desire being to cultivate a close and lasting relationship between all those with whom we have to do with in undertaking our daily work. We trust these motives of ours will be appreciated by you and receive your heartfelt support, for it is important that men whose interests and sympathies are in common should be united in the bonds of brotherhood and mutual regard. If unity is strength, it must be of first importance to those who follow a similar employment to be united together in such an organisation as ours, whose objects are the protection of its trades interests, the support of its members when thrown out of employment, the relief of the sick, the care of the aged, and, when the last great call is made, to render support to the widow and fatherless, and other benevolent objects of a like character.

Each individual member is expected to fully realise his position as a unit of our organisation, and to try and grasp the idea that the success of all mainly depends on the efforts of individuals acting with loyalty to the principles they have pledged themselves to carry out.

Regular and systematic payment of your contributions will foster habits of regularity and be beneficial to you as an individual as well as to this Society, and if you do your part in your promises, we will redeem ours, and the Society will protect and shield you in time of need.

In conclusion, I would enjoin you to be a loving husband, a tender father, a good neighbour and a strict observer of every moral and social duty, honouring your parents as you in your turn expect to be honoured. May you rejoice at all times in the lessening of human suffering, in the alleviation of human sorrow, and in the elevation of your fellow-men. Always let charity and wisdom guide you in your efforts, remembering that in aiding others in distress you are elevating yourself and that it is better to give than receive.

May you long be spared to uphold the objects and principles of our Society, and in the name of the members and officers of this branch permit me to wish you a long continuation of health and happiness.

201

At the conclusion of the address the Past President should take the new member (or members) outside the room and instruct him in the method of addressing the chair when entering. Having instructed him he shall knock three times at the door and upon being admitted shall, after seeing the door closed, address the President, after which he shall take his seat with the members.

ADDRESS AT THE
CLOSING OF THE MEETING
OF
EACH BRANCH OR COMMITTEE

Worthy Officers and Brothers,

having concluded the business of this night, I hope you will part in peace and friendship with each other in the true spirit of brotherhood, until business or duty again calls us together.

I therefore declare this branch legally closed.

Appendix Two

Extracts from Essays on Piece-work 1857

In 1857 the Boilermakers' Society organised an essay competition among its members to expose the evils of piece-work. A number of the submitted essays were subsequently published. Extracts from them are set out below.

ESSAY 1

... Is it not time, I say, to arouse ourselves to a sense of our duty and proclaim throughout the order, that we, the United Society of Boiler Makers and Iron Ship Builders, are fully sensible of the war that is waged against us, and are determined no longer to bend beneath its yoke? No one, worthy brothers, can have worked in places where piece-work is carried on, without being aware that an ill-feeling exists amongst the men, and that they are dissatisfied and often at variance with each other, whilst the evil blood which is generated amongst them is apt to go off with the least spark. I will not venture to say that they are all alike; no, far from it; but hearing of the high rate of wages those men are getting that are on the system, they are often led off by their eagerness and thirst for gain, never thinking of the sort of men that are ever on the alert to take their places, so that it is easily seen that with all their gain they do not obtain wisdom. I remember, worthy brothers, about three years ago. whilst I was working at Leeds, the masters, or at least the trustees, tried the game on there; but a general meeting was called, and I am happy to state that the subject was rejected, and I cannot say that it was ever tried again, at least whilst I was there.

Worthy brothers, surely there is not one amongst us who is not aware of the terrible war that is waged against the Society at large by that most obnoxious and baneful crushing system of piece-work ...

ESSAY 2

. . . Now it is a well-known fact that there are very few men who like working day-work in a boat yard, because they are never sure of making full time, they may work one half the day and then be compelled to go home through bad weather, with their clothes wet to the skin, this I have known to be the case three or four days in a week, so that if a man were ever so willing to work, he is unable to earn sufficient to maintain himself and his family in a respectable manner. And if the men cease work and take shelter for a short time until the storm abates, they are found fault with by the foreman or the master, who tell them plainly that they cannot afford to pay them to stop skulking there, they must either work in the rain or go home; the result is that the men agree to work piece-work, so that the master may lose nothing through their waiting for a few hours occasionally, and that the men may have an opportunity by a little extra exertion in good weather of making up for their lost time in bad weather. Then comes the evil. There are some men who, when on day-work, will do scarcely anything, but when on piece-work will work like niggers, doing as much work in one day as they ought to do in three days. I have known of cases where men have done two days' work, between the hours of six in the morning and twelve at noon (six hours), they have then left their work to go on the spree, and perhaps the work they had done would one-half have to be cut out again through not being done in a workmanlike manner. Then comes a reduction of prices, a dispute, and perhaps a strike; for the master considers it unreasonable for a workman to demand such a price for his labour as to enable him to earn three days' wages in ten hours, although he, the master, may be able to pay the same, through having made a good contract himself . . . But there is another system of piece-work which is greatly practised, but scarcely ever complained of, but which is injurious to the workman in every point when fairly rooted out, I mean the system of piece-masters or foremen, who take the whole of the work by contract from the masters, and then employ the men upon the day-work system, driving and tyrannising over them from morning till night, so as to get as much out of them as it is possible for human nature to part with, and even then, perhaps, not have given satisfaction, especially if a man happens to be of a rather weak or delicate constitution, and unable to keep pace with others who have a constitution like a horse, and whose reasoning powers are very much the same; who think of nothing but going ahead to gain a foreman's favour, even though by doing so they might sacrifice the comfort of the whole of their fellow-men, and ultimately ruin themselves; thus enabling a foreman to enrich himself or make away in luxury or extravagance that which honestly belongs to the workman, and which they probably might have enjoyed if they had considered their own interest, and been determined not to be used as tools to suit any contract by which they would be robbed of both ease and interest . . .

204

Now, with respect to the system of piece-masters, I consider it to be a pernicious system throughout; it reduces a man to the position of a mere machine or beast of burden; from morning till night he is expected to work, work, work incessantly. He has no will of his own, but must do just as he is ordered, whether it be right or wrong; all the freedom he enjoys is before or after the hours of labour, and I doubt there are very few men who are ever in a mood to enjoy much rational recreation after working ten or twelve hours per day for a piece-master boiler maker. It is such as this, in many instances, that drives men to the tap-room, (not to take a glass in moderation to recruit their strength or revive their spirits), but to talk over the sufferings of the day, and to drown care in a 'big jug'. Thus, many a good man has become an habitual drunkard, and so far reduced in the social scale as to lose all spirit and self command, and at last becomes a disgrace to society, and a mere tool for the foreman who employs him . . .

ESSAY 3

. . . Let us enquire for what particular purpose the great bulk of our funds are kept? It is gratifying to see the progress we are making with regard to the funds, but it would be much more gratifying to see some good done with those funds. There is one article to which I would particularly call your attention; namely, Rule first, 'The protection of our Trade'. We have no protection, it is nothing more or less than a benevolent society. If this be an error, I shall feel much obliged to any brother who can correct it. There are certainly a few who receive some benefit, but those that really deserve it never receive a penny. To what better use can the funds be applied than redeeming our trade from its present condition, and that by supporting those brethren who attempt to withstand the tyrannical oppression of their employers?

ESSAY 4

. . . Then there are men who are introduced into the trade by piece-work that have no right to belong to it. This is especially the case in the boat yards, in fact, the major part of our remarks refer to that branch of the business, for we have long thought of, and long hoped for, a radical reform in that department; and we do most sincerely hope that the day is not far distant when the boat yards will bear a comparison with any other branch of the trade. But to return to the subject in hand. Have you not often, like ourselves, seen men coming into a yard in the capacity of helpers, and in a short time they have been riveting? Now this is not as it should be. We wish well to every man – God forbid that we should wish otherwise. But still, if we have a trade, let us keep it free from the encroachments of any and of all who presume to come to work at it without having a right to do so. The way to accomplish this is to

205

do away with piece-work, for it is the cause of our brothers losing a great amount of time. Then, while they are absent, the masters, who are desirous to get on with the work, put these illegal men in their place, and when they find that they answer their purpose, that they are sober and attentive, and do the work (as they often do) for less money, their aim is to get rid of our men as soon as possible, and keep the others on in their place. In this manner these men creep into the trade, while we and our children are thus defrauded of our rights and privileges. The supporter of piece-work may raise an objection here, and say, it is not piece-work that is to blame in this case, but the men's own intemperate habits. We admit that this is the direct cause in this instance; but we ask, on the other hand, what is the indirect cause? Is it not piece-work? We have endeavoured to show, in a former part of this paper, that the great inducement for men to lose time is held out in the fact that they are enabled to make it up again. We do not mean to assert that all the time lost is caused either directly or indirectly by the system of piece-work, far from it; but, though we admit this, we will still contest the point with the supporters of piece-work, and affirm what we are competent to prove, that it is owing to piece-work, and to piece-work alone, that many are now earning their bread by the trade of boiler making and iron ship-building who have no right to do so . . .

It must be evident to all, that if piece-work injures the trade, it must of necessity also injure the Society. We find that wherever this system is carried out, the favoured few perform the work that all should by right have a share of. As a natural consequence, a great number are thrown out of employment, and they are by stern necessity obliged to come on the Society for donations; this acts as a drain upon the funds, and we find at the close of the year, when we come to balance our accounts, that the sum paid to members on travel or at home in donations, is enormous, and tends greatly to cramp the Society's operations . . .

ESSAY 5

. . . Too often do we know men to make double or treble time; but, alas! not so often as the employer who pays it and marks it well. For mark the words of an employer, who, when paying the money, said: 'I am either robbed now, or when they were at day-work; for if justice were done, there could not be such a difference.' This remark is well worthy the consideration of the men; it is them that suffer by it in the end, and more especially when there is a depression of trade . . .

Appendix Three

The Introduction of a Full-time Executive Council

The decision in 1895, taken by the rank-and-file lay delegates of the General Council of the Boilermakers' Society, to provide for a full-time regionally elected Executive Council to replace the previously locally elected lay Executive Council, was the culmination of a long campaign to curtail the power of the then General Secretary, Robert Knight. Robert Knight's authoritarian, but highly efficient control, of the central administration, his views on industrial peace, his opposition to militancy, and his campaign against the socialists and the new unionists in the TUC, had all contributed to a groundswell of revolt among active members inside the Society. This revolt found a response among the wider membership when they found that their actions in a number of disputes with employers did not always find the sympathetic response from the General Secretary which they felt they had a right to expect. The decision of the ASE to elect a full-time Executive Council gave Robert Knight's critics in the Boilermakers' Society an example to follow. The documents reproduced below give some idea of the resistance of Robert Knight and of the 'old' Executive Council to the proposed change introduced by the General Council.

> Executive Council Minutes of 30th July 1895 (this was the 'old' locally elected lay EC).
> 'Resolved that the General Secretary be instructed to prepare for the Monthly Report a few reasons against some of the alterations of rule by the General Council.'

> Statement issued in August 1895 by the 'old' EC when circulating the minutes of the General Council.
> (The statement was almost certainly drafted by Robert Knight.)

> '. . . we herewith send two copies of these minutes for each branch.

207

Full instructions respecting the voting are given on page 3 which we hope all our branch officers will please carry out.

'The votes must be taken on the propositions at branch meetings called for the purpose, and not at aggregate meetings.

'We have received many letters from branches requesting us to take *a special vote* of the Society on one important change which the late General Council proposes to make in the constitution of the Society, namely, the establishment of a permanent Executive Council at this office. We have not thought it wise to accede to this request, as all the principal propositions are placed before you in the pamphlets for your approval or otherwise.

'With regard to this proposed permanent Council as named on page 4 in the pamphlet we may be permitted to call your attention to one or two matters connected therewith.

First: There is not half work at this office to employ seven more permanent hands, and what they are going to do we are completely at a loss to know. Whoever may be the fortunate members to be elected to such a position they would certainly have a very easy time of it, and if you vote in favour of the proposal it will be the first time in the Society's history that you have favoured the establishment of sinecure offices.

Second: We do not approve of the method of election. The Society is to be divided into seven districts, and each of these separate districts are to elect one to represent them. You have here an element of division in the Society that may ultimately cause disunion, which is dangerous. You may thus make each Executive Councilman the creature of a faction instead of a representative of the Society. And to favour his own district he may be willing to sacrifice the Society's interests as a whole.

Third: The additional expense by the appointment of a permanent Executive Council will be very great. The salaries alone for these will amount to £1,001 per annum. Now, taking the average cost of Executive work for the past ten years it amounts to £354 per year. It is true that during the past two years the cost has been considerably heavier than this, but this has been owing to the very large amount of time spent by the Executive Council in considering the extraordinary number of applications for grants from the benevolent fund. But we may fairly expect that the worst is now past, and that we shall fall back to our normal expenditure. If we take the future cost of the present system of working, the average will not exceed £500 per year. The cost for the first six months of this year amounts to only £266 12s 7d. The extra cost of a permanent Executive Council will, we are certain, be nothing less than £500 per annum. It was advanced as an argument in favour of a permanent Executive Council that the Engineers had one, this is so, but the membership of the Engineers' Society is nearly double that of ours, and they, therefore, may find sufficient employment. It was intended by the promoters of this scheme that the district delegates should perform the duties of Executive Councilmen and delegates, but this fell through.

'The proposed alteration in the new donation rule will increase the expenditure at least 25 per cent under this heading, which, on an average, will mean an additional ten thousand a year to be met. Your liabilities will be continually increasing as the Society becomes older for sickness, superannuation, and other benefits.

'There are many of our branches at the present time could not meet their present expenses if they were confined to their own resources, even at a contribution of 3s per member per week.

'We have taken out the accounts of three branches for the past twenty-five years, and they have not only been unable to pay their way after spending all their income, but they have been dependent on remittances sent to them from this office to the following extent: Bristol, indebted to the society £5,718; Liverpool No. 2, £3,176 and Liverpool No. 4, £2,947. There are many more in somewhat similar circumstances.

'We put you in possession of these facts so that you may know what you are doing, and if your votes are in favour of a permanent Council, we shall take it as a proof that you are all quite willing to pay extra contributions to meet the much increased expenditure.

'If the General Council desire to say anything on the subject they can do so in the next Monthly Report.'

In response to this statement a number of members of the General Council then issued a private circular to all branches, defending the decision of the General Council in favour of a full-time EC and strongly criticising Robert Knight and the 'old' EC. The critics of the General Council were no longer prepared to trust the official machinery of the Society, under Robert Knight's influence, to give them a fair showing. Inevitably, many of the criticisms now being voiced were highly personal. Moreover, even on the 'old' EC at least one member was known to be sympathetic to the General Council's decision. He, however, was being disciplined for writing letters critical of the existing leadership.

In September 1895 the 'old' EC issued a further letter to all branches, strongly attacking the private circular issued by a number of members of the General Council. It read:

'Worthy Officers and Brothers,

'We have been favoured with a circular with the names of the majority of the late General Council attached thereto. There are two manly dissentients, namely, Bro. Jones, of Swansea, and Bro. Cheevers, of Southampton, no doubt these could give you good reason for their refusal to sign such a circular.

'After perusing the circular we ask ourselves the question, what wrong have we done by expressing our opinion on the important alteration

o

proposed by the late General Council in the Monthly Report, and calling your attention to the effects of the same on the Society. We said nothing offensive to anyone, we simply stated facts in connection with the case, and left the question to your judgement.

'But it appears this does not meet the approval of the writer of the circular and those who signed it, so as a matter of course the General Secretary has to bear the brunt of their anger. But let us here say that we were unanimous in placing the question before you, independent of any wish of the General Secretary.

'No doubt you have all heard of buying a pig in a poke. Now it appears to us that if they did not want you to buy the pig, they wanted to smuggle this important question through without "any comment". But why do this? If what they propose to do is *a real reform*, then the more it is discussed the better, and if it will not bear discussion and criticism, then it is not worthy of your support. If we had kept silence as they wanted, and when it became too late you had found a mistake had been made, the cry would have been "what was the Executive Council doing in allowing such to pass without pointing the danger out to us?".

'The writer has laboured hard to make it appear that the permanent Council will not be more costly than the present Council, but he has signally failed. We here repeat what we said in the last Monthly, namely that the average cost of Executive Council work during ten years has amounted to £354 per year, the cost for the first six months of this year amounts to £255 12s 7d, this includes everything. And the present system will not average in the future more than £500 per annum, whereas, the *salaries* for a permanent Council would be £1,001 per annum. In addition, they have made a convenient arrangement that two members out of the seven can be away on missions at an increased cost of 1s per hour for all overtime. Taking these together the expenses would be an increase of considerably over £500 per annum.

'In answer to this the writer says "supposing it does cost £500 a year extra, the members can pay it at one farthing per member per month." This looks very nice but why should you pay this when there is so much else to pay, without any reason or the slightest benefit being derived by the change?

'We now come to a statement in the circular which we say is a most *deliberate lie*. The writer of the circular says, "the General Secretary admitted that a goodly portion of the £295 18s 2d mentioned in the annual reports as grants to members had been received by the Executive Council".

'We are told that there is honour amongst a less dignified class of men than those comprising the late General Council, but the honour is absent in the present case, as anything more untrue than the statement in the circular was never circulated amongst men. If their case requires the assistance of such ignoble conduct it must be a bad one indeed.

'We are prepared to place the books of this office in the hands of any

210

accountant, to prove that no Executive Councilman ever received any portion of the grants.

'But how about their own payment as General Council? Do they remember that they paid those who left before the meeting was over, 6s per day for coming and returning home, in addition to the 12s per day allowed by rule? Do they also remember that at the close of the business, they paid those coming from a distance three days each more than they were entitled to at 12s per day, and the local members five days?

'They want to turn the scale in their favour by an unwarrantable attack on the General Secretary. They say that the permanent Council would strip him of the autocratic power he has *too long wielded*. But supposing for argument sake that this be true (which it is not), how would the election of a permanent Council alter this? This Council would be elected for three years, and if the influence of the General Secretary is so great, he would have less difficulty with seven men than he would with twenty-one, who would under the present system take the reigns of government during the same period of time. The whole thing is illogical.

'If the circular contains the opinion at the present time of the General Council, they must have altered considerably since they passed the following resolution at the last day of their sitting:

Resolved: "That we, the members of the General Council, tender to our Worthy General Secretary, Bro. R. Knight, a sincere and hearty vote of thanks for the valuable services rendered by him to us during our deliberations on the revision of rules."

'The General Secretary no more governs the Society than he did the General Council.

'We again repeat, that there is not work enough at this office to employ seven more permanent hands. We don't now refer to any members of the late General Council, as past experience proves that they possess good staying powers, and that a little work will last them a long time.

'You are asked to vote for reform, but this word, as meant by some should be spelt r-u-i-n. We don't think that within the boundaries of this society is exactly the place to experiment on visionary schemes of so called reformers, or to manufacture sinecure offices for them to propagate their ideas.

'We are, faithfully yours,

M. CHARLTON.
C. LAWS.
J. CORBETT.
J. COOPER.   } E. Council
A. CUTTER.
T. HEWITT.
A. THACKRAY. Chairman.
R. KNIGHT. General Secretary.'

The proposition of the General Council for a full-time EC was eventually submitted to a ballot of the membership and was approved. Strangely, the voting figures were not published in the monthly report of the Society. The result was a bitter defeat for Robert Knight.

A circular inviting nominations for the new full-time EC was issued in April 1896. It read:

NOMINATIONS FOR PERMANENT COUNCIL

'The following is the new rule by which you must be guided:

DUTIES AND POWERS OF THE EXECUTIVE COUNCIL

Constitution – Section 1

'The Society shall be governed by an Executive Council consisting of seven members, who shall have been in the Society not less than 10 years, and in benefit, and not more than 8s in arrears. Each member shall be elected for three years by the members in the district they represent. The three councilmen having the highest votes to sit in the first instance for $4\frac{1}{2}$ years, thus causing an election every $1\frac{1}{2}$ years. After the first election, no councilman shall sit for more than three years without re-election.

Applications for Councilmen

'The applicant must have a thorough knowledge of the Society's rules, and such application to be accompanied by testimonials of character and ability. He shall not be connected with any other business other than that of following the trade at the time of such application. None but past or present officers to be eligible for Councilman.

Nominations and Voting

'When three or more are nominated for this office, the candidate having the highest number of votes shall not be considered elected unless he has an absolute majority over all the other candidates; if the highest candidate has not an absolute majority, the votes shall be again taken on the two highest candidates.

'They shall be nominated not less than 12 weeks, and elected not less than four weeks before taking office. Nominations and elections shall take place on general meeting nights summoned for the purpose.

'Nominations must be sent to this office on or before the 6th day of May. The district for which the candidate is nominated must be stated.

'We hope that all our members will realise the great responsibility that devolves upon them in the elections about to take place. We must have the very best men possible. Character and ability should alone influence the choice of candidates, and favouritism must not count in the election. We must also have men capable of corresponding with employers and branches, and who can assist with the accounts at this office. We want the best men who can be found in the Society, men who can build up. We want evolution, and not revolution.

'Nomination papers will be sent to each branch.'

Appendix Four

Should Trade Unions Incorporate?

Clarence Darrow was a distinguished labour lawyer in the U.S.A. He was a central figure, as an advocate for workers' interests, in a number of famous legal cases. The following article written by him appeared in the Boilermakers' Society Monthly Report in March 1903. Mr Darrow's comments are not only of historical interest but they also have a topical ring.

The demand for the incorporation of trade unions is the last trench of those who oppose organised labour. It is impudent and presumptuous. No friend of trade unionism ever believed in it, or advocated it, or called for it. It is demanded to-day by those interests and those enemies who have used every means at their command to oppose trade unionism, to destroy it, and to counteract its influence.

Before this demand was made, the enemies of trade unionism sought to break up the unions in every manner that employers could conceive. They have resorted to the courts, to public opinion, to slander and to vilification. Trade unionism has made its way in the world against every weapon that the employing class could use. It has gained its present position against every effort of the capitalists and their servants, whether in editorial rooms or amongst the paid attorneys of capitalism.

They have learned now that trade unions can not be destroyed directly, and use this demand for incorporation for the purpose of destroying them indirectly. The demand that trade unions should be incorporated is based upon the assumption that they should be made legally responsible for contracts. It is made by a class of men who have persistently refused to contract with them or to recognize them or to have anything to do with them, except to oppose and vilify them.

When the public reaches the stage of consenting to their existence, then it should also recognize their right to manage their own affairs for themselves. The enemies of trade unionism have no right – in decency – to prescribe rules and conditions for trade unions to accept. If working

213

men have the right to organize, it is for them and their friends to provide the methods for their organization and for their work.

For the capitalists to concede that trade unions may organize but at the same time demand the right to dictate the form of their organization is more impudent than open warfare against them. While here and there certain trade unionists may not understand the purpose of their enemies in demanding incorporation, still it is but thinly disguised.

Those who have fought the organization of labour so long, understand perfectly well the disadvantages trade unions would have if they ever consented to incorporation.

The result of incorporating trade unions is perfectly plain to those who make the demand. If trade unions should ever consent to become incorporated, it would mean their absolute destruction.

The great combinations of capital that have taken the form of corporate existence have done this primarily to escape *personal* responsibility and reliability. They have shielded the interests of their members and protected the property of their owners behind the name of a corporation.

When profits were to be divided, they went to the stockholders. When liabilities were incurred, they were those of the corporation and the stockholders escaped responsibility. Creditors were left without redress because the debts incurred were those of the corporation. The modern growth of corporations has been due entirely to the selfishness and greed of capital. They have masked themselves behind these creatures of the law for their own purposes and not to serve any public need.

The great corporations hire their lawyers by the year. They, of course, deal only in high-priced lawyers, who are trained in all the subtleties of the law and understand the intricate mazes of the court. Their salaries are paid regardless of the amount of service they contribute to their employers. It costs the corporation nothing to be constantly in court. These high-priced railroad and other corporation lawyers would ever be ready to pounce upon the labour corporations at every opportunity that was offered.

There is not a single labour organization that could keep out of the hands of a court for one year of its existence if it ever consented to become incorporated.

All sorts of suits would be brought against labour unions. Suits for real grievances and suits for imaginary grievances. Every court would be kept open for their undoing. The result would be that these labour organizations would be compelled to employ high-priced lawyers. They would be mulcted in expenses, which would be a greater burden than they could possibly sustain. The end would be speedy. A judgement rendered against a corporation and remaining unpaid would call for the appointment of a receiver on a petition in bankruptcy.

There would not be one organization of labour which the employers wished to destroy that could keep out of the hands of a receiver for a year.

No sooner would suits be instituted in the various state and federal courts than applications would be made for receiverships, and these receiverships, according to the usages of courts, would be appointed by the parties who are interested in the collection of judgements and redress decreed by the courts, and the result would be that labour organizations would soon be controlled and owned by the employers, and for their own benefit.

In this way the employers and combinations of capital would easily accomplish what they have all along sought to do; that is, they would control their own business and the business of organized labour, too. In this way they would have the unions entirely in their hands. To submit for one moment to incorporation would mean to submit to having organizations run by the enemies of labour instead of by its friends.

The demands of capitalists for the incorporation of labour unions would exactly parallel the demand of a body of atheists to fix the rules governing the Christian church, or for the Democratic party to dictate the policy of the Republican party.

How the labour organizations shall manage their own affairs is not the business of the corporations or the employers. This new demand for the incorporation of labour unions is not only unjust and unreasonable, but it is impudent and insulting to the last degree.

Events in the History of the Boilermakers' Society
1834–1906

1834 Society of Friendly Boiler Makers formed in Manchester. Branch formed in **Bolton.**

1835 General Council formed from parent branch. Consisted of fourteen **members.**

1836 New branch opened in **Bristol.**

1837 The London Working Men's Association produced the six points which were to become the rallying call of the Chartists.

1838 Messrs Laird and Co. of Birkenhead launched a small steamship with a screw propeller.

1839 First branch opened in London.
First rule book drawn up by General Council of the parent branch in Manchester.
Entrance fee fixed at £1 1s. Contributions were 1s 9d every four weeks.
Prominent member of the General Council was John Roach, who until his death in 1847 was an active Chartist.

1840 Branch opened in **Leeds.**

1841 Branch opened in Belfast.

1842 Branch opened in Bradford.
First delegate meeting of branches introduced primitive form of financial equalisation between branches. Parent branch acted as Executive Council.
New Secretary elected: John Roberts. He was paid 12s per week for evening and Sunday work.

1843 Branches opened in Liverpool, Hull and Newcastle.

1844 Expansion in railway construction. New field of employment for boiler-makers.

1845 John Roberts became first full-time General Secretary.
Annual delegate meeting of branches lasted seven days. Thirty-three delegates represented thirty-five branches.
Name changed to United Friendly Boiler Makers' Society.
Holders-up admitted to membership providing they had worked continuously at trade between ages of 20 and 25.
Strike at a boiler shop in Smethwick (not the first strike, but the earliest recorded strike at the annual delegate meeting).
Strike authorised by EC at Dukinfield. Members urged to 'wage war to the knife'.

1847 John Roberts' pay increased to £2 2s per week.
Annual delegate meeting lasted eleven days.

1848 Annual delegate meeting lasted twelve days. Annual meetings henceforth discontinued. EC empowered to take vote of membership.

New class of membership established, Protective Fund members, ineligible because of age or ill-health to qualify for certain benefits. Subscriptions for PF members fixed at 1s 3d per four weeks.

Dispute benefit fixed at 12s per week for married men, 6d per week for each child under 10 years of age. Single men received 10s per week.

All members urged to oppose piece-work.

Every member required to serve in rotation as branch officer.

General Secretary, John Roberts, resigned.

1849 New General Secretary elected: John Pennie.

New branch opened at Greenock (first branch in Scotland).

1850 Society decided not to participate in engineering union amalgamation discussions.

1851 Formation of the Amalgamated Society of Engineers. Boilermakers remained aloof.

Membership 1,781, enrolled in forty-five branches.

1852 Scottish boilermakers in the Amicable and Provident Society of Journeymen Boiler Makers and a separate London society of boilermakers both joined the United Friendly Boiler Makers' Society.

Title changed to United Society of Boiler Makers and Iron Shipbuilders.

Membership 2,000, enrolled in fifty-two branches.

District committees established in Scotland and London.

Delegate meeting revised rules. Subscriptions increased to 3s every four weeks. Entrance fees reduced by about 25 per cent. Sickness, funeral and protective funds consolidated into one general fund. Scales of benefit set up in rules for sickness (up to 10s per week), funeral (up to £10), disablement (up to £60), unemployment (up to 8s per week), superannuation (3s 6d per week), victimisation (half pay), and travelling (cheapest fare to another town).

1853 General Secretary, John Pennie, emigrated to USA.

New General Secretary elected: George Brogden.

1856 Delegate meeting revised rules and made clear that 'all funds belong to the whole of the Society'.

EC increased to seven members, to be elected by a branch or group of branches selected every two years by the whole membership.

Essay competition held in opposition to piece-work.

1857 Death of General Secretary, George Brogden.

New General Secretary elected: John Allen.

1858 Trade depression. Unemployment benefit reduced and then discontinued. Society's debts exceeded assets.

Membership 3,453, enrolled in sixty-nine branches.

1859 Trade recovered and benefits restored.

London building trade employers sought in six-months' dispute to crush trade unionism among building workers. Boiler Makers' Society made donation of 1s per member and a voluntary levy of 6d per week per member to assist building trade workers.

1860 Membership approximately 3,500.

1861 Levy of 4d per week per member to finance dispute in London against introduction of foreman carpenter on iron work in ship construction.

1862 EC complained of branches paying strike benefit in defiance of rules.

Delegate meeting amended rules to provide for district committees throughout the Society.

New rule recognised existence of piece-work.

Opposition to any amalgamation discussion with Amalgamated Society of Engineers.

1863 Strike meeting at Hawthorn's, Newcastle, led to burst of trade union activity and recruitment on the Tyne and Wear.

Two members sentenced to three months' imprisonment arising out of a strike at Hull. Conviction quashed on appeal. Levy of 9d per member to pay costs.

1864 Donation of £100 to Staffordshire ironworkers involved in trade dispute. Boilermakers' members voted 3,797 to 901 for a further donation of £100 to be made, to be raised by a 6d levy.

Upsurge of activity, recruitment, claims, strikes and wage increases on the Mersey, Hull and other areas.

National levy imposed to support Leeds members in dispute.

1865 Decline in trade, and employers press for wage reductions. Strikes in many yards in different parts of Britain.

1866 Boilermakers on the Tees supported movement for nine-hour day. Numerous disputes. A number of boilermakers sent to prison for breach of contract.

Nine-hour movement spread to Clyde yards. Over 20,000 shipyard workers locked out. Employers succeeded and trade union organisation virtually collapsed in the aftermath.

Society represented at the United Kingdom Alliance of Organised Trades to campaign for trade union law reform.

1867 EC upheld by branches in controversy with Clyde members following defeat in nine-hour dispute.

1868 Membership reduced in Scotland to 156, enrolled in nine branches. Over 90 per cent of eligible Clyde workers now unorganised.

Funds reduced to less than £1,000 following disputes and trade depression.

First TUC – representative mainly of trades councils.

1869 Boilermakers campaigned for trade union law reform.

1870 Society decided to be represented at the next TUC.

1871 Society sent delegates to the TUC.

Trade Union Act passed by Parliament.

Retirement of General Secretary, John Allen. Granted pension of £1 per week.

New General Secretary elected: Robert Knight.

Engineering and shipbuilding workers won nine-hour day following strike action on North-East coast.

Trade buoyant. Thirteen new branches opened, including one in Constantinople.

Big improvement in Society's administration following the election of Robert Knight as General Secretary.

1872 Members urged to press political candidates for further trade union law reform.

Five gas stokers involved in trade dispute sentenced to twelve months' imprisonment. Boilermakers' Society supported financial appeal to help families of imprisoned workers.

Nearly £200 donated by the Society to the newly formed National Agricultural Labourers' Union.

1873 Big demonstration on Whit Monday in London, supported by Boilermakers' Society, to protest against sentence of imprisonment with hard labour for picketing on sixteen women, wives of agricultural labourers on strike.

Society donated £500 (two donations of £250 each) to the campaign of Mr Plimsoll to improve the standard of seaworthiness in British ships.

1874 Society's members petition candidates at General Election for trade union law reform.

Lockout of thousands of agricultural workers. Society decided by 6,937 to 613 votes to levy 1s per member to assist the agricultural workers.

Delegate meeting replaced by General Council elected by branches on a group basis. General Council to meet once every two years, or whenever summoned by the EC, or at the request of not less than twenty branches. Subscriptions increased to 4s per four weeks.

Decline in trade. Wage reductions at Clyde yards. Strikes in seven yards but most boilermakers were unorganised.

1875 A new law passed by Parliament, the Conspiracy and Protection of Property Act, which went a long way towards meeting trade union demands for law reform.

Wage reductions in nearly all shipyards. Strikes at many yards.

Abortive attempt to establish a Federation of Engineering Trades. Principle of federation supported by Society's members by 8,869 votes to 1,408.

Robert Knight elected to the Parliamentary Committee of the TUC and shortly afterwards elected to the chair.

£16,600 paid out in unemployment benefit.

1876 Further attempt – also abortive – to establish a Federation of Engineering Trades.

Long strike at Dumbarton dockyard ended in a compromise but strengthened Society's influence on the Clyde.

Notices for lengthening of working day in Barrow, Belfast and Ebbw Vale. After prolonged strike, notices were withdrawn at Ebbw Vale.

Bitter controversy between EC and Tyne and Wear branches regarding control of a local dispute. EC view upheld by narrow majority on a ballot vote, 5,642 to 4,771.

1877 District delegate and Sunderland District Committee resign following dispute with EC.

Clyde lockout following wage claim. Long dispute of thirty-three weeks ended in a compromise.

1878 Clyde employers demand wage cuts and longer hours in conditions of trade depression. Strikes in many yards. Workers defeated.

1879 £32,000 paid out in unemployment benefit.

Following defeat of strike on Clyde, hours increased from fifty-one to fifty-four per week.

Employers elsewhere followed the offensive of the Clyde employers. General wage reductions and strikes in many areas.

1880 Head office moved to Newcastle by decision of the members in a ballot vote.

1881 Pressure for wage increases in all districts. Trade very good.

1882 Trade very prosperous. Wage increases in nearly all shops and yards.

Holders-up admitted to membership but with restricted rights.

Bitter dispute on North-East coast with platers' helpers over 'corner' system.

220

Events in the History of the Boilermakers' Society

1883 Membership reached 30,000 and financial reserves exceeded £100,000.
EC warned against shop stewards exceeding powers under rules by calling unauthorised strikes.
Trade declined towards end of year.
Ballot vote rejected eligibility of draughtsmen for membership. Voting was 1,506 to 664.

1884 Trade fell rapidly.
Wage cuts reported every month. Widespread sporadic strikes of resistance. 23½ per cent of membership unemployed. Much higher proportion unemployed in shipbuilding.

1885 Depression continued. Many wage reductions.

1886 Depression continued. 28 per cent of membership unemployed.
Wages still being cut. Now lower in many areas than for twenty years.
Long strike on North-East coast; four wage cuts in less than two years. Strike defeated.

1887 Trade improved. Percentage of members unemployed fell to 21½ per cent.
In four years £170,000 paid out in unemployment benefit.

1888 Trade continued to improve.
Wage increases in most yards. Threats of strike and strike action in many areas.
Harland and Wolff, Belfast, strike involved over 5,000 members. National ballot favoured levy to support Belfast strikers.

1889 Prosperity. Unemployment rate among members fell to 2½ per cent.
Robert Knight opposed proposal for an Eight Hours Bill. Preferred progress by collective bargaining.
Clyde Employers' Association formed, followed by moves towards a national federation of shipbuilding employers.
Donation of only £20 to London dockers in their historic strike. Robert Knight critical of 'new unionism'.
Members balloted in favour of levy to provide £500 to assist Australian workers on strike.

1890 Trade began to slacken.
New offices, Lifton House, opened in Newcastle. Celebrated with demonstration of 7,000 members.
Members voted 19,464 to 484 in favour of a trade union federation in engineering and shipbuilding. ASE remain outside.

1891 Notice of wage reductions by some employers.
Unofficial strike of Clyde members lasting six weeks. Strike defeated. Bitter controversy between EC and Scottish branches.

1892 1,000 members of a Clyde society of holders-up join the Boilermakers' Society.
Wage increases in South Wales steel works following widespread strike action.

1893 Another depression. Unemployment rate among members rose to 16 per cent.
Clyde employers insisted on successive wage cuts, including three reductions in the winter of 1892–3.
Agreements signed for regulation of apprenticeship in boilershops and shipyards.
Society voted for levy to assist Hull dockers involved in a strike. Donation of £800 saved dockers from defeat.

1894   £48,000 paid out in unemployment benefit.

Demands for successive wage reductions on the Tyne, Wear, Tees and Hartlepools led to a new procedure agreement. On a ballot vote it was accepted nationally but not by members on North-East coast. Prolonged dispute with EC and General Secretary.

Agreement for payment of special allowances for repair of oil ships.

Handbook of agreements issued by Society. Members urged to elect shop stewards wherever six or more members were employed.

Under the influence of Robert Knight the Society threatened to disaffiliate from the TUC because of the activities of the socialists.

Ballot vote in favour of disaffiliation from the TUC: 14,241 to 9,078.

1895   Robert Knight and other 'old guard' leaders of TUC conducted vigorous and successful rearguard action against the socialists and the 'new unionists'. Ballot vote now favoured continued affiliation to TUC.

Growing unrest at the authority wielded by Robert Knight led finally to a decision to elect a full-time EC of seven members on a regional basis. Strongly opposed by Robert Knight. Bitter internal controversy.

Wage increases received in many firms.

The case of Flood *versus* Allen. Judgement given in favour of Allen, the Boilermakers' London district delegate.

1896   Robert Knight re-elected unopposed for his last term of office. He had now served twenty-five years as General Secretary.

By 24,173 to 6,349 Society voted against admission of National Society of Drillers and a number of local unions of drillers.

By 14,190 to 11,031 sheet iron workers, mainly on the Clyde, admitted to the Society.

Society opposed admission of unskilled workers' unions to Federation of Engineering and Shipbuilding Trades.

1897   New full-time EC took office.

£600 donation made to Robert Knight by the Society.

London engineering workers, including boilermakers, opened campaign for eight-hour day.

Formation of Engineering Employers' Federation. London employers resisted demand for shorter hours. Tens of thousands of workers locked out.

Robert Knight argued that shorter hours was a national issue and that the initiative should have been taken in shipbuilding. Relations between Society and ASE became very strained. Ballot vote strongly supported EC attitude by 25,433 to 3,403. Boilermakers' Society withdrew from London eight-hour day committee.

Heavy majority on a ballot for 6d levy to support quarrymen in North Wales involved in dispute.

£200 sent to assist striking Hamburg dockers.

1898   Small societies of London boilermakers and Wear boilermakers admitted to membership.

By 29,068 votes to 1,036 members favoured a 3d levy to assist South Wales miners involved in a dispute.

1899   Robert Knight resigned at the age of 65. By 17,041 to 15,830 votes he was retained as 'consulting secretary' at a salary of £3 10s per week.

Top candidate in first ballot for new General Secretary, Mr F. A. Fox of South Wales, withdrew to become Secretary of South Wales Federation of Ship-repairers.

Mr D. Cummings, Yorkshire district delegate, narrowly elected General Secretary.

222

Society supported TUC resolution inviting co-operation of socialist, co-operative and trade union organisations to secure labour representation in Parliament. Members decided, however, by 6,880 to 3,157 votes not to be represented at the labour representation conference.

Members voted by 31,690 to 1,719 to send £200 to assist Danish workers locked out by their employers.

Members voted for levy to assist strike of American boilermakers.

£20 sent to Austrian textile workers involved in a dispute with their employers.

1900 Beginning of the Taff Vale case.

British shipbuilding output nearly 70 per cent of world output.

Membership exceeded 47,000.

Subscriptions amended by General Council according to class of membership. First-class members to pay 3s per fortnight.

Office of consulting secretary abolished. Robert Knight dissatisfied. Internal controversy about retirement arrangements.

By 24,953 votes to 8,918, admission of London and District United Society of Drillers rejected.

By 31,104 votes to 1,685 members approved donation of £200 – after initial donation of £20 – to Calais lace workers locked out by their employers. Calais lace workers had earlier sent money to Britain in the 1897 engineering dispute.

By 33,390 votes to 610 members approved donation of £100 – after an initial donation of £20 – to assist a strike of London lightermen.

1901 Society's delegates at TUC supported resolution urging unions, in light of Taff Vale case, to affiliate to Labour Representation Committee.

United Kingdom shipbuilding output at record output of 1,800,000 tons.

Draft of new apprenticeship agreement at first rejected by members and then later accepted by ballot vote.

1902 Members voted by 25,581 to 6,995 in favour of political representation, and by 26,478 to 8,905 to affiliate to Labour Representation Committee.

James Conley, Clyde district delegate, becomes first member of Boilermakers' panel of Parliamentary candidates.

Trade declined. Wage cuts in many shipyards.

Numerous demarcation disputes.

Clyde branches played big part in massive demonstration in Glasgow against Taff Vale judgement.

Admission of drillers again rejected.

1903 A number of branches formed in South Africa at end of Boer War.

1904 Unemployment rate among members rose to 15 per cent.

Wage cuts on North-East coast both at the beginning and at the end of the year.

1905 Manchester demonstration of at least 600 boilermakers in favour of labour representation.

Mr D. C. Cummings elected chairman of TUC Parliamentary Committee.

Trade began to revive.

Mr D. C. Cummings re-elected unopposed as General Secretary.

Admission of drillers again rejected.

Mr D. C. Cummings produced commemorative survey of Society to celebrate the seventieth anniversary (1904) of its foundation.

£100 sent to assist victims of Tsarist oppression in the 1905 Russian Revolution.

By 4,990 votes to 1,693 members agreed to affiliate to General Federation of Trade Unions.

223

1906 TUC urged support for General Election candidates pledged to support a new Trade Disputes Bill.

General Election victory for Liberals. About thirty MP'S elected under the auspices of the LRC. Two boilermakers, James Conley and James Hill, both poll well but were defeated.

Trade Disputes Act passed by Parliament.

Movement for wage increases. Eight-week strike on the Clyde, finally settled in 1907. Ten-week strike on the Tees and at Hartlepools.

Weekly pay agreement on the Clyde.

Membership approximately 52,000.

Mr D. C. Cummings served as President of the TUC.

Index

Accident benefit (*see* Benefits)
Admiralty Dockyards, 61
Agricultural Labourers, Friendly Society of, 35 (*see also* National Agricultural Labourers' Union)
Allen, John, 21, 44, 55, 70, 82
Allen versus Flood, 137–8, 144, 195
Amalgamated Society of Engineers (later Amalgamated Engineering Union and Amalgamated Union of Engineering Workers), 9, 11, 30, 50, 60, 64, 66, 69–70, 83, 91, 113, 119, 124, 131–3, 176–7, 180, 186–7, 189–90
Amalgamated Society of Railway Servants, 143, 147
Amicable and Provident Society of Journeymen Boiler Makers, 51
Apprenticeship, 122, 155–6
Arch, Joseph, 86
Armstrong, Sir William, Mitchell & Co., 123
Artificers, Statute of, 31
Asquith, H. N., 148
Australia, 35, 120, 191, 193
Austria, 142, 191

Barrow, 9, 90, 95
'Beehive', 74
Belfast, 41, 54, 65, 95, 112, 154
Bell, Richard, 143
Benefits, 22–3, 42–5, 51–5, 64, 67, 69–70, 84–5, 90, 93–4, 98, 101–2, 112, 120, 171, 174, 182–3
Bilston, 54
Birkenhead, 54, 64–5, 90, 164
Birmingham, 77
Birmingham Political Union, 38
Blackburn, 17
Blacksmiths, 27, 44, 66, 135, 189
Blair & Co., 89
Blyth, 135
Bolton, 17, 21, 54, 59
Boulton, Matthew, 28
Bradford, 30, 41, 54, 72–3, 164, 194

Bristol, 21, 54–5, 165
Brogden, George, 53, 55
Brotherton, Harry, 11
Brown's John, Clydebank, 189
Building trade dispute 1859, 57–9, 191
Bury, 50, 54, 59

Caird & Co., 98
Caledonian Shipbuilding Co., 10
Campbell-Bannerman, Sir H., 150–1
Carlisle, 118
Chalkley, Albert, 11
Chalmers, John, 11
Chartism, 37–8, 40–1, 193
Chatham, 60
Chepstow, 54
Chipping Norton, 79
'Closed shop', 108
Clyde, 9, 29, 50, 65–9, 85, 89–90, 94, 97–9, 105, 108, 111, 113–4, 119–20, 134, 147, 154, 173, 175, 189–90
Clyde Employers' Association, 118
Clyde Shipbuilders' and Engineers' Association, 66
Churchill, W., 148
Cole, G. D. H., 33
Combination Acts, 31–2, 35
Conciliation agreement, 130
Conley, James, 147–8, 152
Connolly, J., 139
Conservative Party, 80, 141, 148–9, 151–2
Confederation of Shipbuilding and Engineering Unions, 10–11
Conspiracy and Protection of Property Act, 1875, 80
Cooper, James, 17
Constantinople, 84
Corner system, 110–11, 188
Cramp, William & Sons, Philadelphia, 160
Crewe, 54
Criminal Law Amendment Act, 1871, 80